DUTY AND CITIZENSHIP

The Correspondence and Political Papers
of Violet Markham, 1896–1953

SOURCES FOR MODERN BRITISH HISTORY

General Editors: Kathleen Burk, John Ramsden, John Turner

REAL OLD TORY POLITICS: The Political Diaries of Robert Sanders, Lord Bayford, 1910–1935
Edited by John Ramsden. 1984

THE DESTRUCTION OF LORD ROSEBERY: From the Diary of Sir Edward Walter Hamilton, 1894–1895
Edited by David Brooks. 1987

THE CRISIS OF BRITISH UNIONISM: The Domestic Political Papers of the Second Earl of Selborne, 1885–1922
Edited by George Boyce. 1987

LABOUR AND THE WARTIME COALITION: From the Diary of James Chuter Ede, 1941–1945
Edited by Kevin Jefferys. 1987

THE MODERNISATION OF CONSERVATIVE POLITICS: The Diaries and Letters of William Bridgeman, 1904–1935
Edited by Philip Williamson. 1988

THE CRISIS OF BRITISH POWER: The Imperial and Naval Papers of the Second Earl of Selborne, 1895–1910
Edited by George Boyce. 1990

MY DEAR MAX: The Letters of Brendan Bracken to Lord Beaverbrook, 1925–1958
Edited by Richard Cockett. 1990

PATRICK GORDON WALKER: Political Diaries, 1932-1971
Edited by Robert Pearce. 1991

PARLIAMENT AND POLITICS IN THE AGE OF BALDWIN AND MACDONALD: The Diaries of Sir Cuthbert Headlam, 1924–1935
Edited by Stuart Ball. 1993

DUTY AND CITIZENSHIP

The Correspondence and Political Papers
of Violet Markham, 1896–1953

Edited with an introduction by
Helen Jones

Introductory matter and commentary © Helen Jones 1994
Correspondence and papers © The British Library of Political and Economic Science; The National Library of Scotland; The Royal Geographical Society; The University of Capetown

All rights reserved. This book may not be reproduced in whole or in part, in any form (beyond that copying permitted by Sections 107 and 108 of the U.S. Copyright Law and except by reviewers for the public press), without written permission from the publishers.

British Library Cataloguing in Publication Data

A copy of the catalogue entry for this publication can be obtained from the British Library

ISBN 1-872273-03-3

PUBLISHED BY THE HISTORIANS' PRESS
9 DAISY ROAD, LONDON E18 1EA
Printed in England by Antony Rowe Ltd

Contents

Acknowledgements		vi
Introduction: Violet Markham, 1872–1959		1
1	Home and Away, 1896–1913	23
2	War Work, 1914–1918	57
3	Women Without Work, 1918–1939	99
4	The Home Front, 1939–1945	148
5	Creating Good Citizens? 1945–1953	183
Index		199

Acknowledgements

The bulk of Violet Markham's papers are deposited with the British Library of Political and Economic Science (BLPES) at the London School of Economics. I am extremely grateful to Dr Angela Raspin and her colleagues at the BLPES for all their help. I should also like to record my thanks to Leonie Twentyman Jones of the University of Cape Town. Unless otherwise indicated all documents quoted or cited in footnotes are from the BLPES collection. Other correspondence cited is held at The National Library of Scotland (NLS) in the Haldane papers; at the Royal Geographical Society (RGS) in the David Gill papers, and at the University of Cape Town (UCT) in the Newton Thompson papers (BC 643) and Patrick Duncan papers (BC 294). I am grateful to all the institutions mentioned above and to Violet Markham's relatives for permission to quote from her papers.

The text has been reproduced as closely as possible to the original. Most individuals are identified on their first appearance, with the exception of those who played no definite part in the public world. Violet Markham has been abbreviated to VM.

The author is extremely grateful to the Isobel Thornley Bequest Fund Committee and the Scouloudi Foundation in association with the Institute of Historical Research for their generous financial support which has finally enabled The Historians Press to publish this volume.

Liverpool
August 1994

Introduction
Violet Markham, 1872–1959.

Private and public worlds

Violet Markham influenced national and local politics in Britain for over half a century.[1] From the First World War onwards she sat on numerous government committees; between the wars she chaired the Central Committee on Women's Training and Employment (CCWTE); from 1934 she was the statutory *woman* member of the Unemployment Assistance Board (UAB) and after 1937 she was its Deputy Chair. The Armed Forces and Foreign Office periodically made use of her expertise in their education programmes, and for fifty years she dined and corresponded with the great and the good both in Britain and abroad. In 1917 she was appointed a Companion of Honour, in 1936 she received an honorary Litt.D from Sheffield University and in 1938 an honorary LL.D. from Edinburgh. In 1952 she received the freedom of Chesterfield. She was a Fellow of both the Royal Historical Society and the Royal Geographical Society. All this was achieved with little more than a year's formal education. Throughout her life she supported a political party which wilted under her. She was never an MP or career civil servant. Her husband provided her with no entrées into political circles or high society, and her career as a national figure was launched on the back of a political dinosaur, the anti-suffrage campaign. How, then, were her career and influence possible, and what views did she bring to bear on her activities? The answers to both questions are closely linked.

Three interlocking areas of influence shaped Markham's activities. First, her family and domestic circumstances, her commitment to Liberalism, and her views on the role of women in society influenced the causes with which she became involved. Second, her class position, financial independence and personal contacts provided her with opportunities for manoeuvring herself into positions of potential influence. Third, she possessed personal attributes,

[1] I am grateful to Andrew Blaikie, Christine Hillam and Philippa Levine for their comments on an earlier draft of this introduction.

such as being a good public speaker and an effective committee member, which ensured that she was able to exploit her opportunities to the full. These areas were not discrete but intermingled with one another; rather like the pieces in a child's kaleidoscope, they periodically shifted and rearranged themselves in complex new patterns under the stimulus of changing events. During the First World War the kaleidoscope underwent more vigorous and intricate agitation than at most other times. Family influences on her attitudes gradually weakened as she matured, but her views on 'citizenship' and 'duty' (underpinned by appropriate education) which she held to be important, for both herself and others, remained unchanged. The constant juggling of her class and gender interests against a changing social and political backdrop makes for a complex and interesting character on the stage of twentieth-century British social and political history.

Violet Rosa Markham was born in 1872. She was the youngest of the five children of Rosa and Charles Markham. At the time of her birth the family was living near Chesterfield and her father was Managing Director of the Stavely Coal and Iron Company.

Details about Markham's early life may be culled from her autobiography, *Return passage*, published in 1953 when she was 81 years old.[2] While her autobiography is undoubtedly useful for establishing places, dates and names, it needs to be handled with care if it is to be used to establish what influenced the attitudes of the young Markham.[3] Markham tells us that both her parents were enthusiastic Liberals (her father stood unsuccessfully as a Liberal Unionist in the 1886 General Election) but they had little else in common and, with their very different personalities, home life was tense. This was an understatement. In 1924 Markham confided 'I saw a great deal of unhappiness & unrest in my younger days'.[4] Markham did not hurl herself speedily into marriage. This may well have been an attempt to avoid a repetition of her earlier home life, or what she regarded as her sister's unfortunate marriage.[5] In 1917 she reflected that 'In days long past the

---

[2] Violet Markham, *Return passage: The autobiography of Violet R. Markham, CH* (Oxford University Press, Oxford, 1953); see also Jane Lewis, *Women and social action in Victorian and Edwardian England* (Edward Elgar, Aldershot, 1991). Chapter 5 has a useful chapter on the earlier part of Markham's life which emphasises the importance of ideas of citizenship and duty for Markham. Lewis compares Markham with a number of other women: Octavia Hill, Helen Bosanquet, Beatrice Webb and Mary Ward.

[3] For a discussion of the potentialities and pitfalls of using women's autobiographies and biographies see Kathleen Barry, 'Biography and the search for women's subjectivity', *Women's Studies International Forum*, vol. 12, no 6, 1989, pp 561–577; *Gender and History*, vol.2, no 1, 1990, whole issue.

[4] VM to Joyce Newton Thompson, a friend living in South Africa, 24 December 1924, UCT BC 643 B 18. 27.

[5] VM to Sir David Gill (1843–1914), astronomer; in 1879 appointed HM astronomer at the Cape of Good Hope. 20 August 1903, RGS.

thought of a man about my room was intolerable to me.'[6]

Markham recalls that as well as jointly nurturing a young Liberal, each of her parents influenced her in their own different ways. Markham's autobiography gives the impression that her mother had a profound influence on her beliefs in her early years: her mother's views contributed to Markham's scepticism of the Christian religion and of votes for women. From both these attitudes she was later weaned. In 1902, at the age of thirty, she became a committed Christian as a result of hearing Herbert Hensley Henson's sermons at St Margaret's, Westminster. He was a controversial liberal theologian who attracted, and convinced, Markham by his rigorously intellectual approach to Christianity.[7] During the First World War she came around to the view that women should be given the parliamentary vote. In her youth Markham, like her mother, was a francophile; by middle age she was a rabid francophobe.[8] Markham's mother had been deeply suspicious of Germans but, after the First World War, Markham developed a respect for them when she lived in Cologne with her husband who was a demobilisation officer with the British army of occupation.[9] Years later, Markham recalled of her mother: 'For society she cared little or nothing, — home & books fulfilled all her needs.'[10]

Brought up surrounded by servants with whom she developed close emotional ties, the domestic servant 'problem' was a subject always close to Markham's heart. It is one of the few examples of her acknowledging that the organisation of life in the private sphere plays a significant part in women's ability to function in the public one. In adult life she found domestic servants indispensable and during the Second World War marvelled at middle-class American women's ability to manage without domestic help. Throughout the inter-war years Markham chaired the Central Committee on Women's Training and Employment, which prepared unemployed working-class girls for domestic service. In the 1930s, as a member of the Unemployment Assistance Board, she took an especial interest in domestic service

[6] VM to Sir Patrick Duncan (1870–1943), from 1910 South African Unionist party MP; in the 1920s and 1930s he served in various governments; 1937–1943 Governor-General. Easter Saturday 1917, UCT BC 643 B18.1.

[7] V. Markham, *Return Passage* (1953) pp 90-91; Herbert Hensley Henson (1863–1947), in 1900 appointed Canon of Westminster and Rector of St Margaret's, and in 1917 appointed Bishop of Hereford; 1920–1939 he was Bishop of Durham.

[8] See for instance her comments about the French immediately after the First World War and during the Second World War.

[9] Markham first started to learn German in 1903 when she accompanied her sister, Geraldine Hole (who was recovering from a long illness), to the spa town of Kreuznach. VM to Sir David Gill, 20 August 1903, RGS.

[10] VM to Elizabeth Haldane (1862–1937), social reformer especially interested in education and health; first female JP in Scotland, author and critic. 20 January 1919 NLS 6028 ff 5. I have not included this comment in Markham's correspondence.

for unemployed women, and during the Second World War she co-authored an official report on the subject. In the 1930s, and in the early days of the Second World War, Markham's letters to her sister are full of grumbles about her own servants.[11] Given that the bulk of employers would have been middle-class and the employees working-class, it was predominantly middle, not working, class women who would have benefited from a greater supply of domestic labour.[12]

Markham was educated at home, apart from eighteen months spent at a girls' school when she was 17–18 years old. By now, the late 1880s, secondary schooling for middle-class girls was widespread. It was also increasingly common for such girls to sit the Cambridge higher local examinations, a right they had won over twenty years previously. Although her mother was enthusiastic about education, and Markham performed well at examinations (and occasionally a girl did sit public examinations at her school), Markham was not entered for any of them. She records neither frustration nor explanation for this omission. The most useful lessons for Markham may well have been those in elocution, for she felt that it was these lessons which helped her in public speaking in later years. After leaving school she went to live with a Parisian family before returning to the family home.

Markham found it hard to settle down to a life of domesticity. The muffled cries of frustration from an intelligent woman without a sense of purpose in life can be heard with the turning of almost every page of her diary. The outcome is predictable: a middle-class woman from provincial England takes up the good cause of public works. The opportunity to see precisely how this outcome was reached makes the inclusion of extracts from Markham's diary from this period worthwhile. The diary provides us with an insight into exactly how different influences were knitted together to produce the familiar pattern of unpaid charitable work. Unease with her own empty life, cooped up in the manor, was juxtaposed with the miserable existence of the poor on her doorstep. The influence of the family's liberalism[13] was sharpened by her reading of social critics such as John Ruskin. These influences on Markham were coupled with one of the few public openings available to a middle-class woman without higher education or training and

---

[11] See 19/30 and 19/31, from which I have not included extracts as they are rather repetitious.

[12] The employment of servants was, however, not an exclusively middle class preserve. See Edward Higgs, 'Domestic service and household production' in Angela John (ed), *Unequal opportunities: Women's employment in England, 1800–1918* (Blackwell, Oxford, 1986), pp 125–150, especially 133–136.

[13] Many Liberals were at this time committed to a wide-ranging package of reforms, although Markham did not recall labour conditions ever being discussed at home, except in the context of condemning strikers.

led inexorably towards workhouse visiting and thence to a seat on a School Board.

Markham did not find that a public role automatically resolved her frustrations; indeed in some ways it increased them. It was not until 1897 when she took up School Board work and began to feel that she was having some positive influence on the School Board children's lives that she started to feel some degree of personal achievement and a greater sense of her own worth. For over thirty years, she remained almost continuously involved with the Chesterfield Education Authority.

One event in 1901, when Markham was 29 years old, transformed her life. A friend of her father's left her a pot of gold with which she established a Settlement in Chesterfield and took a house in London.[14] With a base in London and financial independence, she could now exploit the contacts she was establishing (mainly through trips abroad), and begin a career on the metropolitan stage which would turn her into a national figure.

Markham's interest in establishing a Settlement reflected much the same influences as had led her to take up local charitable work. She did not hold with the views of the Charity Organisation Society which emphasised the link between poverty and individual failing. She remained concerned about the type of training received by those who went into social work and, along with social workers such as Elizabeth Macadam,[15] Markham helped to shape the nature of social work training at the end of the First World War.[16] Her belief in the importance of non-state social welfare remained with her and, after a lifetime of government work, she voluntarily set up and ran a canteen in a blitzed area of south London. Her governmental activities should not be seen as evidence of a conversion to a belief in universal state welfare. For Markham, state and private welfare went hand-in-hand. At a time when she was involved in increasing the power of the state, she was reaffirming the contribution of individual, non-state welfare.

Markham did not sever her local ties: the Settlement work, her local education activities and campaigning for her brother, Arthur, Liberal MP for Mansfield,[17] all helped to ensure that Markham frequently returned to the dusty highways and byways of provincial England. But, it was on the metropolitan and national stage that Markham's career now developed.

The belief that a sense of duty, coupled with an appropriate education, was necessary to mould the good citizen was now firmly ingrained in Markham

---

[14] From the late nineteenth to early twentieth centuries, middle-class men and women moved into 'Settlements' in working-class areas of cities in order to try and improve the social conditions of the local poor.

[15] Macadam was a Liverpool social worker who lectured at the University, campaigned for family allowances and lived with Eleanor Rathbone.

[16] See correspondence in 2/3.

[17] Arthur Markham (1866–1916), Liberal MP for Mansfield 1900–1916.

and it remained with her throughout her long public life. It helps explain why she held anti-suffrage views (in her mind in the late 1890s, and made public a decade later). It was her belief that votes for women would inevitably increase the number of inexperienced and ignorant voters which led her into the anti-suffrage camp. In 1912, Markham proclaimed to an anti-suffrage rally at the Albert Hall that a woman's citizenship was as great and as real as any man's, but as men and women possessed complementary talents, they should have a different share in the management of the country; women's share should be in the local government field 'with its splendid opportunities for civic betterment and the uplifting of the race.... Here her powers of citizenship and service can find the fullest and noblest expression.'[18] (She did not, however, take the logical step and argue that men should be disenfranchised from local government and only allowed to participate in national politics). She claimed that most women did not want the vote, although what they wanted was irrelevant, for it would not increase the efficiency of the state for women to have the vote. Markham later claimed that her mother's anti-suffrage views had a profound influence on her own; her mother's views may indeed have reinforced Markham's, but she was never putty in the hands of others. Markham's correspondence at this time bears eloquent testimony to her anti-suffrage convictions. Even though many suffragists were only demanding that women be given the vote on the same terms as men (that is, they were not necessarily asking for all women to be enfranchised), Markham was never willing before the First World War to take the risk of an extended franchise embracing the least educated and lowest class elements of society: when her class and gender interests were in conflict, the former won hands down. It is no coincidence that it was at this time that Markham's interest in the education of working class girls was blossoming.

Markham was converted to votes for women during the First World War, and her subsequent public career never suffered from her earlier anti-suffrage campaigning. Many of those who were part of the 'Establishment' and wielding influence in high places, where committee membership was decided, would no doubt have been fellow anti-suffragists before the war. In any case, Markham always maintained close friendships with women and men from a wide range of political backgrounds. After Markham had changed her mind over votes for women, her views on women's issues always remained conservative — she continued to believe that women and men should ideally take on different social and economic roles.

There were contradictions in Markham's advocacy of the anti-suffrage cause with its implications for middle-class women's activities. Markham enjoyed airing her views in public: she not only corresponded frequently

---

[18] 28/92 i; *The Times* 29 February 1912.

with the press but she also spoke in public. This latter activity did not always meet with the approval of other anti-suffragists, and in 1912 she received stern criticism from some of them for addressing the major anti-suffrage Albert Hall rally.

One of the most important arguments of the 'antis' was that women should confine themselves to political work at the local level, and not busy themselves with national, or even worse, imperial concerns. Yet, Markham, a Liberal Imperialist, was deeply interested in imperial affairs. In 1901 she confided to Sir David Gill 'I can honestly say that it is S. Africa alone which has ever made me long for the influence which comes from place & power....'[19] She wrote of the British 'It is their fate and their mission to govern.'[20] On her holiday travels around the empire she made contacts which helped her launch a career in the imperial capital. In 1895 she visited Cairo for a few weeks, where Lord Cromer was the Consul-General.[21] A few years later they were to work together in the Anti-Suffrage League. Markham became fascinated with the British administration in Egypt. This visit, coupled with her reading of Lord Milner's *England in Egypt*[22] helped to turn her into an enthusiastic imperialist. Four years later, in 1899, Markham visited South Africa — leaving just a week before war broke out. Here she met Lord Milner, along with numerous others, in particular, John Buchan and Leo Amery, with whom she formed life-long friendships and who were to be part of the social and political circle in which she was soon to move.[23] It was Alfred Lyttelton's wife, whom she first met in South Africa, to whom she owed her first public position in London as honorary secretary of the Personal Service Association.[24] On a return visit to South Africa in 1912 she met her future husband, James Carruthers, at that time a regular army officer. She wrote books about South African history and current affairs,[25]

---

[19] VM to Sir David Gill, 11 February 1901, RGS

[20] Violet Markham *South Africa, Past and present* (Smith, Elder & Co., London, 1900).

[21] Lord Cromer (1841–1917).

[22] Lord Milner *England in Egypt* (Arnold, London, 1892).

[23] Lord Milner (1854–1925) was High Commissioner to South Africa at the time of the Boer war and later a member of Lloyd George's wartime coalition; John Buchan (1875–1940), writer, Director General of Information under the Prime Minister 1917–1918, Conservative MP for Scottish Universities 1927–1935, and 1935–1940 Governor-General of Canada; Leo Amery (1873–1955), journalist, Conservative MP for Birmingham South 1911–1918, Birmingham Sparkbrook 1918–1945; he served in various Governments between 1919 and 1945, usually in posts connected with imperial affairs.

[24] Alfred Lyttelton (1857–1913), Liberal Unionist MP for Warwick and Leamington 1895–1905, Conservative MP for St George's Hanover Square 1906–1913, 1903–1905 Secretary of State for the Colonies.

[25] Violet Markham *South Africa, Past and present* (Smith, Elder & Co., London,1900); Violet Markham *The new era in South Africa, with an examination of the Chinese labour question* (Smith, Elder & Co., London, 1904); Violet Markham *The South African scene*

lectured on South Africa, and in 1903 she was 'digging up various people in London & impressing on them that we can't afford to relax any vigilance in S. Africa.'[26] In 1901 Markham was interested in establishing a service for women wishing to move from one country of the empire to another because 'This would be a practical exhibition of sympathy between the women of the Empire.'[27] In 1913, after her return from South Africa, she wrote long letters to Sir Patrick Duncan about South African politics.[28] In 1905 Markham had set out for Canada in order to see more of the British Empire and, in particular, to see for herself how a new country handled social problems. There she met Mackenzie King and another firm friendship began.[29] Markham spent the two summers prior to the outbreak of the First World War abroad. She returned in 1914 just before war was declared.

Time and again, we see Markham's private friendships intertwining with her public work: one often reinforced the other. Her friendship networks frequently influenced the type of public work with which she became involved. The women with whom she started her Settlement in Chesterfield were friends. Gertrude Bell, a prominent member of the Anti-Suffrage League, was a close friend of the family.[30] It was a friend, Sir Robert Morant, who first introduced her to central government work;[31] Sir George Riddell, who sat on the National Relief Fund (NRF) with her, was a close friend during the war,[32] and May Tennant, Director of the Women's Section of the National Service Department (NSD), was also a dear friend.[33] Tom Jones, with whom she worked on the UAB, was such a close friend that she dedicated her autobiography to him.[34] When sitting on the UAB in

(Smith, Elder & Co., London, 1913).

[26] VM to Sir David Gill, 22 November 1900; VM to Sir David Gill, 3 December 1903, RGS.

[27] VM to Sir David Gill, 8 March 1901, RGS.

[28] Violet Markham's correspondence with Duncan is in UCT BC294.

[29] William Lyon Mackenzie King (1874–1950) Canadian politician, 1921–1925, 1925–1948 Prime Minister of Canada.

[30] Gertrude Bell (1868–1926) traveller, archaeologist and after the First World War Oriental Secretary to the High Commissioner of Baghdad.

[31] Sir Robert Morant (1863–1920), civil servant, 1903–1911 Permanent Secretary at the Board of Education, 1911 appointed chairman of the National Health Insurance Commission and in 1919 first Secretary of the new Ministry of Health.

[32] Sir (from 1920 Lord) George Riddell, newspaper proprietor and close friend of Lloyd George.

[33] May Tennant (1869–1946), Treasurer of Women's Trade Union League, in 1891 appointed one of four Assistant Commissioners on the Royal Commission on Labour. In 1893 appointed one of first women Factory Inspectors from which post she resigned in 1897, a year after her marriage; founder member of CCWE and its Treasurer from 1914 to 1939; during First World War welfare advisor at War Office and in 1917 appointed Director of Women's Section NSD.

[34] Tom Jones (1870–1945), was Deputy Secretary to the Cabinet from 1916 to 1930.

the 1930s, Markham enjoyed weekend house parties, which included Tom Jones, where the problems of unemployment were discussed. On a number of occasions Markham used her contacts to get her views across to the most influential people of the day. During the First World War she had a hot-line to Frances Stevenson at 10 Downing Street, so Markham's views on the National Service Department may well have been advertised on the Prime Ministerial bedpost.[35] In the mid-1930s, when she wanted her opinions on unemployment taken seriously, she revived her acquaintance with Neville Chamberlain,[36] who was now Chancellor of the Exchequer. She tried to get Cynthia Colville, Lady-in-Waiting to Queen Mary, to influence the Queen and thereby the King over unemployment. Friendship with journalists also had its advantages. When Markham was appointed to the NSD, J.A. Spender Editor of the *Westminster Gazette* told her 'I will certainly do my best to shield you from the malicious criticism to which everyone is exposed in these days....'[37] Her correspondence bears out a comment she made in her autobiography: 'Work and friendship have taken the sting for me out of two world wars....no friendships are so sound and so happy as those based on work.'[38]. Interestingly, although Robert Morant and Tom Jones were both civil servants for whom she had enormous respect, her feelings for them did not influence her overall low opinion of civil servants. From the First World War onwards derogatory comments about civil servants pepper her writings.

During the war a number of men and women got their first big opportunity as they were swept up into central government work. Markham was to be one of them. Sir Robert Morant[39] who, with his wife, had become a close friend of Markham since they first met in 1912, recommended that she serve on the NRF's Executive Committee.[40] The commmittee's prestige was provided by the many eminent figures who initially sat on it, but as they drifted away Markham seized the opportunity and carried on with the donkey-work. She was now 42 years old and the fact that the opportunity for such serious work did not present itself until she was mature may well have been to her advantage. She had always moved with great ease in the company of grey-haired men, such as Lord Cromer, Lord Derby, Sir Robert

---

He then became the first Secretary of the Pilgrim Trust.

[35] Frances Stevenson was Lloyd George's secretary and mistress.

[36] Neville Chamberlain (1869–1940), Conservative MP for Birmingham Ladywood 1918–29, Birmingham Edgbaston 1929–40. 1917 Director of National Service. 1922–3 Postmaster-General, Feb–March 1923 Paymaster-General, March–August 1923, 1924–29, 1931 Minister of Health, 1923–24, 1931–37 Chancellor of the Exchequer, 1937–40 Prime Minister.

[37] J.A. Spender (1862–1942), journalist, to VM, 1 February 1917, 4/4.

[38] Violet Markham, *Return passage* (1953), p 150.

[39] At this time chair of the National Insurance Commission.

[40] Other women on the committee included Lady Kerry, Pamela McKenna and Mary Macarthur.

Morant and Lord Milner.[41] From sitting on the NRF other work was to develop — most directly The Central Committee on Women's Employment[42] which the NRF spawned under Mary Macarthur's influence,[43] and in 1917 Markham was appointed Deputy Director of the Women's Section of the National Service Department (a sorry tale for all those caught in its web).

Markham's war work provided her with a permanent niche in post-war administration, brought her into close touch with the problems of working-class women's paid work, and led her to call for higher wages for working-class women. She sat on the CCWTE, an Industrial Board and a Trade Board. Indeed, the work undertaken by women during the war prompted Markham to change her mind over women's suffrage. She argued, along with others, that during the war women had contributed to the survival of the state as never before, and that they had thereby proved their worth. Even before the war, women had entered the labour market, not just from economic necessity, but also to find personal satisfaction. Marriage, she argued, was not necessarily the aim and object of women's lives. As a result of the high number of men killed in the war many women would be denied the option of marriage. So, a whole nation of girls had to be brought up with very special ideas about duty: as men had made the supreme sacrifice in war, so the single women would have to sacrifice normal personal happiness. Hence the importance of making girls see what paid work could mean in their lives. Markham's concern was as much with the stability of society as it was with the personal happiness of the women, as she feared that a large number of thwarted, restless, discontented women would be a most painful and even dangerous social problem. Markham may have been drawing conclusions from her own youth when she suggested that work outside the home, widening mental horizons through an appreciation of great art and good literature, and work for others would deepen women's value of life. This, she believed, could help fulfil the demand for a more adequate expression of citizenship which had grown out of the war.[44]

By the First World War a shift had taken place in Markham's attitude towards working-class women's behaviour: in the 1890s she displayed a highly judgemental attitude towards women with illegitimate babies in the workhouse, but by 1914 she was in favour of granting separation allowances

---

[41] Lord Derby (1865–1948), Conservative MP for West Houghton 1892–1905, 1900–1903 Financial Secretary at the War Office, 1903–1905 Postmaster General, October 1915 appointed Director of Recruiting, 1916 Under-Secretary of State for War, 1916–1918, 1922–1924 Secretary of State for War, 1918–1920 Ambassador to Paris.

[42] After the war this became the Central Committee on Women's Training and Employment (CCWTE).

[43] Mary Macarthur (1880–1921), Secretary of Women's Trade Union League 1903–, friend of Markham.

[44] 13/1 VM's Notes on women's work in war, probably written in 1915.

to women who lived with soldiers, even if they were not married to them. She was not taken in by all the wild scaremongering about sky-rocketing illegitimacy rates or the immorality of women in the Services. However, the change wrought by war on Markham's attitude towards working-class women was not a straightforward one. Although professing that working-class women's fields of employment should be expanded, and their wages raised, in practice Markham confined herself to pressing them into domestic work. Her ideas about widening opportunities for middle-class women received more concrete expression. She pressed for more women in senior civil service posts, and she sat on a committee which recommended the amalgamation of the men's and women's sections of the Factory Inspectorate because she optimistically assumed that this would improve women's promotion prospects. She was also involved in making recommendations to the Lord Chancellor's office about the appointment of the first women JPs.

While keen to see more opportunities for women's employment, Markham wished to see gender differences maintained. She was initially very doubtful about women wearing para-military uniform, even in wartime. Markham was not especially enthusiastic about standing in her dead brother's Mansfield constituency in the 1918 General Election (as a Liberal without the coupon) and she was not slow to use an argument detrimental to the women's cause as a let-out clause: she informed the voters that if elected she would submit herself for re-election in two years time because if they made the 'novel, and very sporting venture' of electing a woman, they should have the chance of getting out of the bargain if they did not like it.[45] She was against an election, anyway, because no one could yet speak clearly about future problems, the Forces could only vote in a fragmentary way and until demobilisation there was little choice over candidates. She also commented in private that 'Parliament is no job for a married woman.'[46]

Despite working for the expansion of middle-class women's employment opportunities, she never wavered in her belief that women's chief joy in life was procreation. She saw the absence of children of her own as something for which she needed to seek compensation, and she found it in writing books.[47]

After the war, there was a brief break in Markham's administrative work with working-class women's employment as she went to live in Germany

---

[45] *Mansfield Chronicle*, 21 November 1918. The coupon was a letter from Lloyd George and Bonar Law to candidates whom they endorsed. Liberals in Asquith's camp did not receive the letter.

[46] VM to Cyril 'Tommy' Newton Thompson, husband of a friend of Markham, 14 November 1918, UCT BC 643 B 18. 17,

[47] See her letter to Elizabeth Haldane (1862–1937), social reformer especially interested in education and health, first woman JP in Scotland, author and critic. 8 January 1925, NLS 6030 ff 8.

with her husband, then serving with the British army. Markham mixed with senior military personnel, met and began to like Germans, and travelled widely elsewhere in Europe. Here is the one occasion when circumstances created by her husband were to influence Markham's public work. (It had implications for her work after the Second World War because her fluent German, coupled with her belief in education for citizenship, meant that she was an obvious candidate for the Foreign Office to send over to Germany to lecture to women on the subject of citizenship). Living in Germany stimulated her interest in foreign affairs. In 1921 she published *A woman's watch on the Rhine* which was based on her own experiences.[48]

Sir Arthur Salter, who had overseen her work on the CCWE during the war, was now living in Paris as Secretary-General of the Reparations Commission and it was as a result of discussions with him that Markham put a good deal of faith in the League of Nations, although she remained sceptical about international junkets. Markham frequently lectured on the League of Nations and kept up her travels around the world. In 1923, at the instigation of Mackenzie King, she was to represent Canada at a meeting of the International Labour Organisation.

Back in Britain, Markham resumed her local government work, became vice-chair of the education committee and from 1927 to 1928 was Mayor of Chesterfield. In 1925 she wrote 'I am enjoying my municipal work & feel it really worth while. After the futility of political life in recent years I feel the dustbin splendidly concrete. However small the scale *something* happens.'[49] Markham is best remembered from these years for chairing the CCWTE and then for her work on the UAB. She showed a concern, typical of many Liberals, for the plight of the unemployed.

Whereas the First World War had presented Markham with her first entrée into central government work, by the Second World War, Markham was an old hand. She continued her public work in areas of long-standing interest, as well as taking on new projects, such as running a make-shift canteen and sitting on the Government's 18b Advisory Committee which decided the fate of aliens and fascists. Her work on the UAB continued as did her exasperation with civil servants. Although the CCWTE folded early in the war her concern over the domestic servant problem continued at both a personal and a formal level. As in the First World War, she investigated the morals of women in the Forces, and again dismissed double-standard scaremongering in what became a famous comment at the time 'virtue has no gossip value'. She no longer expressed the same faith in men that she had had in her younger days. Her old animosity towards the French was given

---

[48] She also published a book on twelfth century French architecture and a biography of her grandfather.

[49] VM to Joyce Newton Thompson, 15 July 1925, UCT BC 643 B 18. 31.

a new lease of life in the war and, along with many of her compatriots, she displayed a sudden enthusiasm for the Soviet Union. Her attitude towards the Germans was ambivalent. After the war Markham's involvement with Germans was revived as she spent a brief period in Germany talking to German women about the importance of their becoming active citizens. Her interest in foreign affairs continued at a time when many of her friends and acquaintances were looking to a new world order.

Education for better citizenship always remained high on Markham's agenda, perhaps because it was the first point at which her personal fulfilment and an external activity met in perfect harmony: it was a marriage made in heaven. For Markham, education was as important for herself as it was for those at whom she directed her energies. When Markham first started School Board work she herself began a course of reading on education. When converted to votes for women during the First World War she would have liked enfranchisement to have been based on a test of citizenship. She argued that the rights of citizenship should rest on education not race. She condemned the 'indiscriminate' handing out of votes and political privileges to a race 'unfitted to use them'.[50] Educated citizens, so Markham claimed, would not tolerate social evils, such as drink and vice, overcrowding, and poor industrial conditions.[51] When she stood for election in Chesterfield she told the electors 'I look on education as the master key to good citizenship.'[52] She aimed at bridging the gulf between the complexity of political problems on the one hand and the knowledge and experience of the average elector on the other. In 1930 she suggested to a small group of friends meeting at her home in London that if they looked at the concrete problem of how citizenship could be stimulated among large groups, such as people living on the new housing estates, some general principles might emerge.[53]

One of her last public activities was to go out to Germany to talk to German women during the British Occupation, precisely on this subject of education for active citizenship. Her principles travelled well, across countries and two world wars. Before the First World War she argued in *The South African Scene* for better educational opportunities for the Black population of South Africa. In 1953, when reflecting on the South African situation, she commented that 'civilisation' rather than race should form the basis of citizenship. Civilisation was achieved through education. Her public attempts to promote citizenship, as reflected in her writings, produced

[50] Violet Markham, *The South African Scene*, p 269. This comment referred to Black people, not Whites.
[51] 13/1 notes for a lecture to a Liberal summer school in the 1920s.
[52] VM's election address in UCT collection.
[53] Keith Middlemas (ed), *Thomas Jones: Whitehall diary vol 1 1916–25* (Oxford University Press, London, 1969), VM to TJ, 13 February 1930.

almost perfect symmetry; they opened and closed her public life.

Markham personified the auto-didact, conscious of the links between her own reading and thinking and her public activities, and she advocated such an education for others. Here we see personal conviction having implications both for her own role in women's issues, and for the role she believed other women should play in society. Markham's personal frustrations led her into public work which aimed at improving the supposed shortcomings of other's lives. Her talk of a sense of duty in the home spilled over to talk of public duty, both for herself and for the working classes. She advocated paid work for women as a compensation for the husband shortage. Yet, at the same time, Markham recognised that work was not necessarily a consolation prize for those who lost out in the marriage stakes. After all, her public work actually snowballed after her marriage. Neither marriage in 1915 nor widowhood in 1936 impinged on Markham's public activities. In 1915, soon after her marriage, she wrote 'where a man is big enough & forebearing enough to let a woman have plenty of elbow room as regards her own work & opinions the adjustments are not difficult at all.'[54] Markham was irritated by women who held public positions as a result of their husband's status. In 1920, when the appointment of women JPs was being discussed, Markham hoped to 'avoid getting the list too aristocratic. I get dreadfully bored with the type of woman who "presides" just because she is her husband's wife'.[55]

A maverick Liberal

While Markham's personal experiences shaped her public outlook and her commitment to liberalism, her connections with Liberal party politics were not as straightforward as might be assumed at first glance. Markham was a lifelong Liberal. Born and bred in a political hothouse, as already mentioned, she campaigned publicly for her brother, Arthur, a Liberal MP, and after his death she stood in his constituency as the Liberal candidate (without the coupon) in the 1918 General Election. Markham discussed a range of Liberal policy issues with Liberal women, such as Elizabeth Haldane and Hilda Runciman. She wrote and spoke for the Liberal cause and, despite private waverings and uncertainties, she remained committed to the party throughout her life.

But Markham was no party clone. She never fitted neatly into the mould of a Liberal party woman. Nineteenth-century Liberal women based their arguments for women's involvement in the rough and tumble of political life on moral and religious grounds. Like so many other politically active women around the Western world at this time, they believed that women

---

[54] VM to Duncan 18 March 1915 UCT BC 294. D7. 1. 10.
[55] VM to Elizabeth Haldane, 29 March 1920, NLS 6028 ff 84.

had a distinct role to play in raising the moral tone of national politics. Before the First World War they focused on the great women's issues of the day, such as divorce law reform; women's treatment under the National Insurance Bill; labour, maternity and educational legislation, and votes for women.[56] Here, as an anti-suffragist, Markham parted company from the bulk of Liberal women. Liberal women worked with suffrage societies, the National Union of Women Workers, the Women's Cooperative Guild and the Women's Local Government Society. Apart from the last of these, Markham gave such organisations a wide berth. She showed little interest in issues explicitly pertaining to women, except educational ones, and initially she had little sympathy for organised Christianity. While actively involved in the politics of the parish pump, Markham was fascinated by foreign and imperial affairs. She read widely, travelled abroad extensively and formed her own opinions on foreign issues. Yet, as an anti-suffragist, she wished to deny women any formal influence over these issues.

After the First World War Markham was probably swimming more with the ebbing tide of her party than before the war, when her anti-suffrage activities and imperialism had brought her into close contact with many Conservatives. During her 1918 General Election campaign she displayed a commitment to long-standing Liberal principles in the policies she advocated: free trade, the repeal of the Military Service Acts, social reforms, especially those connected with education, a national minimum wage, the extension of Trade Boards, graduated taxation and the ideal of the League of Nations. She pledged support for ex-servicemen and the claims of labour, and listed specific policies for women, such as equal pay for equal work, better training for women, and the continuation of women in paid work.[57] Markham was offering the electors a typical hustings à la carte menu, with tit-bits to appeal to a wide range of palates, but those policies relating to women did reflect the areas she had become closely involved with during the war, and which were to continue to occupy her for many years.

The activities of Liberal women in the inter-war years have received less attention than those of Labour or Conservative women so it is important to establish the context and points of reference for an active Liberal woman, such as Markham.[58] After the First World War, Liberal women were constantly restating the relevance of liberalism for women; Liberal party policies

---

[56] Linda Walker 'Party political women: A comparative study of Liberal women and the Primrose League, 1890–1914', in Jane Rendall (ed), *Equal or Different: Women's politics, 1800–1914* (Blackwell, Oxford, 1987), pp 176–190.

[57] *Mansfield Chronicle*, 21 November 1918.

[58] For Conservatives see Beatrix Campbell, *The iron ladies: Why women vote Tory* (Virago, London, 1987); for Labour women see Pat Thane, 'The women of the British Labour party and feminism' in Harold Smith (ed), *Twentieth century feminism in Britain* (Edward Elgar, Aldershot, 1990), pp 124-143.

were seen as having a positive effect on every aspect of all women's lives. There was, however, another aspect to the agenda which meant that women active in the Liberal party were primarily pressing for middle, rather than working, class women's interests.

Campaigning for women's interests, as perceived by Liberal women, was integral to their attempts to halt the decline of the Liberal party; women's interests were explicitly put forward. The aims of the Women's National Liberal Federation, as amended in 1920, were first, to promote Liberal principles in government; second, to promote 'just' legislation for women, to remove their legal disabilities and to protect the interests of children; third, to advance political education; fourth to promote women's Liberal Associations and finally, to bring into union all women's Liberal Associations.[59] 'Just' legislation included housing legislation because women were the ones most closely confronted with the problems of overcrowding and unsuitable homes. In 1923 it was argued that free trade was particularly important to women because under a protectionist system housekeeping money would not go as far. Foreign policy was viewed as directly touching the lives of women because it could affect levels of taxation as well as food prices.[60] Changes in rural life were seen as being of especial importance. Liberal women wanted an extension of agricultural education to women and for women workers on the land to be better paid.[61] It was thought that women should have the opportunity to become small-holders of land. In the winter of 1930 it was argued that the nation needed a contented rural population and good home-produced food; this would never be achieved unless women had the opportunity, through training, to become efficient partners in building up agricultural life.[62]

What was not always made explicit was the way in which policies put forward as being in all women's interests were primarily in the interests of middle-class women. The *Women's Liberal Magazine* was quite clearly aimed at such sections of society, with advertisements for maids' uniforms and holidays on the continent. Some of their policies did, of course, largely affect working-class women, such as the 1924 demand for pensions for widows with dependent children so that they were not condemned to the Poor Law with its inadequate payments and stigma,[63] the demand for industrial councils in a range of trades and industries in order to regulate wages, hours and conditions of labour,[64] and public works' schemes to re-

---

[59] *Women's Liberal Magazine*, 20 October 1920.
[60] *Women's Liberal Magazine*, July 1923.
[61] *Women's Liberal Magazine*, June 1925.
[62] *Women's Liberal News*, December 1930.
[63] *Women's Liberal Magazine*, January-February 1924.
[64] *Women's Liberal Magazine*, July 1924.

duce unemployment.[65] However, the balance of concerns tilted decidedly towards middle-class women.

Liberal women's advocacy of voluntary sterilisation or segregation for those dubbed 'mentally deficient' or 'defective' by Liberal women was a blatantly classist policy because those most likely to be so labelled were working, not middle, class.[66] This is one important example of the way in which Liberal women's views fitted in with the dominant ideas in society, and militated against working-class women. The view of good health which received 'official' support and which was reflected in the nature of the health services, emphasised the importance of an individual's, especially women's, behaviour and lifestyles. We will see later how Markham's views of working-class girls and women vacillated between, on the one hand, being highly judgemental and on the other, being critical of the assumption that individuals were responsible for their poverty and unemployment.

One of the most explicit promotions of middle-class women's interests by Liberal women, and a subject especially close to Markham's heart, was that of domestic service. Strong arguments were put in favour of regulating domestic service, not first and foremost to relieve the unpleasant working conditions of many working-class girls, but rather to make domestic service more attractive and so solve what was thought to be a major problem for middle-class women, a domestic labour shortage.[67]

Other non-party women's organisations, such as the Open Door Council, whose philosophy was close to that of the Liberal party, also fought ostensibly for all women's interests but in practice for those of middle-class women. Such organisations opposed protective legislation for women because it hindered the job opportunities of middle-class women. A 'fair field and no favour' was also carried over into arguments against protective legislation for working-class women's jobs, but there is little evidence of support from working-class women for such a policy. Although these organisations campaigned for equal treatment for men and women under national insurance and national health insurance, they threw most of their energies behind campaigns against the dismissal of teachers on marriage, the exclusion of women from certain medical schools, and against single women being given pensions from the age of 53 because this would have adversely affected women's chances of obtaining responsible positions.

After the First World War Markham did toy with the idea of joining the Labour party, although after the Second World War when she was unceremoniously demobbed from her work on the Assistance Board, she took great

---

[65] *Women's Liberal News*, March 1933.
[66] *Women's Liberal Magazine*, July 1924; *Women's Liberal News*, March and May 1932.
[67] *Women's Liberal News*, June 1930.

umbrage at the Labour government, and certainly would not have joined its party. In her youth and old age she was in many respects closer to the Conservatives than Liberals, and despaired at the quality of Liberal politicians. Why, then, did Markham never actually abandon the party but remain wedded to liberalism as a creed? She never needed to join a party which had a chance of being elected to government because her political career and influence were independent of the fortunes of any political party. Her principles never had to be compromised by democracy. She only briefly flirted with the idea of a parliamentary career in 1918; she never had much faith in the electorate, and she disparaged the machinations of Whitehall.

Resolving the demands of both class and gender interests was viewed as unproblematic by those women who put their middle-class interests first. Tensions only existed when this did not happen. It was far more difficult to put working-class, and gender, interests first. This not only caused tensions within the Labour party but also a split within the women's movement. Ironically, the split is also testimony to the vitality and varied activities of politically active women. The divisions between women remained unresolved, and the experience of war and the welfare state settlement did nothing to alter this fact, but it was largely ignored until the feminist critiques of the late 1960s and early 1970s. As in the early post-First World War years, the re-emergence of high profile feminist campaigning in the late 1960s and early 1970s was to lead to splits, not only on class but also on ethnic lines; such divisions can be as much a sign of the vitality of politically active women as of their weakness.

A liberal feminist?

Debating and corresponding with well-informed (and often politically active) friends from wide-ranging perspectives and age-groups, her family's influences and her own personal experiences all combined together to produce rich soil for the growth and development of Markham's views.

A simple definition of classical liberalism would emphasise that a person's status in life should be determined by *his* own individual ability and skills. Towards the end of the eighteenth century liberalism was refined to include the other half of the human race with Mary Wollstonecraft arguing that society should judge women by the same yardsticks as it applied to men.[68] Markham's Edwardian views would have gone only so far as a pre-Wollstonecraft mark-one version of liberalism; she did not accept that women were equal to men in ability or skills. It was the experience of the First World War which brought her views up to the turn of the eighteenth century. (The experience of working with men actually seems to

---

[68] Mary Wollstonecraft, *A vindication of the rights of women* (Penguin, Harmondsworth, 1985, first published in 1798).

have brought her views about turn, so that in her later years one gets the impression that she rarely finds men up to the standard of women!)

In the post First World War years, with Markham agreeing that women should have the vote, she had more in common with liberal feminists than had been the case before the war, and many suffragists and suffragettes were now, like Markham, deeply concerned about international relations and involved with the League of Nations. Historians have labelled inter-war feminists as either 'traditional' or 'liberal' feminists on the one hand and 'new' or 'welfare' feminists on the other. 'Traditional' feminists strove for women to be treated like men in the labour force and campaigned primarily around women's equal rights with men in the 'public' field. They tried to underplay the significance of biological differences between men and women, and opposed protective legislation for women and children in the workplace, arguing for 'a fair field and no favour'. The 'new' feminists, in contrast, emphasised the differing experiences of men and women, precisely because of their biological differences. They focused on women's role in the 'private' sphere and their needs as wives and mothers.[69]

Markham does not fit neatly into any of the feminist categories. She believed that biological differences were important, but she also campaigned for changes in women's employment opportunities. After the First World War she abandoned her anti-suffrage position, and like many suffragists and suffragettes she was deeply committed to international peace and put her faith in the League of Nations. Like liberal feminists, she pressed the state to facilitate changes in the public sphere and worked for women to have equal rights with men in public life. Whereas welfare feminists, such as Eleanor Rathbone, campaigned for the state to intervene to support (mainly working-class) women in their role as wives and mothers, Markham showed no interest in supporting working-class women in the private sphere by, for instance, campaigning for family allowances, or for birth control information to be made available to them.[70] Historians have given far more attention to those feminists who fit roughly into a welfare feminist category. One important contribution of Markham's papers is to draw our attention to an equally potent influence, that of liberal thought, on women's actions during this period.

Markham herself always drew a clear distinction between her own two worlds and never let her marital status impinge on her public activities: one

---

[69] See Olive Banks, *Faces of feminism: a study of feminism as a social movement* (Blackwell, Oxford, 1986), pp 163–179; Jane Lewis 'In search of real equality: Women between the wars' in Frank Gloversmith (ed), *Class, culture and social change: A new view of the 1930s* (Harvester, Brighton, 1980) pp 208–239.

[70] VM to Joyce Newton Thompson, 15 July 1925, UCT BC 643 B 18.31; Eleanor Rathbone ((1872–1946), Independent MP for the Combined English Universities 1926–1946, involved with social work and leading campaigner for family allowances.

should note the symbolic retention of her maiden name for public work and the adoption of her married name in private. She did recognise, however, the influence of the private sphere on women's experiences in the public world. It was for this reason that she took a consistent interest in the 'problem' of domestic service, because she wanted to free middle-class women from the burden of domestic chores. To a large extent she viewed working-class women as a tool for the emancipation of middle-class women. Despite many years of public work in the field of working-class women's concerns, Markham's personal and class interests outweighed her gender interests throughout her life. For this reason it would be difficult to place her firmly in any of the feminist camps.

Some feminists would have been horrified at the thought of being tarred with the same brush as Markham. Although Eleanor Rathbone, a fellow Liberal, showed amazing generosity of spirit in campaigning for Markham in the 1918 General Election soon after Markham had given up her anti-suffragist views, other feminists never changed their minds about her. In 1954 Sylvia Pankhurst wrote 'Is it not possible to protest against the broadcasting, if not also the honouring by a seat on royal commissions, of that foul traitor — who, while suffragettes were hunger striking, appeared on the Albert Hall platform, surrounded by reactionaries like Lord Cromer and Lord Curzon, protesting against women having the vote? She has had her reward for her treachery to women. A protest should be made to the BBC by every woman who values her citizenship.'[71]

In her lifestyle Markham displayed many of the characteristics which have been identified with late nineteenth and early twentieth century feminists.[72] First, Markham married relatively late in life and her marriage imposed no restrictions on her public activities. Second, she was widely read, a writer and educationalist. Third, she formed close emotional ties with women (but also men) and she had a close network of friends who bridged her public and private world. Fourth, her own experiences as a woman affected her public activities.[73] But, none of this made Markham a feminist. A woman promoting her own interests is not necessarily wearing a feminist badge. How far did Markham promote other women's interests? Before the First World War she campaigned against women gaining the vote, but offered some help to working-class girls in her settlement. Markham advocated new job opportunities for middle-class women and traditional ones for working-class

---

[71] David Mitchell, *The fighting Pankhursts* (Cape, London, 1967), pp 332–33; Sylvia Pankhurst (1882–1960), suffragette and socialist.

[72] Johanna Alberti, *Beyond suffrage: Feminists in war and peace, 1914-28* (Macmillan, London, 1989) and Philippa Levine *Feminist lives in Victorian England: private roles and public commitment* (Blackwell, Oxford, 1990).

[73] Philippa Levine, *Feminist lives in Victorian England* (1990), identifies the above lifestyles with feminists at this time.

women. Moreover, while she continued to believe that biological differences between men and women meant that women and men were ideally suited to separate roles in life, nevertheless she recognised its impracticality and encouraged the employment of women in paid work. But, one never has the sense that it is her critique of the gendered nature of society which is firing her imagination or dictating her actions. In the 1920s, Markham uses the term 'feminist' in both a positive and a negative sense. We are not left with a single picture of Markham, so much as a series of silhouettes. This reflects both Markham's personality and the impression emerging from her edited papers.

Editorial explanation

Markham was involved in a host of activities over a long period and she received letters on a wide range of subjects. An attempt has been made to impose some degree of coherence and unity on this edition of her papers by focusing on Britain. Comments about other countries have only been included if they contribute to our understanding of Markham's general outlook. Where material is tediously repetitive, only a few comments have been extracted. So, her repeated criticisms of the French and sudden praise for the wonders of the Soviet Union during the Second World War have been severely pruned. Domestic details which do not add to our understanding of either Markham or the politics of the period have been excluded.

Problems of selection inevitably create problems of balance, but there is already imbalance in what Markham chose to write about either in her diary or letters, and in the content of letters she received. Markham only occasionally recorded her thoughts in a diary, hence the only diary extracts included here are from the late 1890s. Two rules guided the selection of material. First, material is included if it relates to social and political attitudes and developments. Second, material is included if it reveals Markham's own attitudes. This means that there is material which was written neither to, nor from, Markham, and occasionally extracts from memoranda have been included. Of course, there is a third and irrational rule running across the other two, that material has been included if I happen to find it interesting.[74] Any pretence at objectivity would be spurious.

There is a further problem of balance between either letting the papers speak for themselves or of providing close analysis of them. This edition of Markham's papers is not intended to be an exercise in butterfly collecting, of merely selecting, labelling and highlighting the exotic. An attempt has been made, therefore, to place the papers in context at the beginning of sections.

Finally, an edition of papers contains all the pitfalls of a biography, such as giving centre stage to an individual who was not necessarily pivotal to

---

[74] On these grounds tittle-tattle about the British royal family has been excluded.

the events discussed, but at least an awareness of the drawbacks can help to overcome them. The justification for this edition must lie not merely in an attempt to right the balance between the endless number of editions of men's papers which have appeared, but in the intrinsic value of seeing the development of one influential and interesting woman's attitudes and in linking these to some of the most momentous events of twentieth-century Britain. Markham's career offers a reminder that influences brought to bear at one period may be the result of attitudes formed in a very different era: a woman who was already an adult when Gladstone was Prime Minister was still active in the public world during the life-time of Attlee's post-Second World War Labour government. This edition of papers is attempting to inject a 'human interest' element into what is often lifeless administrative history; to make the links between women's history and mainstream, traditional history; individual biography and social change; and people's private and public worlds.

1
Home and Away
1896–1913

In 1896, when these diary extracts begin, Markham is 24 years old. She is still living at her parents' home, bored and without occupation. Soon, she will become involved with local government work. Local government was regarded as a sphere of activity particularly suited to the supposed qualities of middle-class women, an extension of their caring and nurturing role in the family. In 1869 the municipal vote had been granted to single, rate-paying women, and over the next three decades women's local government franchise was gradually extended.[1]

2 November 1896   17/3

Mother & I had an argument about the tenants but she had the best of it as secretly I sympathised with what I tried to condemn. In her place I know it would make me quite as wretched to take the money these poor old men and women bring out of a little bag. Mother promptly returns half of it & I am sure I should want to do the same when I think of how much I have & how little they. But of course such behaviour is hopelessly wrong & demoralising. I always find the fact that generosity is much easier than justice a very hard nut to crack....

12 November 1896   17/3

Markham was reading a book on Persia.

How nice to be a man and able to visit these outlandish countries.

---

[1] The best study of women in local government is Patricia Hollis. *Ladies elect: women in English local government, 1865–1914* (Clarendon, Oxford, 1987).

15 November 1896

One of the curates preached well & demanded reform in the sanitary condition of the Town. He remarked — I think truly — that when a man's home is but a filthy hovel he turns naturally to the comfort of the public house....

28 November 1896

....Mother made a good bit today at lunch remarking the modern girl without education is the odious product of the age.... [This week] I have felt bored and désoeuvrée without occupation.

29 November 1896

Markham is trying to write an article on the social and economic conditions of an iron foundry.

It seems rather absurd for me to be dilating gravely on capital & *labour* about which I can understand so little.

24 December 1896

Markham had spent the last four days sending off presents and cards.

Xmas.... Now it's all over and I can rest a little with the consciousness of having tried in my poor imperfect way to make things pleasant for my less fortunate neighbours....

25 December 1896

Mother & I walked to the workhouse and saw the old folks having their dinner. I dread these occasional visits to the Union. The faces of those old men and women haunt me for days; they look like people who have gone out of life & have nothing left to hope for or to fear. They wished me a Merry Xmas & I felt half choked in replying. All the Xmas decorations on the walls seemed such a mockery. Merriment & happiness in the New Year can scarcely be their lot. It was intensely pathetic....

29 December 1896

....We went to the Workhouse entertainment, a dreary mortification of the flesh which is probably very wholesome but is essentially exceedingly depressing. Yet daily I feel more compelled to take some active part in the work of this town. Life up here is pleasant, intellectual & selfish. I ought to be up & doing as a member of the community & help if I can in the public business of the place I live in. Poor Law work would suit me best. I can't be mixed up with Church concerns. I hate the idea of the whole thing & yet I feel duty points that way....

5 January 1897

It's odd how things come about in this world. Only last week I was consulting with Mother as regards taking up some Poor Law Work. Today comes a request from the Ladies' Board that I should join them in their business. I am to have a Chesterfield district and shall be glad to do what's wanted not because I like it but because I think I ought....

7 January 1897

....More & more do I begin to feel drawn [towards charitable work] & certainly the wish to spend a few weeks in the East End & work there with the Charity Organisation is constantly forcing its way into my mind. But of course there would be many difficulties. Still the training would be splendid. Well I must feel my way gently & see how I prosper on the Workhouse Board before tempting more ambitious flights. If I could only get hold of the subject I should like to occupy a place on a School Board but that of course is quite in the future....

16 January 1897

Markham is despairing of her attempts to write a novel.

A quiet day's work marked by a determination I made to become a Guardian at the first opportunity. Philanthropy will perhaps find an outlet for efforts which seem wasted at present on literature. I should feel more contented to have some object in life which bore tangible fruit & was of use to someone. And these poor people begin to attract me. One feels the infinite pity & pathos of their lives.

2 February 1897 17/3

I attended the first meeting of the Ladies Committee. I thought the proceedings vacuous to a point which was really comical. These good ladies are no doubt excellent for visiting purposes but I imagine their meetings might be held but once a quarter with no loss to anyone. They talked for 20 minutes about an extra arm chair in the ward & then put it solemnly on the minutes & dissolved.

4 February 1897 17/3

.... The House of Commons passed the Second Reading of the Women's Franchise Bill last night. The Times slates them properly for a flippant unworthy discussion on the subject.

11 February 1897 17/3

I had a great afternoon's inspection of the Workhouse with Mrs Edmunds who took me round. It was very interesting if depressing but I was struck by the utter absence of moral sense among the paupers. They were all of the lowest type & the girls with illegitimate babies seemed to have no idea of shame in connection with their trouble. Without moral sense there seems to be nothing to take hold of with these people.

24 February 1897 17/3

.... Well last night the Chesterfield School Board made me a Manager.... It will give me occupation and some interest in the Town and I hope I shall be able to do the work properly....

25 February 1897 17/3

My introduction to School Board duties has not been long delayed. Dr Booth took me round the Durrant Board New Brampton & St Helen's Street Schools today. It was really most interesting & the children were much pleasanter in appearance than I expected. The teachers were all affable & seemed glad to have a woman on the Board. Of course we had not time to stay long at any place. Our visit was but a preliminary skirmish but I found two small matters all the same which I was able to see after.

1 March 1897   17/3

....I careered round Industrial Schools & the Brampton Board Schools & attended to small matters there. I suppose it's one of the small ironies of late that a person who prates as loudly as I do about Imperialism should be thus occupied by the politics of the Parish Pump....

2 March 1897   17/3

....I went to the Ladies Meeting at the Union. The proceedings were vacuous as usual but after our deliberations we decided to send some washing out....

3 March 1897   17/3

I did a round of inspection at the Workhouse. It is curious how much less distasteful the work becomes as one goes on.

7 March 1897   17/3

There had been a spate of illness, and Markham was worried about her mother's health.

....I am getting sick of doing my duty even in the indifferent perfunctory way I perform that office. I am beginning to inwardly clamour for a rest from all the bother & worry of the last six weeks.

26 April 1897   17/3

I visited the Workhouse & its dreary inmates....

3 May 1897   17/3

An utterly vacuous day. My existence of late seems passed in doing nothing....

4 May 1897   17/3

I went to the Ladies Meeting today. We actually passed a resolution about a stove & after such a glut of work we shall require a month's rest I suppose. I drove to the Industrial Schools in the afternoon....

5 May 1897

Markham spent the afternoon in Board schools

....much struck by their efficiency. The children seem happy & orderly....This school work begins to interest me much. I think the teachers like a lady manager as they talk to me more easily than to the men....

24 May 1897

I visited the Brampton Board Schools....I heard complaints of the half timers. They do their work unsatisfactorily being tired & gain undesirable habits of language and manner in the factories....

1 June 1897

....There is certainly a terrible monotony about life here which only reading & study can render endurable....

17 July 1897

Markham entertained the school board teachers to tea with a band, dancing and croquet.

....it gives me infinitely more pleasure to entertain these sort of people than one's own class....I always feel more pity for the dreariness of the lower middle orders than for the harder struggles of the working man....

3 October 1897

Markham's 25th birthday

....I am ever haunted by the thought am I making the best of life now it is at its height, & conscience answers no. There is a terrible aimlessness & lack of purpose about my existence....

7 October 1897

....It seems so absurd candidates for the School Board should come forward with a religious instead of an educational programme. Surely what we should seek is the moral development & training of the children, not the victory of any particular sect or creed....What one wants in the Schools is the moral training of the Bible intelligently taught & illustrated....

18 October 1897   17/4

....I visited Brampton School and was shocked to find how many hours work the half time children do. I noticed some of them looking pale & washed out & no wonder! Up at six am, at the pill box factory from 6.30 to 8.30; then breakfast & back to the factory from 9 a.m. till 12.30 p.m. In the afternoon they have to come to school from 1.30 p.m. to 4 p.m. (N.B. The Factory & School work alternates morning & afternoon each week). For this amount of labour they receive the splendid wages of 1/6 per week. Some of the children after school hours actually return to work from 4 to 6 p.m. & by this they gain another 6d per week. It seems terrible to think of little girls between the ages of 11 & 13 engaged in such business. What constitution or physique can they be expected to have with such a strain made upon them at such an age. More than ever am I convinced in regard to this school work that the evils of the present day do not arise from too much education but too little. The most stupendous amount of nonsense is talked with regard to Board Schools by people who have never seen the inside of a classroom. How often am I told the impudence the independence the flightiness of servants arise from their Board School training! I thought so at one time myself but now I see differently. On the contrary it is the Schools which keep some sort of restraint over the children which knock into them some ideas of duty, obedience & self restraint. The trouble arises from the fact that they are released too young from the School influence & left at the age of 13 or 14 to run about wild in the streets & unlearn every lesson they have been taught. As for the impudence it arises I feel sure from the spirit of the times, from the cheap literature, political independence & above all the easy means of communications, cheap trips etc which have filled a class with unrest and new ideas impossible fifty years since. To blame education for the social revolt of the lower orders is absurd. The educational influence of the Board Schools has been a restraining and a civilising one. And what home influences have the teachers not to struggle against.

24 October 1897   17/4

Arthur Charlie[2] and I had a long discussion over the strike and the tyranny of the Trades Unions....

2 November 1897   17/4

Workhouse committee meeting. We discussed the propriety of pauper children having bread & jam & butter all at once, but felt such an important

---

[2] Her brothers

matter altogether too weighty for us to take in hand. These meetings are fatuous & no mistake.

11 January 1898

Markham stood for election to the Chesterfield School Board.

....saw the printing of my electioneering literature....

Markham argued that primary education should fit children so
that they may worthily sustain their rights and dignities as English citizens.

24 January 1898

The day of Markham's election

....the whole business has disgusted me. If this is the public opinion on which we rely so much may it not be of all opinions the least reliable and the least thoughtful! Liberal though I am, there are times when the ignorance, the apathy, the utter lack of discrimination in the class to whom we have handed over the governing power fill me with despair. There is of course only one remedy that is education & plenty of it. And by education I don't mean only mere reading & writing but the developing of a sense of responsibility & the knowledge of the practical duties which devolve from the possession of the franchise. I was delighted with Jock [a dog] who with a fine hatred of the proletariat growled at the mob and worried the heels of every voter who came within reach.

26 January 1898

Markham was holding the balance between four churchmen and four dissenters; there was a problem over who should be chairman.

Really I do think it humiliating for my masculine colleagues to feel they are at the mercy of one girl....

1 February 1898

....What folly it is for women to engage in public life. One of two evils must overtake them. Either they become more or less unsexed & callous in their dealings with men, or else they remain women & at the same time do their work properly but with a mental wear & tear in the latter case which is a tremendous strain on their endurance. Certain women can do men's work perhaps but *always* with double the fatigue double the exertion both mental & physical....

3 February 1898   17/4

Markham gave a dinner party for her executive committee and canvassers.

.... It's infinitely more pleasure to entertain these simple big children who are so genuinely delighted by their out[ing] than one's own blasé friends.

9 February 1898   17/4

Markham travelled up to London with Lady Pender, whom she found clever

but like all clever women she has fads[3].... I was delighted to find her opposed to this absurd Woman's Suffrage Bill & we both agreed it would be fatal to the best interests of the country if such a measure ever became law....

9 April 1898   17/4

Markham was now sitting on seven committees.

.... all this local work which takes up my time so much is it of use to anyone? I doubt it greatly.

13 May 1898   17/4

Markham, on holiday in Belgium, was reading Gustave Flaubert's Madame Bovary.

.... One remark struck me as very true 'La femme riche semble avoir autour d'elle pour garder sa vertu tous ses billets de banque comme une cuirasse dans la doublure de son corsage'.

---

[3] She was a vegetarian and anti-vivisectionist

22 June 1898   17/4

Markham was visiting schools.

....I was shocked at some of the Departmental returns I saw as to the employment of children after hours. One little girl of 8 who goes nursing 2½ hours each day & 12 hours on Saturday receives the magnificent pay of three half pence a week. It is perfectly disgraceful such things can be.

9 July 1898   17/4

I had a long afternoon at the Workhouse. Truly it is a depressing place, not so much for the sadness & sorrow it contains but for the utter lack of moral sense which marks its inmates....

14 July 1898   17/4

Markham had been to see La Dame aux Camelias *by Dumas at the theatre in Sheffield*

....I know Dumas is reproached for exciting so much sympathy for a class beyond the ban of society but surely if any class needs pity that is the one & if he shows that such women may be good & noble at heart is it not true that this could often be the case?

9 May 1899   17/5

Arthur and Charlie came to see Markham and her mother off before they left for South Africa, a trip which it was hoped would improve a period of poor health for Markham.

....How they smoothed over that horrible parting moment I shall never forget. But these men are so much cleverer & more capable than women & can do things we poor creatures never can. I never realised more fully than I did today the heights of masculine superiority when the men are kind & good!

After her return from South Africa Markham began lecturing on the 'South African native question' and publishing on South African affairs.

25 January 1901   RGS
VM to Sir David Gill

I have lost my seat on the School Board. It's a long story, but briefly the Board egged on by me had made bye laws keeping the children at school as long as possible. Two employers of labour who own respectively a pottery & a card board box factory where they sweat children for 1/6 a week wages raised a cry that we were 'depriving parents of their children's earnings'. The cry caught on. It has resulted in the complete overthrow of the old 'Progressive' Board; I adorned the bottom of the poll & a majority of new members have been elected pledged to undo all our work. Three if not four out of these six men are utterly illiterate, two can, without exaggeration barely sign their names. On personal grounds I care little or nothing about my defeat, but on public grounds I care a good deal. It's very discouraging & disheartening to feeel one's work lasting over four years is as good as ruined & that interests one has so much at heart handed over to the tender mercies of an ignorant reactionary body....

11 February 1901   RGS
VM to Sir David Gill

I can honestly say that it is S. Africa alone which has ever made me long for the influence which comes from place & power ....

In 1901 Markham was left some money by a friend of her father's. With some of the money she started a Settlement and a girls' club in Chesterfield. She was also much preoccupied at this time with the situation in South Africa.

8 March 1901   RGS
VM to Sir David Gill

Markham would like the Daughters of the Empire Guild linked to emigration schemes, so that it might provide a service for women moving between countries such as Canada, Australia and UK.

This would be a practical exhibition of sympathy between the women of the Empire.

8 August 1902   RGS
VM to Sir David Gill

.... here in Chesterfield I am very busy trying to start a Settlement & Girls' Club in a low part of the town where civilising influences are few & far between.

11 December 1902   RGS

VM to Sir David Gill

....I have been going around factories & potteries of late & am appalled at the conditions under which people labour. How any decency or self respect can survive such degrading surroundings is I think wonderful ....There is much that is profoundly saddening in our social system today with our two extremes of extreme wealth & extreme poverty; *both* so degrading & demoralising to the people concerned. I should like to preach a crusade for greater simplicity of life & better spirit of work & a more universal charity & sympathy between & among our classes....

16 January 1903   RGS

VM to Sir David Gill

....the Club is doing very well & I find real happiness in the work....the girls seem happy & I think are fond of the Club. You will be impressed to hear I am going to discourse to them one night soon on ASTRONOMY! & am laying in oranges & knitting needles by way of scientific equipment. I take them for these 'talks' in the reading room & they seem to like them. One wants to make them realise something of the great world, historical & natural which lies beyond the dire limitations of their lot.

3 December 1903   RGS

VM to Sir David Gill

I am digging up various people in London & impressing on them that we can't afford to relax any vigilance in S. Africa.

During the early years of the century Markham worked closely with her brother Arthur, a local Liberal MP. She was a Liberal Imperialist and social reformer. Markham was now spending more time in London and had converted to Christianity under the influence of the liberal theologian, Canon Hensley Henson, Rector of St. Margaret's Westminster. Her anti-suffrage sentiments can be gleaned from her diary entries but, now in 1908, she starts to campaign publicly for the cause.

Two major developments in women's political rights took place in the late nineteenth century: women organised a campaign for the parliamentary vote and certain women were gradually granted the vote in local elections. In 1866 the first organised suffrage committee was founded. Organised opposition to the suffrage campaign began in 1889 when Mary (Humphry)[4] Ward

---

[4] Mary Ward (1851–1920), novelist and social reformer. She liked to be known by

drafted, with the help of Louise Creighton, a *Protest Against Women's Suffrage*, signed by a number of prominent individuals in response to a private member's Bill to establish the parliamentary vote for women. In 1908, in response to the Liberal Prime Minister, Herbert Asquith's, undertaking that if an amendment extending the franchise to women was moved in the proposed reform Bill, the government would not oppose the amendment, Mary Ward formed the Women's National Anti-Suffrage League (WNASL), usually shortened to ASL and later known as the National League for Opposing Women's Suffrage (NLOWS). It survived until 1918 when some women were granted the vote. It was women's right to vote in parliamentary elections, not women's participation in local elections, against which anti-suffragists campaigned; the latter was positively welcomed by some anti-suffragists, who wanted a positive or 'forward' policy, but it was opposed by some of the anti-suffragist men (from 1910 in control of the organisation), who wanted to fight purely against women's right to vote in parliamentary elections. Divisions plagued the anti-suffragists, and the position of strong-minded anti-suffragist women, such as Markham and Mrs Humphry Ward, became increasingly untenable as they bowed to the opinions of the men.

Markham was one of the most prominent anti-suffragists, not because of her social position, but because she was one of their few effective public speakers. The climax of the campaign, both for Markham, and the whole movement, came in 1912 when she addressed an anti-suffrage rally in the Albert Hall. Soon after, she left the country and returned only shortly before the outbreak of the First World War. It was the experience of war which was to change her views, as well as those of a number of other anti-suffragists, on women's right to vote in parliamentary elections. Many years later Markham was to reflect on the reasons why she had opposed votes for women: the influence of her mother, who was strongly opposed to votes for women; female suffrage implied adult suffrage and this would double the number of inexperienced and ignorant voters (although in fact many suffragists only asked for women to be given the vote on the same terms as men, so maintaining the class bias); women made little use of the municipal vote; the claims suffragists made for the impact of the vote were exaggerated and although Markham had doubts about her stance because of the reactionaries involved in the anti-suffrage campaign, they were nevertheless 'so charming and so intelligent'.[5] Markham's most public activity before the war was her anti-suffragist campaigning, but she continued to show an interest in local affairs and especially the education of girls.

---

her husband's name, Humphry. Like Markham she was a great believer in education for the working classes. See too the letter her daughter wrote to Markham on 29 June 1947.

[5] Violet Markham, *Return passage*, pp 95, 97.

19 March 1908
Adeline Cashmore to VM

Cashmore is writing to Markham about the continuation schools with which she is involved.

There is no subject that our girls like so much as Hygiene.... The care and management of Infants also comes into hygiene & is exceedingly popular & quite the most useful thing that can be taught to a class of girls who are growing up & who never lose time about having an infant to manage or mismanage. I don't find either that the girls giggle or get silly over it if they are at all properly managed.

To leave hygiene I suppose cookery is the other most important thing to teach.... Laundry is a good subject to teach if it is not taught in the Elementary Schools. Dressmaking is generally liked but not really one of the most essential things. [But, night schools were often a failure she thought because] the home is too often in the background instead of the foreground....

10 March 1909
Lord Cromer to VM

....I should like to explain to you rather more fully the limits of my argument. My case is that when the Suffragists ask for votes in order, *inter alia* that they may acquire for women the full right to work as hard as they please and as long as they please, under the same conditions as men, they are demanding something which is not in the true interests of women, of children, or of the race in general....

Lady Chance, however, has really shifted the issue. I think I can state what she really means perhaps rather better than she has stated it herself. She assumes, without doubt rightly, that there are a number of poverty-stricken women, many of whom are mothers. She then maintains that it does more harm, both to the mothers and to the children, whether born or unborn, that the women should be half-starved than it does to allow them to work to the neglect of their own health, and to the risk of the lives of their children, and thus gain a sufficient amount of money to enable both them and the children to be properly nourished. As an argument in favour of votes for women this is, of course, quite valueless, but, on the other hand, naturally every reasonable person will concede that it shows a state of things which is, to say the least, deplorable. We then, however, entirely get off the votes for women question and come on the general ground of how to deal with the poor, which is one amongst the numerous and vitally important social problems presented for solution to the present generation.

Neither I, nor, I presume, anyone else is prepared to come forward with a cut and dried plan for dealing with this matter; one can only fall back upon generalities, and express in general terms sympathy with the cause which Lady Chance wants to plead, however unskilfully she has pleaded it, and profess readiness to consider any reasonable proposals for amelioration. Only I repeat that the evidence that we have as yet of the wishes of the Suffragists so far from inducing the belief that the granting of Parliamentary votes to women would solve these social difficulties, points in a diametrically opposite direction, whilst it is certain that in dealing with other matters which are not, strictly speaking, of a social character, the granting of the vote to women would almost certainly produce disastrous results.

23 September 1909? 26/30 Part 1
Lady Jersey[6] to VM

Unfortunately from the very first — in the days of the 'Provisional Law' of the ASL this question of a 'Forward Policy' has been a bone of contention. Mrs Humphry-Ward [President of the ASL] and Mrs Lionel Tennyson — not to mention the present Hon. Sec. Mrs Somervell have been strongly in favour of some such policy as you sense — on the other hand Lady Haversham [member ASL] & Mrs Clarendon Hyde [member ASL] & others have been equal strong against anything of the kind. Between ourselves one main reason which forces me into the Chairmanship — the last thing I desired — was the wish to keep the peace between these views, and to get the thing (A.S.L) started *somehow*. If you will look at Constitution you will see that I (b) *very* vaguely shadows forth some sense of the desirability of an active as against a purely negative policy — this was the most which the 'negatives' would concede. I have refrained from taking sides as being the only method of keeping things going.

Almost a year ago Mrs Humphry Ward tabulated a motion to bring forward 1 (b) in the Committee with a view to action but it was postponed from time to time in favour of more pressing matters and ultimately she let it slide in view of the impossibility of securing any sort of unanimity about it in the Committee.

.... [I] fear that you will find that she is a little disheartened about this 'Forward Policy' being tacked on to anti-suff: much as she wishes it.

[6] Lady Jersey (1849–1945), in 1901 helped found the Victoria League of which she was President for 26 years, chair, Anti-Suffrage League and prominent society hostess.

29 September 1909　　　　　　　　　　　　　　　　　　　　　26/30 Part II
Mary Ward to VM

I entirely agree with you as to a *positive* policy.... for anti-suffragists. But I am afraid I don't think a woman's council of the sort you propose could be worked. It is too big and vague, and I don't myself see that it would have much more authority and effect than the conference of the N[ational] U[nion of] W[omen] W[orkers] or it would be like convocation which only represents a fraction of the possible voting body.... What has always seemed to me to be possible is some representative body arising out of Local Government. If we *could* only push forward the representation of women on County & Borough Councils — if we could get some 300 or 400 women elected throughout England, then these women meeting every three years might choose a permanent Local Gov[ernment] Committee, analogous to the Departmental Committees which play now such a large part in legislation. It might be strengthened by representatives of three or four Government Offices, with which it would be in close touch —the Home Off[ice], the Education Office etc — And I can quite imagine the government of the day being extremely glad to consult such a body on all matters concerning women and children. I can even imagine, a Resolution of the House of Commons, directing that on certain scheduled matters its opinion should be taken — You see it would have an elective basis under the existing law. And the fact of such a Committee's existence would give great additional interest to local elections. The women candidates for Lancashire for instance would be elected with reference to it, & factory questions in particular, & so on —

I have talked this over with a good many politicians who think the idea feasible. Lord Cromer in particular if I remember right was attracted by it.....

11 October 1909　　　　　　　　　　　　　　　　　　　　　　26/30 Part I
St. Loe Strachey[7] to VM

I think your distinction between local government and the central government is a perfectly sound one, and for this reason. County Councils do not make peace or war nor do they legislate, that is, say the supreme word as to how the country is governed. That supreme word spoken by Parliament may involve (1) war with a foreign foe; (2) civil war. Remember the case of the American Civil War. If women vote and sit in the Parliament which speaks this final word they may force men to fight against their will. All men are potential fighters. That is, under the common law the sovereign State may call upon every male citizen to resist invasion or to put down rebellion.... A

---

[7] St. Loe Strachey (1860–1927), Editor and proprietor of the *Spectator* 1891–1925

County Council claims no such sovereignty and is simply an administrative body and therefore as I have said your distinction is perfectly sound.

As to your second point, taxation without representation, I answer by really the same argument. Indeed in this business there is only one argument. Sovereignty has got to rest somewhere in every State. In a modern democratic State like ours it rests with the majority of the male inhabitants. In my opinion, and for the physical force reason, it can rest nowhere else. Taxation without representation to my mind only applies to those who are possessed of a share of the sovereignty. I cannot agree with women trade unionists with votes are in a stronger position than women trade unionists without them, or if they are, it is only because politicians let themselves be blackmailed by the male trade unionists. I am no enemy of trade unions, but look at this fact. There are no trade unions among male or female domestic workers and yet the rise in wages among domestic servants, male and female, has been much greater than in the case of the industrial workers.[8]

As to a representative women's council competent to debate and discuss, I should have probably said yes three years ago. It seems to me however that recent events have shown the extreme danger of women acting together. They seem to suffer from a kind of moral and intellectual contagion of a very dangerous sort. I was having tea with Margot Asquith[9] last Thursday and she gave me a really apalling account of the threats which she has received apparently from quite sane women. They threaten to throw vitriol over her and her husband and what is still worse to kidnap or injure her small children. Just fancy, too, Connie Lytton[10] being arrested for throwing stones at [Walter] Runciman's[11] motor car like any street cad. You probably know her and what a gentle harmless creature she is in normal circumstances. If fifteen years ago when I used to see a good deal of Lady Constance a medium had prophesied that she would ever be in gaol or would throw stones at a motor car I should have said unhesitatingly — 'This shows what bosh spiritualism

---

[8] Wages of domestic servants did rise in the second half of the nineteenth century. It is difficult to calculate the worth of free board, lodgings and uniforms but, in 1909, domestic servants were still relatively badly paid.

[9] Wife of the Prime Minister.

[10] Constance Lytton was a suffragette who felt that she had been treated leniently when arrested because of her social position. The next time she was arrested for her suffragette activities she posed as a working-class woman. She wrote about her experiences: Constance Lytton, *Prisons and prisoners: Some personal experiences* (Heinemann, London, 1914).

[11] Walter Runciman (1870–1949), Liberal MP for Oldham 1899–1900, Dewsbury 1902–1918, Swansea West 1924–1929. St Ives 1929–1931. Liberal Nationalist for St Ives 1931–1937. 1905–1907 Parliamentary Secretary Local Government Board, 1907–1908 Financial Secretary to the Treasury, 1908–1911 President of the Board of Education, 1911–1914 President Board of Agriculture and Fisheries, 1914–1916 and 1931–1937 President Board of Trade, 1938–1939 Lord President of the Council.

is. Whatever else happens that will never happen'. Honestly, instead of a great debating club I would much rather see some organisation by which the administrative departments could establish councils of women whom they could consult, not women elected with exciting elections. Honestly I dread an outbreak of hysteria amounting almost to madness in the case of a large section of women unless we set our minds determinedly to yield nothing to their outcries. I am afraid just now I am all for refusing any concessions whatever....

PS Please don't think from this letter that I am anti-feminist — I am just the reverse. None values the influence of women more than I do or puts women higher as regards the part they play in the State.

2 December 1909 26/30 Part I
St Loe Strachey to VM

....I by no means say that rebellion can never be justified, but I am sure that no well ordered State can afford to justify rebellion and treat it as a normal diet. From the citizen's point of view rebellion against the moral law is sure to lead to terrible suffering among the women. They are the people whom in the main it protects and who have so poor a time if a return is made to primitive savagery. Under Socialism and free love women must and do sink to the level of the squaw or the kaffir's wife. Mankind has slowly and painfully evolved an elaborate system of protection for the women, called the family, and now half the women of the world want to throw it all away. If I were a cynical man and if I wanted to enslave the physically weaker half of the human race I should feel inclined to say to them: 'So be it; It is you who will suffer, not me. What you are really doing is to put yourself at my mercy.'

1 October 1911 25/12
VM to Hilda Cashmore[12]

I too am going to be desperately busy this winter between the Personal Service & the Victoria League. The P.S. is going to try & clear up *one* area of London; as for the VL I have embarked on a forlorn hope of trying to persuade the working man in the North of England that the Empire is a system of governments of great political & economic importance & that it doesn't mean jingoism flag wagging & aggression....I want to get town planning taken up on an inter Dominion scheme; also the care of Infant life and the treatment of consumption.

[12] Established a Settlement at Chesterfield with VM, and worked in others in Bristol and Manchester.

17 December 1911   26/30 Part II

Mary Harcourt[13] to VM

I feel that it would be an excellent thing to have some 'Liberal Anti Suffrage' Meetings as otherwise we are always met with the taunt that 'we are of course working with the forces of reaction'.[14]

12 January 1912   26/30

John ('Jack') Hills[15] Conservative MP, to VM

The Campaign Committee of the Anti-Suffrage League, of which I am Chairman, are extremely anxious that you should address some meetings on the subject. They desire this for many reasons, but more particularly because you are a Liberal and because of your well-known power of speech.

25 January 1912   26/30

John Hills to VM

There was to be a major anti-suffrage rally at the Albert Hall, at which Markham was to speak.

I am told privately that, though there will possibly be interruption of the Cabinet Ministers' speeches, there will be little if any of the other speakers and none of any woman speakers. This sounds quite in accord with the tactics hereto displayed and is probably true.

7 February 1912   26/30 Part II

Mrs Mary Ward to VM

If you support my doings in West-Marylebone, and I think you will, — will you write a little letter to Lord Cromer tonight to say you do so? I am sure it would have great weight with him, and we shall probably have rather an angry discussion when the Executive meets tomorrow.

The facts, as far as I am concerned, are as follows: – In a very full meeting of the L.G.A. Committee the Aims that I enclose were carried and endorsed, with a further addition, which will be found in the Minutes, i.e. that while

---

[13] Wife of Loulou Harcourt (1863–1922) Secretary of State for the Colonies.

[14] In her autobiography Markham commented on doubts which she occasionally experienced about her anti-suffrage views because of their close links with reactionaries: Violet Markham *Return passage* (1953) p 97.

[15] John Hills (1867–1938), Conservative MP for Durham 1906–1922, Ripon 1925–1938. 1922–23 Financial Secretary to the Treasury.

we might support moderate Suffragist candidates by speakers, literature, and canvassing, we might not support any but Anti-Suffragists *with money*.

We have strictly held to this in the case of Dr Jevons,[16] having done nothing but write a letter supporting her, and doing some canvassing through members of the Committee. The real point of dear Lord Cromer's annoyance is that Lord Greville had proclaimed himself an Anti-Suffragist. Lord Greville came to see me, and I understood that he had been in favour of the Conciliation Bill[17] — 'taxation with representation' — but on Lord Cromer's personal letter had consented to go to the Albert Hall. He is not, however, a member of our League, nor is Miss Jevons a member of any Suffrage Society, and her Agent assured my daughter [Dorothy] that she was inclining very much to the Anti-Suffrage side.

At the same time, the Municipal Reformers have behaved extremely badly in the matter of this Marylebone seat. They are perhaps naturally indignant that Miss [Susan] Lawrence[18] should have deserted them as she did on behalf of a Minority Report policy, but they could easily have found a lady who was both a strong Municipal Reformer, and highly qualified for the work of the Council. Directly I saw the vacancy, I telegraphed to Miss Tomes, who is a strong Anti-Suffragist, a Municipal Reformer, a C[harity] O[rganisation] S[ociety] worker, and has been for some years training Care Committee workers under the Council. She went at once to the Municipal Reform Offices, and found that Lord Greville had been adopted. Then we heard of Dr. Jevons, and that Charles Booth strongly supported her. Dorothy went to see the Booths, and I had a telephone conversation with Mrs Booth. They both declared that Miss Jevons was exactly the woman who ought to be on the Council, and gave a most interesting and favourable account of her. Then I hastily summoned a meeting of the L.G.A. Committee, and we got 5 persons, including myself. We decided that we couldn't spend any money in supporting Miss Jevons, as she was not a declared Anti-Suffragist, but that we could issue a letter supporting her, and this, as Chairman, I accordingly did. Lord Greville's Agent has complained strongly to Lord Cromer; I have written a letter to the *Times*, which appears today, and there we are!

Now, personally, I believe (a) that Dr. Jevons won't get in, so that Lord Greville's injury will not be great. But (b) I am pretty certain that if Dr. Jevons makes a good stand, we shall have secured a bargaining position with the Municipal Reformers, and it will be, of course, quite easy to secure it with the Progressives. I have been in correspondence with Mr. Hayes

---

[16] Standing against an anti-suffragist.

[17] Which involved limited women's suffrage.

[18] Susan Lawrence (1871–1947), 1900 Member of London School Board, 1910 Conservative Councillor LCC, soon to convert to socialism. Labour MP for East Ham North 1923–1924 and 1926–1931. 1929–1931 Parliamentary Secretary Ministry of Health. 1930 Chair of Labour Party.

Fisher[19] and have told him that our Local Government Advancement Committee feels itself in possession of the nucleus of a considerable organisation in London, and that we want to make a bargain with both parties — if the thing must be done on party lines, as apparently it must — to secure an equal representation of women; at least 10 women on the Council, and 4 or 5 co-opted women on the Education Committee. Then we might get the work done which is absolutely indispensable. I am, as you know, in very close touch with the L.C.C., through the 20,000 of their school children who are now in our Play Centre, and I can testify strongly to the need for more women, with more time, for the educational work of the Council. Our demonstration in this election will be a token to the Municipal Reformers that we must have more consideration for women on their side. It won't be more than a demonstration, but as such, it will be important.

29/30 part II

AIMS OF THE LOCAL GOVERNMENT ADVANCEMENT COMMITTEE
(1) To spread a knowledge of the duties and opportunities of local government among women, with a view to showing that a large proportion at least of the improvements in our social life, the need for which is so constantly urged by the Suffragists as a ground for claiming the Parliamentary vote, can be obtained by a proper use of the powers women already possess, in and through Local Government.
(2) To distribute literature, and employ speakers to spread the views of the Committee....
(3) To promote the candidatures of women, at municipal and other elections, whether by literature, public meetings, or grants of money in aid of election expenses.

9 February 1912 26/30 part 1

Lord Cromer to VM

.... There are, for the purposes of the present argument, three types of Municipal voters. In the first place, those who very unwillingly accept the idea that women should take part even in Municipal work, and will vote against a woman merely by reason of her sex. I cannot say that I have come across any voters of this type, and I fancy they are very few, but there may be some.

---

[19] William Hayes Fisher (1853–1920), Conservative MP for Fulham 1885–1906, and January 1910–1918. 1902–1903 Financial Secretary to the Treasury, 1915–1917 Parliamentary Secretary to the Local Government Board, 1917–1918 President of the Local Government Board, 1918–1919 Chancellor of the Duchy of Lancaster.

At the other end are the extremists, amongst whom I am afraid I must class Mrs Humphry Ward and yourself — although I do not doubt that you are quite unaware of the fact — who invite the ratepayers to vote for a woman merely on account of her sex, quite irrespective of her opinions on other questions.

Between these two extremes lie the mass of voters, that is to say, people like myself, who would gladly see more women on the Municipal Councils, but who will vote Progressive or Moderate according to their views on these issues, without reference to the question of whether the Candidate who represents their views is a man or a woman. It is really quite hopeless to expect that these voters should give up the whole of their opinions on other subjects merely in order to increase the number of women on the Councils.

You will probably hear from others what happened at the meeting of the Executive Committee yesterday. Briefly I may say that a Resolution was passed debarring the branch which deals with this particular question under Mrs Humphry Ward's Chairmanship from pledging the Association as a body either to support or oppose any special candidate. Further, a Committee is to be appointed to try and patch up some compromise. I feel quite certain that they will not be able to make any satisfactory arrangement, for the same issue is sure to crop up again in some other form. Pray remember what has happened on this point. Lord Curzon,[20] Lord Northcote,[21] myself, and I think every man with any political experience warned the members of our Association that it was impossible to mix up these two questions together, that is to say, the question of resisting the granting of the Parliamentary vote to women, and pushing the employment of women on Municipal Councils. I do not mean to say that there is not a connection between the two subjects. On the contrary, the connection is very distinct, and personally, in common with, I believe, most of the men of our League, I sympathise with the objects which you and Mrs Humphry Ward have in view, but I hold very strongly that it is perfectly impossible to run the two ideas by the same Association. The moment you come to close quarters with a political issue and have to decide which Candidate the Association as a body is to support a difficulty similar to that which has arisen in the case of Lord Greville and Miss Jevons must always arise. There is only one possible solution of this question, and that is that our League should devote itself exclusively to the object for which it was formed, that is to say, to resist the Parliamentary vote for

[20] George Nathaniel Curzon (1859–1925), traveller, Conservative MP for Southport 1886–1898, Viceroy of India 1898–1905. Held various government posts between 1891–1924. Took over presidency of ASL (jointly with Lord Weardale) from Lord Cromer in 1912.

[21] Lord Northcote (1846–1911), 1900–1903 Governor of Bombay, 1903–1908 Governor-General of Australia.

women, and that in respect to the other issue it should either be dealt with by a separate Association, having its own funds and its own management, or else that each individual member should be free to act as he or she thinks fit, without in any way pledging the League as a body.

10 February 1912 26/30 Part I
VM to Lord Cromer

.... Your letter has left me in the frame of mind not uncommon among sinners — that is to say chastened, but I fear at heart impenitent.... I certainly should not support any woman presenting herself as a candidate for Local Government merely on the score of her sex. I should support her purely on the score of her qualifications. My sympathies with Dr Jevons' candidature were due to the fact that I believe she possessed qualifications of a special kind which would have been of great value to the work of the County Council. I might also say that I dissent strongly from the principle and practice of selecting candidates for Local Government on the grounds of their political opinions. A man's or woman's views about Tariff Reform or Home Rule have nothing whatever to do with their capacity for dealing with housing, sanitation, or education. I have had too much practical experience of Local Government not to realise how much of the Municipal life of the country is stultified owing to this very reason. The most impossible people are thrust on to local bodies merely because they are ardent Liberals or ardent Conservatives. I am an ardent, not to say rabid, upholder of the party system in Imperial politics so I am not prejudiced against the party system as such. But I do not think it is a system which works well in Local Government and I am anxious to see it broken up. Generally speaking women who serve in Local Government deal with social facts and are not concerned with the exigencies of the party machine.

Pray forgive this long dissertation, but it seems to me to go to the root of the position which Mrs Ward and myself hold in the matter. We believe in women's work and influence in Local Government and we want to see that work and influence extended. Further we are bound to dissent from the action of the Municipal Reformers in West Marylebone in filling up one of the few women's seats held on the Council by a man. We feel this the more because quite apart from Dr. Jevons it would have been possible for them to have found an excellent candidate in Miss Tomes, a lady who is a strong Municipal Reformer, a strong Anti-Suffragist, and otherwise a highly qualified social worker. I know nothing of Lord Greville so speak of him quite impersonally, but it is difficult to avoid the conclusion that either Dr Jevons or Miss Tomes by virtue of their special knowledge of social work would have made a more valuable contribution to the general work of the Council. All women who are interested in women's work will feel they have been rather badly treated in this matter of West Marylebone. I humbly submit that this is not a very desirable state of affairs to provoke at a time of so much feeling. I have always as you know held the view that our League should have a positive as well as a negative policy, but it should not confine its work merely to opposing the Parliamentary franchise for women. It should also point out the directions in which women's work and energies could most profitably be used.

I know you do not agree with this point of view and I feel it may be presumptuous of me to press it upon you. Your great personal kindness to me on all occasions, however, emboldens me to do so. I cannot but feel it would be a real disaster for our cause if we give even the least impression however unjustified of being anti-women. There is a large centre opinion which I feel it should be our object to conciliate and detach from the Suffragist side. But to do this we must show that we do take positive views of women's work and do not meet the whole feminist movement with a blunt non possumus. I hope and think it is not impossible to reconcile the two principles within the same organizations though I am sorry to hear you hold a contrary opinion....

11 February 1912   26/30 Part II
Mary Ward to VM

So many thanks for sending me your most excellent reply to Lord Cromer. But alach! — it is no use. We cannot persuade him; & the present Director, Captain Creed [Director, ASL] *l'homme necessaire* of the moment is wholly illiberal and bigoted in such things, & simply believes that all the L.G. movement is doing harm! We must maintain it of course, but I fear in a changed form, and we must look to an absolutely independent committee for the support of women candidates.

13 February 1912   25/12
VM to Hilda Cashmore

If it [the COS] can be induced to reconsider its principles or rather to review them in the light of present facts and experience it might be of incalculable value to the whole principle of voluntary work.... Those of us who believe as you and I do in the principle of voluntary work and the importance of having voluntary societies running alongside the State ones have no wish whatever to see the COS go under. It would be such a splendid thing if it could reform itself and reform itself from within. And I repeat I believe there is a great body of opinion inside the Society who would welcome the change if only the depressing cast iron formulae of the Central Office might be relaxed.

14 February 1912 26/30 Part II
Mrs Mary Ward to VM

So many thanks for your letter of yesterday. It really helped me through. We had first of all a meeting of our L.G.A. Committee in the morning which entirely refused to confine itself to mere speeches and meetings in the air, without support of candidates, and passed instead a resolution asking the Executive to allow them to present a list of five candidates from either party, and to give their consent to the support of the list. I did not vote in either division, though I drew up the resolutions. I did not see any finality in either of them, but thought it a good thing to let the Executive know that we were not prepared at once to have our only practical outlet cut away.

Then in the afternoon there was a meeting at my house of the Special Committee appointed by the League Executive, and all the three men upon it — Mr Heber Hart, Mr C.E. Mallet[22] and Mr Mitchell Innes, were so strongly of opinion that while officially connected with the League we should never be allowed to support individual candidates, and that endless friction would be the result of any attempt to keep up the official connection, — this being the view both of Mr Mallet and Mr Heber Hart the two Liberals, and of Mr Mitchell Innes the Unionist, and of dear Gertrude Bell [Hon Secretary of ASL] who put in words of wisdom from time to time — that I felt we must probably accept a dissolution of the official tie, and make the best terms we can. So I shall summon another meeting of our own Committee before the next Executive, and I hope carry them with me and with the Special Committee in a final settlement....

Meanwhile you will be amused to hear that the sequel of all the flood and fury on dear Lord Cromer's part is that in consequence of my letter in the *Times*, I have had a letter — this is private — from Captain Jessel, the Chairman of the London Municipal Reform Union, and more responsible than anyone else, as he points out, for the choice of candidates on that side, asking me for the names of qualified women likely to be acceptable to the Municipal Reform party, and saying in the strongest way that they are most anxious to have not only co-opted women, but *Councillors* The rest of the letter is an explanation of — I might almost say an apology for — their proceedings in Marylebone....

25 February 1912 26/30 Part II
Lucy Terry Lewis[23] to VM

I hear that Mrs Ward is dissociating the Local Government Advance-

---

[22] Sir Charles Mallet (1862–1947), Conservative MP for Plymouth 1906–December 1910. Financial Secretary to the War Office January to December 1910.

[23] A member of the Local Government Advancement Committee.

ment Committee from the Anti-Suffrage League.... Capt Creed (the 'man in charge') deliberately set himself against Local Gov[ernment] matters from the first joining forces over this with the two pro-consuls. I warned Mrs Ward but at the time there was no thought of allowing Captain C[reed] to be 'Dictator'.

On 28 February[24] Markham was one of the main speakers at an anti-suffrage rally at the Albert Hall, attended by roughly 20,000 supporters. Her speech, which The Times, *a strong opponent of women's enfranchisement, considered 'admirable' brought forth 'immense applause'. Markham rested her case on a number of linked grounds: men and women had different talents which meant that they should play different roles in the management of the state — women's role was in local government; many women did not want the vote; if women were given the vote, it would have to apply to all women, but many suffragists were willing to exclude working-class women in the Conciliation Bill; the average political experience of the average woman was bound to be less than that of the average man; men would continue to provide the business spirit in the world, and the work of the Imperial Parliament would be beyond the practical experience of most women. Finally, Markham queried why more women were not involved in local politics and did not make better use of the rights and votes they already possessed.[25] When Markham made her anti-suffrage speech at the Albert Hall, there were very few women local councillors. It was difficult for women to get adopted as candidates in winnable seats; many men still did not believe that women were suited to even local government work and women could therefore be an electoral liability. Local elections were often seen as a dress rehearsal and stepping stone to a parliamentary career, so women's position in local government was weakened precisely because they could not stand and vote in parliamentary elections. Outside London there was a property qualification which would have prevented some women from participating in council work.[26]*

? 1912   26/30 Part II

VM to Women's Local Government Society

My attention has been drawn to a statement issued by your Society dealing with some remarks of mine at the Albert Hall about the work of women in Local Government.... I am a member of the Women's Local Government Society and have nothing but respect and admiration for its work. Had your Committee thought fit to communicate with me before sending its

---

[24] Markham incorrectly dated this 12 February in her autobiography: Violet Markham *Return passage* (1953) p 98.

[25] *The Times*, 29 February 1912.

[26] Patricia Hollis, *Ladies elect* (1987).

manifesto to the press I might have saved them from the false position of publicly condemning one of their own members without any enquiry and of completely misconstruing a speech obviously read in a hasty and imperfect manner.

I must give the most emphatic denial to the fiction circulated by Suffragists and endorsed by your statement that I made any general charge about the indifference of women to social work and the affairs of their less fortunate neighbours. My remarks on the subject at the Albert Hall were directed to one special point and one special point only, namely, the question whether in the absence of the Parliamentary vote women as *ratepayers* were bereft of any channel of public expression and service. I showed that the great field of Local Government lay open to them and that it was practically neglected, only 21 women serving on Town Councils, 3 on County Councils, and that 232 Boards of Guardians had no woman member. I then asked why as *ratepayers* women tolerated slums, insanitary dwellings, infant mortality, etc., and 'was it not humbug to say they were denied all share in the national life when a small minority excepted they had shown so little practical interest in causes concerning the sick, aged, destitute, etc.,' The question of the activities of women in general social work never entered into the argument at all. I was not nearly or remotely referring to voluntary effort but to the work of women as ratepayers. I can assure your Committee that I am perfectly familiar with the work carried on by the long list of admirable voluntary Societies they enumerate. I am not aware that Suffragists at their public meetings dilate on the excellencies of such bodies, and it is a little unreasonable to suggest I should have ranged over the whole wide field of philanthropy in a brief speech dealing with the political status of women. I did however make a reference in general terms towards the end about the bands of devoted workers who were giving of their best in public service without thought of profit or reward. Your manifesto is however silent about this remark....

So much for the charge of seeking to hinder and belittle the efforts of the 'army of devoted women'. As regards the more special issue of the numbers of women engaged in Local Government; you are good enough to say that my figures are correct 'so far as they go'. It would be strange if they were challenged by your Society seeing that they were taken from its own annual Report. You complain that I did not give figures showing the total number of candidates who came forward. The complaint seems to me somewhat captious, but taking your own figures 85 candidates for Borough and County Councils seems a modest total out of the million odd women ratepayers who are qualified to sit and vote for such bodies. You then enumerate certain difficulties which beset the path of women in Local Government — expense, apathy, etc., and you speak of the work of your own Society in seeking to remedy this 'state of ignorance'. I have before me as

I write an admirable leaflet issued by your Committee called 'An Appeal to Women'. This leaflet calls on all women to use their municipal votes wisely and well and concludes with the warning that they will be responsible if the work of their Council is done badly and extravagantly. The leaflet then sets out a list of the powers and duties of Town Councils which I am interested to find covers every point I raised at the Albert Hall. With all this I am in hearty agreement but I am at a loss to understand the process of logic which makes it fit and proper for Suffragists to draw attention to a 'state of ignorance' and appeal to women to use their municipal powers wisely and well, yet denounces an Anti-Suffragist as an enemy of her sex when she ventures to say the same thing.

Again, Suffragists attack me because I did not explain in minute detail to the Albert Hall audience the complicated point that though married women are qualified to sit and vote for London, Borough, and County Councils, and Parish and Urban Councils outside London, the question of coverture still exists for Town and County Councils, some married women having established their right to vote and others having failed to do so. I spoke of a field of equal rights and opportunities with men and I hold to the statement. All women who would have been enfranchised under the Conciliation Bill already possess full municipal rights. The electoral system is full of anomalies so far as men are concerned and if on one point there is still an anomaly to be redressed as regards the position of married women municipal voters that one anomaly seems a feeble excuse to put forward for the apathy of other women ratepayers who are qualified in every respect. Even so this argument breaks down completely so far as the Boards of Guardians are concerned. Women married or single are qualified for such bodies on a residential qualification, and in spite of this fact more than a third of all the Boards in the country are without a woman member. If a larger proportion of Suffragists had some practical experience of Poor Law work they would realise the sinister significance of those figures.

Women have had the municipal franchise for over forty years: they have been qualified as candidates for seven. During that time no great municipal reform movement has sprung from the women ratepayers of the country. Your own Society has been at work for nearly twenty years and the fruits of its labours are not considerable. The fact that women have done splendid work in other fields does not affect my point that they have neglected the municipal rights within their reach. As against this thousands of women have flung themselves with ardour into the campaign for the Parliamentary vote. Is it for your Society to condemn me for holding the view that their energies would have been better employed in supporting and encouraging the candidature of women in Local Government, in improving their position where it requires improvement and generally in vitalising and cleansing the life of our great towns....

? *March 1912* 26/30 Part II

VM to Mrs Mary Ward

....I am completely reconciled to the separation of the Local Government Committee from the National League for Opposing Woman's Suffrage; indeed, on reflection I am prepared to go a great deal further and should prefer to see it become an independent Anti-Suffrage organization run by Anti-Suffragists and inspired by Anti-Suffrage ideals, affiliated with the N.L.O.W.S. and on close terms of friendship with it, but withal an independent body with independent funds.

I am satisfied that in view of the difficult personalities on the N.L.O.W.S. Executive Committee and the opposition there has always been from an influential section to a progressive policy this is the only sound basis for the work. Any other scheme renders us liable to harassing restrictions and criticism which might seriously jeopardise our activities....

If we are tactful the organisation of this new Society could be made a demonstration of strength not of weakness to the Anti-Suffrage cause. There must be no talk of cleavage, dissensions, quarrels, or schism: no; our position must be that the Anti-Suffrage work has developed to such an extent that this new organization has grown out of it as naturally as a Colony springs from the Mother Country. It is a sign of vitality and strength if Anti-Suffrage Societies multiply in the same way as the multiplication of the Suffrage Societies prove the strength of their movement....

Granted then that a new Society for the promotion of Local Government work among women is to be started what are to be its principles? My feeling would be to make those principles as positive as possible all along the line; to dwell primarily on the needs of Local Government and the opportunities for service that it offers rather than an Anti-Suffrage propaganda *as such*. In the first place I should give it a positive name 'Society for the Promotion of Municipal Service among Women'. The Committee, supporters, subscribers of the Society would all be Anti-Suffragists; 'affiliated to the N.L.O.W.S.' would appear on the writing paper so there could not be the smallest doubt as to who and what we were and the ideals for which we were standing. The aim of the Society should be to encourage municipal work among women and to bring Anti-Suffragists out in that field. So far we are all agreed. Now I come to the point which is the real crux of the situation — what is to be our attitude to Suffragists doing good work in Local Government? I am perfectly clear as to my own position on this point. I could join no Society which would in any way harass, oppose, or throw obstacles in the path of women who are first rate workers with special knowledge of social questions but who incidentally may be Suffragists. I could not join any Society which promoted the candidature of an inferior Anti in opposition to that of a capable Suffragist. Finally I could not join a Society which involved the smallest obligation upon me as *an individual* to refrain from supporting the candidature of Suffragist friends for any given public office

I quite recognise as a Society that we cannot support the candidature of professed and ardent Suffragists in Local Government. But we can refrain from opposing them when otherwise excellent and desirable women; we can refrain from putting up less good Anti women to contest their seats. We can leave them a perfectly clear field.

Practically I do not believe much difficulty would arise; the field is so wide, the workers so few that we could surely dispose of our women in localities where they would not run up against other women. And I feel we should leave ourselves the widest discretionary powers as to who we do or do not support. It seems to me most important that we should not hamper ourselves with tests.... It would be absurd if we were pledged to give no help to an excellent woman because at one time or another she subscribed in a luke warm way to a Suffrage Society.... Again there are women of special qualifications whose election to municipal bodies on public grounds is most desirable quite apart from their opinions. We ought to be able to judge such cases on their merits and not to be prohibited from dealing with them if in the opinion of the Committee their election would promote the public good.

....We Anti-Suffragists believing municipal work to be the alternative to the parliamentary vote naturally desire to educate and bring out women on those lines. But the claims of the work itself as well as Anti-Suffrage principles have to be weighed and from that point of view we do not want to interfere with good women whatever their opinions who on Town and County Councils, Boards of Guardians, etc., might render yeoman service to the community. I believe this policy if adopted would be not only generous but politic....

My own belief is that a Society of this kind would attract many waverers who might find it difficult to join the N.L.O.W.S. but who could reconcile the work now proposed with their inclinations and consciences....

6 March 1912 NLS 6023 ff103-106
VM to Elizabeth Haldane

....I have felt & feel my alienation on this question [women's suffrage] from three parts of my friends & fellow workers more keenly than I can well describe.... there is not one element of gratification in it—only a sense of disagreeable & compelling duty against which I can't trespass. Obviously there is so much to be said for the Suffragist position.... But to me the assertion of *equality* between men & women is not what I want, equality if you will but equality in *diversity*. I feel so very strongly about the spiritual aspects of life for which women ought to stand in their public work & I cannot see how that spiritual quality could survive the obligation to take part in the rough & tumble on even terms. I dont think I *could* go through the work of a General Election if I had anything nearly or remotely to gain from it. To me life rests on such vast paradoxes & I do believe that what one renounces is given back with a much truer sense of possession than if possession had been sought direct. It's because I value women's work & influence supremely that I am not content to see them claim the rights of *L'homme moyen sensuel*. When they go into battle I want them to be the Red Cross Legion—fearless where the struggle is fiercest but withal self denying & consecrated....

14 June 1912   26/30 Part I
Loulou Harcourt to VM

The Cabinet have decided, for reasons in which I concur, that it is impossible in our Parliamentary Franchise Bill to touch the qualifications of the *Local Government* Franchise. The two have never been dealt with together in a single Bill and if we were to do so on this occasion it would lengthen the measure so much as to make its passage this Session impossible. I only explain this in order that you may not think that I misled you when I said that your suggestion might possibly find a place in the Government Bill. I do not think, even in the future, that you could substitute residential for occupier franchise for local government, as I do not think that non-rate-paying domestic servants of either sex have a claim to local government votes.

15 June 1912   26/30 Part II
Dorothy Ward to VM

The situation in the A.L.O.W.S. with regard to the White Slave Traffic Bill is, — so far as I know — this. For several weeks the office was much perturbed, receiving letters from Branches & individuals asking what the League was going to 'do', etc. etc. Various members of the Executive wrote to & consulted each other. A really *admirable* memorandum by Lord Charnwood was privately circulated round the Executive (about the middle of May). Lord Curzon sent round a long letter for consideration, a *draft*, with a view to its being circulated round the Branches as a guide for their action. Mother came home from abroad on May 19 & immediately had a long consultation with Lady Jersey. She (Mother) was of opinion that Lord Curzon's draft letter was too hard in tone, in parts, & might rather depress the poor Branches. So she at once set to & drew up two long paragraphs to be worked in, & the gist of which was *sympathy* with all wise efforts to improve legislation for women & children, while at the same time the

Memorandum as a whole expressed the view that as a League and *officially* the N.L.O.W.S. cld not take action with regard to particular Bills. These additions of my Mother's were approved unanimously by the Executive and inserted practically en bloc into Lord Curzon's letter at their meeting on May 23rd — As he was not present the thing had to be referred back to him for final approval, which he gave, & at the meeting of June 6th the Letter was *finally* passed by the Executive, with one or two slight alterations and ordered to be circulated in the Branches. In its final form *I think* it was not sent out as a letter from Lord C. but just as a Memorandum from the Head Office for the guidance of Branches, — but I have not got a copy here and cannot exactly remember about this.... *Personally* I would rather the Executive had gone a step further and *had* passed a Resolution definitely in favour of this Bill. Mother also would have been really glad if they had felt that way, but she saw that the feeling was really quite a *serious* and well-intentioned one, that the League ought not *officially* to go out into the Arena & back up any Bill outside its own province. She has told me more than once that the feeling on the Executive is all in favour of all of us anti-suffragists as individuals saying or doing as much as ever we like in favour of this Bill. And remember that there are two very unanswerable answers to any malicious Suffragist insinuations:1) This Bill was brought in by an *Anti-Suffragist* member (Mr. Arthur Lee).[27]

2) The Memorial to the Prime Minister asking the Govt. to take it up & give it time was signed by members of all parties, *Suffragists and Anti-Suffragists* alike. My brother of course was among the signatories....

June 1912 26/30 Part II

.... the League is pledged to maintain the principle of the representation of Women on Municipal and other bodies concerned with the domestic and social affairs of the community. With a view to the furtherance of this object a 'Local Government Advancement Committee', which until recently was affiliated to the League and of which Mrs Humphry Ward is the Chairman, was constituted some two years ago. Experience has, however, shown that great practical advantage will arise if the work of the League be entirely separated from that of the Local Government Advancement Committee. Arrangements have therefore been made under which the latter body is wholly independent of the League.

As regards the question of the removal of disabilities under which women and children are alleged to suffer, and the amendment of the existing laws in

---

[27] Sir Arthur Lee (1868–1947), Conservative MP for Fareham 1900–1918. 1903–1905 Civil Lord of the Admiralty, 1915–1916 Parliamentary Secretary Ministry of Munitions, 1919–1921 Minister of Agriculture and Fisheries, 1921–1922 First Lord of the Admiralty.

respect to marriage, divorce, etc.... the Executive Committee, as also, we believe, the members of the League generally, would individually approach them in a spirit of marked sympathy and with an earnest desire to support any changes in the law the necessity of which had been clearly shown. The Executive Committee, however, feel that they have no right to utilise the funds or to employ the organisation of the League for objects essentially distinct from those which it was founded to promote.

At the same time resistance to the grant of the Parliamentary Vote to women means the employment of argument and controversy with opponents of many different kinds. We desire accordingly to show, not only that Woman Suffrage would be bad for the community to which we belong, but that existing channels and agencies are sufficient, if rightly employed, to meet the demands for social and ethical reform which may be put forward by our own members or by others.

27 July 1912 26/30 Part II

Gertrude Bell to VM

.... a committee should form itself inside the House of members who would be ready to give special care to all legislation or projects of legislation which covered women. That, at their request, a similar committee of women should be formed to whom they could go for advice & help, & which could also be ready to suggest matters that the M.P. Committee ought to take up.... it must clearly be understood that the committee is not to be used as or means of advocating the suffrage.

Bell wanted both suffragists and anti-suffragists to sit on the committee.

The Albert Hall rally in February 1912 proved to be the highlight of the anti-suffrage campaign, both for the NLOWS and for Markham. In the summer of 1912, Markham left England to spend a few months in South Africa.

2 March 1913 UCT BC294 D7.1.2

VM to Sir Patrick Duncan

.... The fundamental economic fallacy of the average S. African is this crazy illusion that the weakness & demoralisation of the native is a source of strength to the European.... None of these artificial policies will safeguard the superiority of the white man — that is clear to me. It's up to the white man to prove his superiority by his better intelligence & better industry. But paradoxical though it sounds I entirely agree with you that in the development not in the repression of the black we must look for the adjustment of these labour difficulties....

6 June 1913
VM to Sir Patrick Duncan   UCT BC 294 D7.1.4

....I agree absolutely with all you say about the restrictions on the rights of native land purchase. I should not allow natives to buy land for communal tenure but I think it a real hardship to forbid a decent & civilised native to own his own property....

In the summer Markham again left England to travel extensively in China and the Far East. By the spring of 1914 she was back in England.

2
War Work
1914–1918

During the First World War Markham was to change her mind over the women's franchise question, but she did not alter her views on the role that men and women should play in society. This chapter provides further evidence of the way in which the First World War reinforced both Markham's, and others', views about separate spheres and double standards for men and women. Paradoxically, women were, at the same time, expanding their field of activities. This conundrum is highlighted in Markham's correspondence.

The war brought to the fore the double moral standards for men and women, in particular, working-class women. There was an assumption that the experience of war led to a loss of self-control. Concern over the alleged immorality of working-class women prompted the appointment of women welfare officers in factories employing large numbers of working-class girls, and women police patrols in areas where it was feared women would seduce men, or vice versa. These fears were fuelled by the assumption that women's rising real incomes were being spent on alcohol, which in turn would be accompanied by an upsurge in immoral behaviour. This moral panic was not the result of an actual revolution in sexual mores: the illegitimacy rate did increase by 30%, but with fewer births in wartime, fewer women actually had illegitimate babies. Statistics are, anyway, misleading. Before the war many working-class women did not marry until they were pregnant; in wartime men's mobility often made such weddings more difficult. Moreover, it had been widespread practice for working-class men and women to live together as if they were married, without actually going through a marriage ceremony. This widespread practice of cohabitation was to cause much soul-searching over the rights and wrongs of public money, whether collected by charity or the state, being given to the unmarried partners of soldiers and sailors. The organisation of these funds shows how the difference between state and charitable support became blurred during the war. Although the state intervened in people's lives more than ever before, Markham, for one, was keen to emphasise the importance of maintaining a strong charitable ethos in society.

The outbreak of war was accompanied by fears of high prices, unemploy-

ment and general distress. As men enlisted so chaos ensued, not only at the administrative level but also at the personal one, as family life was ruptured. On 6 August 1914 the National Relief Fund was launched, with an appeal from the Prince of Wales, to alleviate distress resulting from the war. On the same day Queen Alexandra appealed for subscriptions to the Soldiers and Sailors Families Association (SSFA); on 11 August the two funds were fused, and help given to the families of soldiers and sailors, as well as to civilians. The rates of separation allowances paid by the War Office had not been raised since the Boer War, and the slowness with which payments were made in the the early days of the war led to hardship and bitter criticism of the system. The army pay offices were faced with a dramatic increase in numbers: on 4 August there were 1,500 soldiers' wives on their books and payments to these women were made monthly. There was no record of marriages 'off the strength' and the decision to abolish this distinction, as well as the call-up of men, meant that within a few weeks 250,000 wives were entitled to separation allowances. (By 1918 1 1/2 million wives were receiving support for themselves and their children, and an equal number of other dependents were also receiving allowances.)[1]

Attempts to set up local representation committees around the country proved difficult because in many places there were no voluntary workers to run them. It was therefore decided that where there were active SSFA branches, they should distribute funds and in the few remaining areas the work should be entrusted to local representation committees. Markham was a member of the executive committee, which on 30 September 1914 agreed that relief should always be appreciably lower than wages. A sub-committee had already been appointed to look into the thorny problem of allowances for the 'unmarried wives' of servicemen, and after much agonising it was agreed that these women should receive help. It has already been pointed out that women qualified for these benefits solely because of their relationship with a man. It was his right to have his wife supported. The idea of male breadwinner and dependent wife was at the heart of the system. Moreover, the man was entitled to this support for his wife, but paradoxically, the women could have the money withdrawn (as happened in 16,000 cases — about 2% of the women) if their conduct was considered depraved. SSFA had always seen its role as a moral one and even after it lost control of the funds in 1917 (following a select committee's investigation in 1915) the government put on the mantle of guardian angel of the women's morals.[2]

---

[1] For another account of working-class women in the war, also written by a middle-class woman, but from a different standpoint to Markham's see Sylvia Pankhurst, *The home front: A mirror to life in England during the First World War* (Cresset, London 1987 edn, first published 1932).

[2] S. Pedersen, 'Gender, welfare, and citizenship in Britain during the Great War', *American Historical Review*, vol.95, no 4 (1990) pp 983–1006.

War Work 59

One group of women in particular, those in the Women's Army Auxiliary Corps (WAAC), were singled out for their allegedly wicked conduct. A committee of inquiry, which included Markham as honorary secretary, visited France in early 1918 and came to the conclusion that the allegations were false; the innuendos continued.

Until the First World War the army viewed women in one of three ways, as nurses, potential carriers of Venereal Disease (VD), or as wives of soldiers.[3] No serious thought had been given to any other role that women might play in total war. Some women had, however, already begun organising themselves along paramilitary lines. In 1907 the First Aid Nursing Yeomanry (FANY) was formed to provide a corps of women who could ride out on horseback and bring in the wounded from the battlefield. In the same year, the Women's Convoy Corps was established to train women for service in wartime, and in 1910 the Voluntary Aid Detachment (VAD) was founded to act as a home defence unit and to provide nursing care for the wounded in times of war. When war broke out, a range of similar organisations sprung up, but the idea that women should play anything other than their traditional wartime role was greeted with horror by many, including Markham. One of the planks of the anti-suffragists' case had been that the defence of the nation ultimately rested on the physical force of men; as only men could defend their country, only men should wield power in national politics and take decisions about making war and peace. Other arguments were now harnessed to the case against women in uniform, some of which appear in Markham's correspondence. In 1915 she made her views known publicly when she entered the fray with letters to the Morning Post.

While at first opposing a paramilitary role for women, Markham supported the employment of women in commerce and industry. In 1917 she became Deputy Director of the Women's Section of the National Service Department (NSD), a job which was to end in acrimonious mudslinging with its Minister, Neville Chamberlain, as well as with the Ministry of Labour. Markham's papers present her case in the affair.[4]

---

[3] Jenny Gould, 'Women's military services in First World War Britain', in Margaret Randolph Higonnet et al, *Behind the lines: Gender and the two world wars* (Yale University Press, New Haven, 1987), pp 114–115.

[4] For a sympathetic account of Chamberlain's role see David Dilks, *Neville Chamberlain: vol 1 Pioneer and reform, 1869–1929* (Cambridge University Press, Cambridge, 1984), pp 199–250.

7 September 1914 25/55

Charles Masterman[5] to VM

National Relief Fund

Very many thanks for your letter, with every word of which I agree; but it is a great advantage to have someone actually engaged in the chaos of the locality also on the Central Committee. How that chaos can be avoided is another matter, but we simply must peg away and not abandon the work in despair.

I agree with you it was a rotten plan to let the S.S.F.A. loose in this fashion. It was not decided by us at all; it was entirely a dodge from the collectors' point of view to prevent separate appeals by the Prince of Wales and Queen Alexandra and practically the condition of a united appeal was that the military side should be run through the Soldiers' and Sailors' Fund.

16 September 1914 1/13

S.S.F.A. to Laurie Brock, Secretary, N.R.F

It is suggested that a mistake, with somewhat far-reaching consequences, will be committed if no real distinction is made between the Wives of Soldiers and Sailors and the unmarried women with whom they have been living, on the following grounds:-(a) It would deal a real blow to the self respect of the women who were married: my information is that those who know the people in the poor Districts best could give an assurance that this is no mere sentimental fancy, and that the married women would feel this most keenly.(b) It would encourage the idea — too lightly held already — amongst the men that, after all, it doesn't matter, and that the women would be looked after just the same.

To meet this difficulty it is suggested that in issuing further detailed instructions about these cases, which it will be necessary for us to do very shortly, we should be in a position to state that the unmarried mother and children should be dealt with by the Association on the basis of the Separation Allowance granted by the War Office to Soldiers' Wives, and that it is not to be expected of us to grant allowances supplementary to the Separation rate, as is the case with those families where the legal tie exists.

---

[5] Charles Masterman (1874–1927), Liberal MP for West Ham North 1906–1911, Bethnal Green South West 1911–1914, Manchester Rusholme 1923–1924. 1908–1909 Parliamentary Secretary, Local Government Board, 1909–1912 Parliamentary Under-Secretary Home Office, 1912–1914 Financial Secretary to the Treasury, 1914–1915 Chancellor of the Duchy of Lancaster. Member of NRF committee.

24 September 1914

1/13

Evidence from Mrs Randall Davidson to unmarried mothers sub-committee I have had more than twenty years experience in connection with work among mothers, married and unmarried.... and have been in constant touch with those handling these problems in their daily duty.

At the present time I have had constant interviews and correspondence with those who are working for the S & S. F. A. and seek advice from the Archbishop and me.

On the particular problem you are trying to solve it seems to me clear — A. The unmarried mothers of soldiers' children and unmarried partners of soldiers' homes are entitled to very definite consideration and must not be left unaided. But the conditions vary in every particular case. B. It would be harmful to the permanent interest and tone of (a) soldiers generally, (b) soldiers' *wives* generally, (c) these unmarried women themselves and (d) the moral standard of the district and e.g. the police if the line of demarcation between the married and the unmarried who ask help were broken down or obliterated. C. That there is no insuperable difficulty in reconciling A and B so as to help women who have a reasonable (though not technical) claim to such aid, while yet maintaining the obligation and supremacy of the marriage tie. D. This reconciliation of A and B cannot be by definite rule of thumb because of — 1. the diversity of the cases to be dealt with — e.g. (a) long-established 'homes' (b) so called homes which are mere sudden and recent 'attachments'. (c) Unmarried partners of *married* men whose wives and families have a claim. (d) women of evil life who are merely manufacturing a claim. 2. Owing to delicacy and difficulty of the personal questions involved. 3. The harmfulness of seeming, by authority, to make a formal rule that a soldier's *unmarried* partner shall stand fully on a par with a soldier's *wife*. E.That the thing can be done by appointing on every Committee of the S.& S.F.A. one or more women of Experience Capacity Quiet judgement Real care for the girls and women who can 1. tactfully investigate each case privately 2. make the necessary application for the relief when it is suitable. 3. get into touch with the soldier himself. 4. bring abiding influence to bear on the woman herself. Experienced workers capable of doing this quietly — tactfully — effectively, are available almost everywhere.

6 October 1914

1/13

James Brown & Sandeman, House Factors, Glasgow to Richard Williamson JP

...in some cases we have found that it has been suggested to some of our tenants who are dependents of soldiers on service, that they should dispose of some of their belongings and go into a single house from a room &

kitchen. We may say that this is objected to by them, as it is not possible to get a single apartment house in a locality at all suitable as to neighbours etc. and the saving in many cases would not amount to 3/- per month.

As a rule any effects they could sell would only realise a few shillings at present, which would not be an adequate compensation for the sentimental value which the dependent would probably put on her own things.

13 October 1914   1/13
R. Williamson JP to Sir George Riddell, NRF committee member

Many of the women are now in a pitiful condition as well as their children. Many of them being in rags, and some of them without boots. The majority of their supporters were reservists, and of course they were called up on the 4th and 5th of August. Practically speaking two months before they got any assistance whatever....

Some of the women have pawned the very boots off their feet to get food. I have a number of pawn tickets in my possession. One of the cases reported to you yesterday had to borrow a skirt and shawl before she could come and report to me.

14 October 1914   1/13
Mona Wilson, National Health Insurance Commissioner for England, to Charles Masterman

I went to Glasgow on Friday, 9th October, in order to make enquiries with regard to the alleged unsatisfactory administration of the local branch of the Soldiers' and Sailors' Families Association....

I came to the conclusion that criticisms of the organisation and methods of the Soldiers' and Sailors' Families Association were by no means confined to Mr Williamson and the Trade Council and that these criticisms touched other questions besides the attitude of the Soldiers' and Sailors' Families Association toward the cases of unmarried mothers.

.... [Mr Milwain, the local Secretary] told me that the visitors were not instructed to press the women to go out to work although we received various complaints of this.... Some of the social workers strongly objected to the opening of an employment agency specially for soldiers' and sailors' wives as they said that in normal cases they should not require to go out to work and it was already extremely difficult for women who had been working before war broke out to secure employment. This point was emphasised by one of the women whose case we investigated.

The Soldiers' and Sailors' Families Association's visitor had represented to her that she ought to try and get work although she pointed out to them that she had two children, one of $2\frac{1}{2}$ and a baby whom she was nursing.

She did not want to leave these children all day and also thought that it would be 'doing another woman out of a job', as it was difficult enough for unmarried women to find employment.

Mr. Milwain states that he had arranged in the first instance with the Charity Organisation Society for the use of their district offices and the aid of their officials and voluntary workers for the purpose of taking down applications for relief .... A good many of the Soldiers' and Sailors' Families Association workers are also connected with the Charity Organisation Society. These workers are probably better trained and more efficient than the rest but it is not improbable that this close connection with the Charity Organisation Society is partly responsible for the general attitude of the Soldiers' and Sailors' Families Association towards women as recipients of charity rather than as entitled to the allowances given to them.

In Kitchener's Army cases applicants are required to give rank and regiment of their husband. If they fail to do so the Soldiers' and Sailors' Families Association will not help them, but if such cases are relieved by the Charity Organisation Society or the Parish Council the Association will refund the amount expended when the necessary information is received. It is probable that in a number of cases the women have not been in a position to furnish this information at the outset and have consequently received relief from either the Charity Organisation Society or the Poor Law.

.... Some of the social workers complained to us that some women were receiving far too much and others too little and it appeared to us that there was no adherence to the scale and little uniformity of procedure, as in some divisions the workers decided cases as they pleased, in others the Divisional President gave directions in all cases....

.... I am satisfied that the treatment of these cases by the Soldiers' and Sailors' Families Association had been unsatisfactory.... One of the visitors told us that there had been a great deal of confusion about the case of unmarried mothers and he had only received instructions that day (October 12th) that they were to be dealt with by the Soldiers' and Sailors' Families Association. Some of the workers whom we saw objected to helping these cases. A Divisional President said that she was not now helping them on the same scale as the wives and thought it would be undesirable to do so. Another informed us that she had not helped a case where there were no children as she did not consider the woman eligible for help.... It was evident that no pains were taken to avoid exposing the fact that the women were unmarried; in fact, some of the workers we spoke to evidently regarded it as unnecessary and absurd to spare them in any way. The visitor whom we came across was insisting on putting the woman's maiden name on the food order, although she had lived with the man for eleven years and was known as his wife, until it was represented to him that this was unnecessary and after some demur he altered it....

Mr Milwain speaks of food allowances for groceries, coal or milk as one of the special ways in which help is given. Complaints were made to us both by social workers and by the President of the Trade Council that these tickets ought to be reserved for cases in which the woman could not be trusted with money and that they were given much too freely.... I was informed by a Branch President and by a social worker that in certain Divisions food tickets were used for practically all cases. This appeared to be the main grievance of the Trade Council, because they thought it an insult to a respectable woman....

I was not satisfied that in all cases the Soldiers' and Sailors' Families Association were giving the women reasonable assistance in obtaining the right allowances from the War Office. In one case no allowance had been received for the children and the woman stated that the Soldiers' and Sailors' Families Association lady had refused to write for her as she was tired of writing to the War Office. A similar complaint was made to us in another case.

A Minister whose visitors were working for the Soldiers' and Sailors' Families Association mentioned to us the case of a woman with a nice home to whom he had given a letter to the Soldiers' and Sailors' Families Association asking them not to send an unskilled visitor to see her as in that case the visitor would be likely to think that she was too comfortably off to require help with her rent. The clerk to the Parish Council told us of a similar case in which the husband who was a territorial had been married two years and had a comfortable home and the Soldiers' and Sailors' Families Association visitor had told the woman to pawn the furniture. We visited a woman ourselves to whom the visitor had said that she still had a good deal left which she could 'put away'....

I do not wish to minimise the great difficulty of the task which the Soldiers' and Sailors' Families Association had undertaken in Glasgow, nor do I think that the Representative Committee would at the outset have been in a position to undertake it. They have had an enormous number of cases to deal with and the Presidents and Vice-Presidents have been working very long hours; but at the same time I am satisfied that there is a marked lack of control, and of uniformity among the Divisions.... It is also clear that a number of the workers whom they have been employing have been untrained. They do not appear to have given them definite instructions or to have made any attempt to weed out unsuitable workers. I think also that the general attitude of the Soldiers' and Sailors' Families Association has been a mistaken one. I was much struck by the remarks of the clerk to the Parish Council, a gentleman whom no one would accuse of undue sympathy with either bookmakers or socialists. He said that his staff had received so many complaints and had themselves heard such unsuitable questions asked by the Soldiers' and Sailors' Association visitors that they had written him a confidential report on the subject. His feeling seemed to be generally shared by the social workers whom we interviewed.

I do not wish to express any opinion as to the purity of Mr Williamson's motives, but I think that he has been quite justified in calling attention to the way in which the unmarried mothers were dealt with by the Soldiers' and Sailors' Families Association, and that good resulted from his action. We were present when Mr Williamson was interviewing some women, and it was clear that he merely wrote down what they told him without any attempt to investigate the truth of their statements. It is, therefore, probable that a considerable number of the cases sent on by him to the Soldiers' and Sailors' Families Association will turn out to be capable of explanation or even fraudulent....

Other investigators found the SSFA doing creditable work under difficult circumstances.

5 November 1914 1/12
Portsmouth Services Sub-Committee to E.H. Kelly

....I should explain that we are not narrow-minded on the subject [of unmarried mothers]....

We fear that these instructions, as issued, may tend to legitimise immorality at a time when people are likely to have less self-control than usual, and this would seem to us to be a disaster....

In the Portsmouth Command we expect to have some 23,000 troops during the Winter months. At any time the town is full of temptations. We can only *imagine* the consequences of the Government's and Committee's action next year, and the number of unmarried dependents who will be left.

I think we may say on the whole that the unmarried women who apply to us are not as a rule respectable women, who have lived perfectly straight lives otherwise.

A large majority of these cases come from an area where immorality is the rule. The other cases are isolated.

....It seems as if some efforts should be made, when possible to train the women with a view to make them self-supporting later, and that any relief given should be on rather a lower scale than that given to wives.

5 November 1914 1/12
T.W. Hunter replying for Cardinal Bourne, RC to Pamela McKenna, member of N.R.F.

On the ground that no one is entitled in such circumstances to make public a private sin, the administration of relief might in these circumstances proceed in the ordinary way, unless it should appear that the mothers were not fit and proper persons to have charge even of their own children. In such cases the children might be placed in Homes, and the mothers provided for in some other way than under the Poor Law. It would seem that these mothers have a kind of moral claim on the man for support, until either marriage has been effected or the woman placed in such a position that she would not be obliged to apply to the Poor Law for relief....

18 December 1914   1/9

J.S. Middleton[6] to Laurie Brock

I am still receiving complaints from various correspondents in Lancashire that relief is being refused to men who are within the ages of enlistment....

6 February 1915   25/58

Robert Morant to VM

....Lloyd George is already very angry at having heard how many of our best men here have been giving large slices of time away from Health Insurance.... And he has long been cursing 'Morants' supine acquiescence' in the continuance of the unpopularity of Health Insurance! He declares it cd easily have been made universally loved & venerated by 1915....

18 March 1915   UCT BC 294. D7. 1 10

VM to Sir Patrick Duncan

....For any Radical with strong pacifist sympathies such a conflict as this seems to knock the bottom out of every faith & hope one possessed. One had believed in Christianity & civilisation & in the development of a real sense of brotherhood between nations.... So far as England is concerned I have no shadow of doubt that we took the right path in a most righteous cause & I am all for prosecuting the war with the greatest rigour to a conclusion which will remove the Prussian manace to civilisation.

On her recent marriage to James Carruthers VM comments

....It took me a long time to make up my mind—I have never been a great believer in the marriage of opposites! But where a man is big enough & forebearing enough to let a woman have plenty of elbow room as regards her own work & opinions the adjustments are not difficult at all....

---

[6] J.S. Middleton (1878–1962), From 1904 Assistant Secretary of the Labour Party, and 1934–1944 Secretary of Labour Party. During First World War Secretary War Emergency Workers' National Committee.

13 April 1915
Secretary, Winchester C.O.C. to VM

2/1

I have consulted the Rescue Workers, the Police and the Relieving Officer who all say an increase [in illegitimacy] must come, but no grounds for such rumours as are persistently being circulated. Unfortunately here we are faced with widows and married women having fallen and that is probably due to the billeting in the houses.

23 April 1915
Jessica Smith, Chesterfield Settlement to VM

2/1

.... This awfully difficult and painful question of the number of illegitimate children to be born soon, has occupied us a good deal lately. The fact is that no one knows anything — nevertheless the wildest rumours are about. After the soldiers had been here barely a month someone said that there were 90 expectant mothers in the town! The Rescue workers here to whom I was talking on the subject one day this week, said that Miss Bruce had told her that 400 unmarried girls from Buxton had been sent to Maternity Homes. Miss Scott Smith said it was an absolute impossibility, there were not Homes to take them & it would cost £1000 a sum not likely to be collected by such a small town for the purpose. Anyone who knows anything about girls knows how they will hide the thing to the last minute.

Then the question of women patrols came up a month or two ago, we talked the question over with Mrs Kenneth Bond [wife of a Unitarian Minister] (who is acting as woman police court missioner) and with Miss Twelves of the Adult School and British Women's Temperance Assn, who had been asked to investigate conditions — Chest/d & having made all enquiries from the police & others & looked about for themselves came to the conclusion that there was no sign of any appreciable increase of flighty behaviour in the town. Miss Scott Smith (the rescue worker) says it is impossible to make the roughest estimate but she does not anticipate any great increase in the number of illegitimate births here (of course we do not bear a good record in ordinary times in this town). She has made a point of walking round Ashgate country lanes near where soldiers & girls congregate but has seen little silly behaviour she says. On the other hand the district nurse was telling William that she was dreadfull shocked at the behaviour of some young girls in the outlying parts near Hasland — but she is not an educated woman & might easily exaggerate the position from one or two instances — Bruce also takes a lurid view of the situation. No one seems to have seen parties of girls collected round the temporary barracks as seems to have been in some places, and our helpers who leave the Club quite late say that the town is almost as quiet as usual — though since we have been in such darkness it is difficult to know what is going on....

Though I have quoted Miss Scott Smith — *privately* — I don't think very much of her judgment. The soldiers have only been here about 4 or 5 months you know. The harm that comes will be, I think, thro' the soldiers that are billeted here rather than thro' these — barracks as there is no real check on their hours.

I do think that one must be very chary about bringing any special legislation to deal with these case. Anything that is done (& the children when they come must be cared for) should be done privately or through charitable agencies. It does seem to me that to advertise all round that illegitimate children of soldiers are different & that the irregularity is less because it is war time & so on is only to encourage the loss of self-control of which we have so little & to ask for imposture.

At the same time it does fall hard on the girls in towns like ours where the custom is so prevalent of marrying just before the birth of the child that their men can't now marry them because they are abroad....

24 April 1915 2/1

Alice Petty to V.M

....I have not come across one single case of the 'war baby' problem and I think that in Derby the precautions were such as to minimize the danger. We have women patrols, and a club for the men to which they can bring their girls....A certain number of educated men and women in the town take it in turn to act as stewards. Then there are endless church and chapel activities and all public houses close at 9 p.m. Of course, a great many little monkeys of girls pursued the soldiers boldly in the streets but they were generally firmly dealt with.

....Of course, all this sort of thing is the corollary of war, when the physical side of life is uppermost and any State action should be based on individual effort as the responsibility of the present position is both individual and collective....

3 May 1915 2/1

Mothers' Union to Diocesan Presidents

Much is being said and written to the Press about the problem of what are called 'War Babies', against which title we strongly protest.

....so far investigation has proved that there has been the greatest exaggeration as to the number of expected illegitimate births....

....no Christians, and still more, Church Workers, can ever condone sin which is sin still whatever the circumstances may be.

Illegitimate births are, alas nothing new, and we know that the present state of the country affords the opportunity for the worthless to exploit their evil doings.

It is therefore absolutely necessary that there should be a steady upholding of constructive teaching on the whole marriage question, using the service for Holy Matrimony as the basis of this teaching but also remembering and practising the need of *reticence*, too often forgotten in these days.

Great confusion of thought has arisen from much emotionalism and wrong sentiment which has appeared in the Public Press, speaking as though present conditions not only justified sin, but almost placed transgressors on a pedestal to be admired.

.... We want you to bring this subject at once before your Members and bring home to them the giant evil that is stalking through the land doing the devil's work.

1915 2/1

Mothers Union

Will you forgive me for saying there is a great danger of the men being damaged and made unfit for the hard and awful work in front of them unless parents and employers try to prevent the girls from getting excited, running wild in the evenings and forgetting their honour, their purity, their self-respect?

So much terrible wrong-doing has happened in some of the places where troops have been, that I feel I must warn you all of the danger and beg the elder women to guard the younger and the girls from their own folly and rashness....

Many of these soldiers will never return home, and the message which ought to be and I am sure often is ringing in their ears is 'Prepare to meet thy God.' It is terrible to think that the folly and sin of any of the women and girls should make these men *less* fit to die and send them away with a guilty conscience and a stain on their soul.

.... be good friends to any of the men you may meet, be kind and wise, give them your sympathy, cheer them and encourage them, and pray for them, but take care that no girls for whom you are responsible or whom you love shall lead or encourage these men to sin against their conscience and against God.

11 May 1915 2/1

The Charity Organisation Society wrote to the press claiming that allegations about rocketing illegitimacy rates were wildly exaggerated.

....what gave rise to the sinister rumours above referred to was not infrequently the noisy and somewhat irregular behaviour of girls in the streets.

4 June 1915 25/75

J.A. Spender[7] to VM

....I have had many warnings during the last few days that to talk at this stage about applying compulsion in workshops is playing with fire. And if that is much to the fore, we shall have a revolt among trade unions, even against the national register. The working people are not unpatriotic, but the idea of their labour arrangements being put under the control of military gentlemen is highly alarming to them, and I confess myself that I am very much unconvinced about its desirablity. I see no reason to think that a hastily improvised system of national workshops would make for efficiency in war....

5 June 1915 25/77

St Loe Strachey to V.M.

....just now even the voice of sympathetic criticism has to be stilled. Otherwise people rush to the conclusion that you are in league with Northcliffe.[8] This is another example of the harm Northcliffe has done. He has given the War Office a far freer hand than anybody however just and virtuous ought to have.

25 June 1915 2/6

VM to Mayor of Chesterfield

....I feel I ought to tell you with what absolute and unqualified disapproval I view any scheme for teaching women combatant or quasi *military* operations in the event of invasion.

....No one feels more strongly than I do what an urgent call there is for women to take up many duties in civil life which will release men for military or munitions work. No one is more anxious than I am to facilitate

---

[7] J.A. Spender (1862–1942), Editor *Westminster Gazette* 1896-1922.
[8] Lord Northcliffe (1865–1922), journalist and newspaper proprietor.

the employment of women in many directions where their services to the State can be invaluable. But playing at soldiering in any form is in my opinion foolish and undesirable.

27 June 1915 2/1

Gertrude Green to VM

.... There is no intention whatever to use the girls or women, who join the movement, for military purposes. In some places shooting is taught; it will not be taken up in Chesterfield. We feel that the use of military titles is misleading and serves no practical or useful purpose. If the organisation can be carried on without these titles it would be preferable. The chief aim and object of the Association is to discipline and train women during their leisure hours, and women of all classes engage side by side in the operations.... Drilling is essential & each member pays a penny per drill. Bandaging, first-aid, camp cooking under difficulties and out of doors, signalling & sewing all form part of the programme. There is a simple uniform, but in some places, Birmingham is one, the uniform has not yet been bought by the members though the movement was started in Jaunary. Another point is that it has *nothing whatever to do with any Suffrage Society*.

30 June 1915 2/6

Mrs R. Hopkins, Colonel, Birmingham to VM

.... Nothing could be more absurd than to think women would be used for the fighting line — they could be nothing but an extra burden & trouble & I should be very sorry to trust myself with the majority of women with Rifles! Anyway that's not the idea at all. We are military in so far that we have adopted the method of organization and discipline of the army & because the military note has gathered together a body of women of all classes who otherwise would still be isolated units & who attracted by that military note are now banded together as a useful organisation — it has given them esprit de corps & a spirit of cooperation (badly wanted) as nothing else could — it has made them obedient & quick & improved their manners as nothing else could — the drill has disciplined them & made them fit in body & mind.... So far we have carried out the following works. Sent $2\frac{1}{2}$ tons of medical stores & a good sum of money to Serbia. Carried out Miss Beatrice Chamberlain's [sister of Neville] National Penny Col. for St Johns & the Red X from house to house for the whole of B'ham.

Are helping at several VAD Hospitals.... in the gardens & doing flowers in the wards. Organizing Canteens for the Munition workers & running one canteen with our own members at the B.ham Metal & Munitions in 3 shifts a day.... & at the latter we take the refreshments round the shops on hand trolleys.

This week the New Munitions Bureau sent to ask if we would help to make known their enrolment of skilled workmen at the Council House which we have done. Some of us are fruit picking — I have sent several to various war works & we have been asked to help in recruiting marches. So you see we are doing a good deal of work — none of what would have been possible if I had not been backed by the 1000 girls in my battalion & there are branches in many other towns under me in all of which I am pushing the useful side in addition to the pleasure of the military one — & of course there are some under London as well. We learn signalling First-Aid, Home Nursing, Stretcher drill, telegraphy, Camp cooking, Fire drill so that in case of need we may be ready. We wear a brown uniform which makes for uniformity of mind & body — teaches suitability of clothes & gives us something to uphold & respect & in the wearing of which we are expected to behave ourselves so that other people may respect us as a body. I should like to add that I am a strong Anti Suffragist so that there is no question of that part of politics tho' we include all sorts.... I am very glad they are going to make this register of men and women as it seems such a pity that all this splendid spirit among us of wishing to help should be wasted & if it could be directed to the right channels it ought to be worth so much to the Country.

no date 2/1

Mrs Grace Dawson-Scott, Founder Women's Defence Relief Corps to VM

Our work is to relieve the defence by undertaking their jobs & thereby reducing to a minimum the disturbance of the country's economic life. We do that civilly and also by getting ready to undertake any home defence the authorities might call on us for. By so getting ready we are working off the dangerous stimulus to the emotions of young folk which the war has given. We always work under the authorities and the mayors in the towns of our branches are generally our patrons.

no date 2/1

Mrs Dawson-Scott to VM

It's an unarmed corps but ready and at the disposal of the authorities.... Of course it's ideal that no women shd be in the neighbourhood of troops. I'm growing however just a bit dubious as to whether the ideal is going to remain possible when it's a matter of home defence. Moreover at the present moment *women's health is being largely benefited* by the various semi-military exercises (I like best to call them 'Good-Citizen') & I hope that will mean that next year when the drain on the men is more felt that they will be stronger and more fit to undertake men's jobs than they are at present. I endeavour to keep the semi-military idea as much as possible in the background & put the civil forward but the former is grasped after by the unthinking who do not see what is coming.... & who find in it an outlet for their roused and stimulated emotions. Its a good & harmless way of working them off (what women don't understand yet is that they have to turn from superfluities (in the employment of their time) to necessities....

no date 2/1

A Lady Guardian, Tunbridge Wells to VM

It is being said in our neighbourhood that we have already over 200 expectant mothers owing to the soldiers coming to Tunbridge Wells, and it is added — 'The workhouse is full of them.' This has been so generally said that people stop me out-of-doors and ask if it is true. My answer I can give is this — We have had fewer, not more, cases of girls in the Maternity Ward, and not one of these have come there from the wrong doing of a soldier in Tunbridge Wells.... I feel very strongly that those who could help the standard of morality now are those who serve on Midwives Boards and Pension Insurance Committee, and we want many more suitable women on these committees before we shall arrive at reform. These things *are* women's work and should not be left in the hands of paid men officials.

6 July 1915 25/75

J.A. Spender to VM

Lord K[itchener][9] is adament about revealing any detail of the preparations. I had a reprimand from the censor the other day because a reporter slipped in the number of a division that the King was reviewing. Among other things this secrecy prevents all criticism of military matters.

10 July 1915 2/6

Mayor of Chesterfield to VM

.... I think the girls' movement is to be on the right lines. I took strong measures some months ago when it was first suggested & two points have been guaranteed to me — 1st that this has nothing to do with Suffragists as such nor is it to be dragged in in any way — 2 It is to be in no way

---

[9] Lord Kitchener of Khartoum (1850–1916), Commander Dongola Expedit. Force 1896, Khartoum Expedition 1898. Chief of Staff South Africa 1899–1900, C-in-C South Africa 1900–1902 and India 1902–1909. Agent and Consul General in Egypt 1911–1914. Secretary of State for War 1914–1916.

a military movement other than the use of drill & nomenclature such as is necessary for the ordering of a body of people — discipline & physical training.

undated 2/6

Mrs Dawson-Scott to VM

....I'm absolutely with you about Khaki and using men's terms for the officers (Col etc) why can't we be more original?

You may be right as to its being a waste of time teaching women scouting; but ....The War Office wanted us all to learn signalling and some of my corps are already being used for despatch riding while as to shooting there is nothing like it for the nerve....

15 July 1915 25/50

VM to David Lloyd George, Minister of Munitions

....Women feel and with justice that they have not yet been given an opportunity of serving the State in a reasoned way. Yet it is clear that if we are to carry the war to a successful conclusion women will have to play an unprecedented part in industry by setting free men for service both in the field and factory.

National registration is a first and valuable step in estimating our resources, but registration of itself will not set one woman to work unless organization is simultaneously provided. I need not enlarge to you on the special difficulties connected with women's labour and the host of knotty problems involved in the transference of labour from trade to trade — let alone sex to sex. Hence the need for definite organization and control on the part of the State.

The suggestion I wish to make is as follows. Could you not set up a representative National Committee for the organization of women's labour (with local committees dependent on it) which would be a feminine counterpart of the Munitions Committee and of course work in cooperation with the latter?

This Committee would have at its disposal the official information and expert staffs of both Home Office and Board of Trade. It could survey the field of employment, lay down the principles and examine the conditions of any transference of labour. It would have definite knowledge as to the posts women could fill and would be in a definite position to call for volunteers to fill them. Such a body if properly constituted and with an adequate representation of women workers would give confidence in Labour circles. Its existence would be a guarantee that the Government recognise the difficulties of special war employment and are alive to the necessity for safeguards.

Mrs. Pankhurst's demonstration is I am sure inspired by most patriotic motives. But while emphasising the desire of women to serve it does not of itself provide the *plan* for setting them to work. Haphazard methods of employment would certainly bring a shower of Labour objections about our ears. The Pankhurst group are not closely in touch with Labour matters and at this time when we all want to work together it seems to me very important to avoid opportunities of friction with the Trade Union organizations.

On 1st July a meeting had been held at the London Pavilion in support of women's war work at which Mrs Pankhurst spoke. A deputation to the Government was arranged and was accompanied by a demonstration in Whitehall in support of women's war work.

19 July 1915 1/9
Laurie Brock to VM

National Relief Fund

I hardly expected that you would be able to come, but the question was so important and the notice of the Chancellor's[10] coming was so short that I thought I had better warn you by wire. The meeting was so poorly attended and it was obvious that they could not come to a final decision. Most of the time was spent in unseemly rangling between McKenna and Long[11] not merely in regard to the merits of McKenna's proposal but in regard to the decisions and intentions of the Cabinet! Fancy the Cabinet ministers arguing hotly before a group of outsiders as to what the Cabinet had done or meant to do. Even our cynical Chairman[12] was shocked. As he [the Chairman] said he had been brought up in the belief that the object of Cabinet councils was to enable ministers to compose their differences in private, but the Coalition quarrelled in public. McKenna kept his temper admirably but somehow he always seemed a little glib, too plausible and too convincing. One couldnt

---

[10] Reginald McKenna (1863–1943), Liberal MP for Monmouthshire North 1895–1918. Financial Secretary to the Treasury 1905–1907, President of the Board of Education 1907–1908, 1908–1911 First Lord of the Admiralty 1908–1911, Home Secretary 1911–1915, Chancellor of the Exchequer 1915–1916.

[11] Walter Long (1854–1924), Conservative MP for Wiltshire North 1880–1895, Devizes 1885–1892, Liverpool West Derby 1893–1900, Bristol South 1900–1906, Dublin County South 1906–January 1910, Strand January 1910–1918, Westminster St George's 1918–1921. Parliamentary Secretary Local Government Board 1886–1892, President of the Board of Agriculture 1895–1900, President of the Local Government Board 1900–1905 and 1915–1916, Chief Secretary for Ireland 1905, Secretary of State for Colonial Affairs 1916–1919, First Lord of the Admiralty 1919–1921.

[12] George Murray, previously Secretary of the Treasury.

escape from a feeling that he was too slim. As for the squire he was really intolerable. You could have lit a cigar from the top of his head. He talked no end of rot, but as usual there were gleams of sound sense. Incidentallly in his excitement he denounced the Bill which his own Dept and his own Under secretary have been in charge of. Part of his speech might have come from an SSFA diehard and the opinions he voiced on the subjects of mayors were most unbecoming to the President of the Local Govt Board, who is in theory the ex officio guardian angel of 'Ossid Itch' and his tribe.

As it was clear that McKenna's proposal would only be carried by the votes of his wife and his ministerial colleagues other than Long he has decided to drop it and amend the Bill.

I am not quite sure what form these amendments will take and the fate of the Bill in the Lords is doubtful. The SSFA have many friends in the Lords and it is not unlikely that they will move to omit from the Bill all references to separation allowance, which would have the effect of leaving us in relation to the SSFA exactly where we are now. The SSFA are so entirely free from any taint of democracy or representative institutions that they necessarily appeal to the instinct of the hereditary legislator. I am bound to add that, speaking as a mere official, I like the SSFA, partly because it is so entirely indifferent to local opinion. When we fix a scale the SSFA generally stick to it. Local committees mostly do not, because they are made up in so many cases of people with an eye on the municipal elector. It rather looks as though the end of the whole thing would only be to create an enormous number of committees without achieving an amalgamation of the competing institutions and overlapping committees which make it so difficult to get anything done....

20 August 1915 25/2

St Loe Strachey to VM

We have got into a situation where defeat is possible, stalemate certain, unless we make a great effort. Are we going to make it on a plan or all haphazard? The present system disorganises all industries, compels us to enlist men when we don't want them and can't equip them for fear that we may not get them when we do want them. And from the military and munitions point of view it gives us no idea to work to, so you can't say how many Divisions you wish to have equipped by next July and consequently what new you should lay down if you don't know whether you will get enough men not only to make up those Divisions but to sustain them.

28 August 1915 4/1

Sir George Riddell

Last night I went to an interesting dinner at Frederick Guest's[13] the object being to promote National Service. I was asked as an independent. I strongly deprecated agitation and suggested that it would be desirable to await a declaration of the policy of the Government. Ultimately they decided to ask the PM to receive a private deputation. All this is confidential, but I thought you would like to know what was happening in this direction.

4 September 1915 4/1

J.H. Thomas[14] to VM

.... First of all Lord Lansdowne[15] is a dear old gentleman but entirely unfitted for this job. On the other hand I could see at a glance all the KCBs that were surrounding us would be simply playing if we went against them. However, for the moment I think we had better let things run, until we have an opportunity of talking over the whole situation.

16 September 1915 25/58

Sir Robert Morant to VM

L-G, I hear, is determined to get Compulsory Service for industry and for Mil[itary] Service within 5 weeks! [D.J.] Shackleton[16] is today seeing Asquith (don't repeat this) Shn's strongest point against Compulsion being that in a given family one son will be compelled to the front and be killed & the other son will stay at Munitions, & the people (he says) won't tolerate such a vast difference in the fates of the two sons, as a result of one happening to be in a particular trade — when all this happens by *compulsion*: it is different when it is by personal option.

---

[13] Frederick Guest (1875–1937), Liberal MP for Dorset East January 1910–1922, Stroud 1923–1924, Bristol North 1924–1929, Conservative MP for Plymouth Drake 1931–1937. Secretary of State for Air 1921–1922.

[14] 'Jimmy' Thomas (1874–1949), Labour MP for Derby January 1910–1931, National Labour MP for Derby 1931–1936. Secretary of State for Colonial Affairs 1924 and 1935–1936, Lord Privy Seal 1929–1930, Secretary of State for the Dominions 1930–1935. General Secretary of NUR 1918–1924 and 1925–1931.

[15] Lord Lansdowne (1845–1927), Parliamentary Under-Secretary of State at the War Office 1872–1874, India Office 1880. Governor-General of Canada 1883–1888, Viceroy of India 1888–1894, Secretary of State for War 1895-1900, Foreign Secretary 1900-1905, Minister without Portfolio 1915–1916.

[16] Permanent Secretary, Ministry of Labour and member of National Health Insurance Commission.

20 October 1915

Bernard Mallet, Registrar-General to VM

I agree with what you say about the necessity of grappling with the subject of getting women into employment more effectively. I cannot see why the Home Office should not set a more comprehensive committee of inquiry on foot. The Home Office seems to be the best Department to deal with it. Gibbon[17] and I were discussing the subject with Lord Lansdowne last night. Personally, I rather agree with Lord Lansdowne's feeling that the only way to get women employed *in large numbers* is to take away the men from the employers. I hope the new recruiting movement will give a great stimulus in this direction.

30 March 1916

Lord Derby to VM

....I confess I am rather sick about things now....I cannot think that [resignation] is the right course to pursue at all events at present!

31 March 1916

VM to Sir Edward Carson[18]

I was a member of both the Jackson and Lansdowne Committees which dealt with the National Register, and am greatly concerned at the general state of chaos into which the Register has drifted. From your remarks in the House two nights ago I am happy to see you realise the importance of all that is at stake....

The Registrar General and the Local Government Board were warned at the time that the system would prove quite unworkable, and the warnings (to which they paid no attention) have been fully justified by the result. Neither Department has any experience of Registration which is a matter quite distinct from the Census. On the other hand the advice of the National Health Insurance Department which has been working on Registration problems for some years and knows all that is to known on the subject, was entirely ignored and thrust aside....

---

[17] Local Government Board.

[18] Sir Edward Carson (1854–1935), Conservative MP for Dublin University 1892–1918, Belfast Duncairn 1918–1921. Irish Solicitor-General 1892, 1900–1905 Solicitor-General 1900-1905, Attorney-General 1915, First Lord of the Admiralty 1916-1917, Minister without Portfolio 1917–1918.

26 April 1916 4/11

Katharine Furse[19] to VM

.... What frightens me most is the absolute lack of foresight among the Military Authorities. They will not train women and we have practically come to the end of good trained women. I think it would be perfectly possible to run some form of organisation for women to work in various departments under the War Office at any rate, but quite agree that it is impossible to rake in munition workers and women on the land, as a national army....

20 May 1916 1/11

H.A. Robinson, Local Government Board, Dublin to Laurie Brock, Secretary NRF

I have received your letter stating that the Committee of the National Relief Fund are doubtful whether the distress caused by the recent Rising in Dublin can be regarded as coming within the scope of the Fund, and asking for further information to enable them to determine this point. As the object of the Fund is the relief of distress caused by the war, I submit that the evidence given by Sir Matthew Nathan[20] and Mr Birrell[21] at the inquiry into the recent Rising leaves no doubt that it was financed and promoted by the German Government as part of the operations against the British Empire....

9 June 1916 25/23

Geoffrey Dawson[22] to VM

Now about Lord Milner. Of course I am always supposed to be biassed when I contend that he is the one man in England who ought beyond any question to be in a War Government. So on this occasion I let the *Morning Post* start the hare, and came into the hunt myself on the following day but I am amazed to find how popular the suggestion is even with the most unlikely people. Of course the *Daily News* and the *Manchester Guardian* crab it today but that was only to be expected. Why don't you write, or get some other prominent Liberal to write a short letter endorsing what I said? I do not think that there is any real prospect that Asquith will entertain it,

---

[19] Dame Katharine Furse (1875–1952), Head of VADs, 1917 first Director WRNS.

[20] Sir Matthew Nathan (1862–1939), soldier, civil servant. 1914–1916 Under-Sec. for Ireland.

[21] Augustine Birrell (1850–1933), Liberal MP for Fife West 1889–1900, Bristol North 1906–1918. 1905–1907 President of the Board of Education, 1907–1916 Chief Secretary for Ireland.

[22] Geoffrey Dawson (1874–1944), 1901–1905 Member of Lord Milner's 'Kindergarten' in South Africa, 1912–1919, 1923–1941 Editor of *The Times*.

but for future emergencies — and we shall certainly need all our strong men before we are done — I think it is useful to get the matter talked about.

7 October 1916   3/34
Adelaide Anderson[23]

Recounting the views of a welfare supervisor in Coventry.

In Coventry, there are a great many little back alleys and passages, also small gardens, parks and heaths, which are open all night which does not help towards the morality of the town. My works are so small that I don't suffer much. The bad women go to a bigger place where they cannot be so found out.

November 1916   3/33
Memo. by Adelaide Anderson and VM

Anderson and Markham had investigated the social conditions of women who had moved to Coventry during the war for work. They found overcrowding, high rents and no recreation apart from that provided by denominational clubs.

Picture Palaces and walking the dark streets are the only alternatives.

[They claimed there was evidence of an increase in VD and] of loose and immoral conduct in recreation grounds and dark streets. We were assured that the pre-war tone of Coventry was a low one, consequently the introduction of large numbers of new workers into an undesirable atmosphere calls for special vigilance. We feel that Women Police of a trained and responsible character would be of real value on the preventive side as we believe that good recreation would be of importance on the constructive side.

2 November 1916   26/30 Part I
VM to Lord Cromer

I have had it in my mind for some time past to write and lay my perplexities about the Suffrage question before you. My views on the whole subject have grown chaotic during the last two years....

---

[23] Adelaide Anderson (1863–1936), one of first women Factory Inspectors 1894. Principal Lady Inspector 1897–1921. In 1921 created a Dame. See Helen Jones, 'Women health workers: The case of the first women Factory Inspectors in Britain' *Social History of Medicine*, vol.1, no. 2, (1988) pp 165–181.

I am entirely with you that it would be a scandal of the first magnitude if this worn out Parliament which has so long outlived its mandate and its welcome were to carry a fundamental constitutional reform without any reference to the electorate. I am most strongly of opinion that the whole question of women's suffrage should remain in abeyance till the country has reverted to normal conditions of life again. But I equally do not feel I could sign a letter affirming strenuous opposition to votes for women in the future because I cannot pretend that the experience of the war has left me unmoved as to the principle of women's suffrage. Even without the modifications of opinion which have answer in my own mind I should not be optimistic as to the practical possibility of sustained opposition in the future.

I do not exaggerate the services of women at this time. I deprecate the excessive flattery of which they have been the objects. But when all reservations are made the war could not have been carried on without them, and after the way they have helped to fill the breach it would as a matter of practical speech making be an uncommonly hard task to stand on a platform and say the things we said in old days.

I have seen a great deal of the industrial side of women's employment during the last eighteen months and one realises all the values are altered. Many preconceived opinions have gone by the board. I have been amazed at the success and efficiency with which women have carried out work which would have seemed incredible in pre war days. The spirit and the patriotism they have shewn has been above praise, far better often than that of the men. As a matter of practical politics I put it to you can we say with one breath that women have helped to save the State and with the next deny them any share in its management? That is my difficulty at the present time.

I do not think my opinions have changed very fundamentally. The man as worker, the woman as home maker remains my ideal of society. But in this difficult world one has to take facts as they are. The conditions of modern life are thoroughly artificial. Little though I like it women are going to play an ever larger part in industry and public life. More and more women are going to be forced by economic pressure into the labour market and will be obliged to struggle single handed for their own bread. They suffer at present from many disadvantages. I am more clear on that point than in old days. I am far from thinking votes will remedy all the abuses but if the State keeps thrusting public duties on women it is not easy to avoid giving them a larger say in the management of affairs.

But having reached the point when I feel I cannot maintain the old anti-suffrage position in its entirety I fall into a new set of perplexities as to ways and means. As a democrat I am profoundly shaken at the moment about the whole theory and practise of applied democracy. The present expression of democracy seems to me hopelessly bad.

The idea of Adult Suffrage fills me therefore with dismay. To multiply all the evils of the present system, to duplicate the ignorance and the weakness of the electorate seems to me a step worthy of Bedlam alone. My mind has been groping therefore after a much more fundamental reform. I want to see the franchise altered and women brought in but not by any measure of wholesale extension. Would you think it absolutely chimerical to press for a complete revision of the basis of franchise — to base the exercise of the franchise on service, citizenship, and education, — not on property which seems to me essentially undemocratic, and not on the mechanical fact of being 21 or 25 years of age? Could we not have some test of fitness and service under which suitable men and women alike could qualify as voters?....

As to the practical and most important point of not having Adult Suffrage introduced by a side issue in this discredited and decaying Parliament might I make a suggestion? It is not of course for me to advise Lord Curzon and yourself but I do not think opposition to women's suffrage as such is the best means at the moment of fighting the scandal of a hole and corner introduction of Adult Suffrage. A great deal of public sympathy and sentiment centres round women at this time.

An anti-Suffrage letter as such I think would be a mistake. My own feeling would be to leave that side of the question entirely alone and get a group of responsible people including well known Suffragists to combat the proposals on constitutional grounds pointing out the wholly immoral character of slipping through fundamental changes in a worn out Parliament with several million electors disqualified.

8 November 1916 26/30 Part I

VM to Lord Cromer

The whole question of women's suffrage has presented itself to me of late in the light of its connection with some of the wider issues raised by the present democratic system. I entirely agree with you that Democracy as such is coming very well out of the present ordeal. Among many doubts and hesitatations I have not lost one grain of faith in my belief in the people. But I am increasingly concerned with the whole latter day expression of Democracy and the political system it has thrown up. The party machines have become wicked and tyrannous instruments, and the politicians who run them are in the main extraordinarily unsatisfactory leaders for a great country. I do not think it possible to continue indefinitely with a system so admittedly unsatisfactory as the one in which we live at present. The premium on ignorance and prejudice is too high as things stand and some way some how we must work towards an expression of Democracy which will mean government by the best, not government by inchoate masses of poeple swayed by greedy and unscrupulous leaders for their own ends.

The failures which are troubling me are clearly troubling large numbers of students of political science. I have been especially interested to find how Syndicalism as a philosophical system is attempting to correct some of the obvious failures of the present democratic system.

From this point of view you will understand how my mind has been working, not towards any large wholesale increase of the franchise but towards some effort to improve the quality of the electorate. If we can have an electorate based in some degree on fitness or quality then there would be an opportunity for the introduction of women voters on reasonable lines. I am of course discouraged to find that with your great political experience you feel the solution after which I am groping to be impossible.... I shall continue to offer unqualified opposition to Adult Suffrage, not so much because it would enfranchise women but because oppressed as I am at the moment by the failures of Democracy the huge increase it would effect in the electorate would intensify all the evils about which I feel so much concern.

As regards the women, in the light of the experience of the war I cannot help feeling they have a real contribution to make in the affairs of the country and I do not despair of finding some channel of expression for them which would avoid the evils of their wholesale introduction as voters....

9 November 1916 26/30 Part 2
Lord Cromer to VM

Very many thanks for your most interesting letter. I quite agree in much of your argument, but I am afraid there is not the smallest chance of your programme being carried out. It would be above the heads of all but a few thinkers.

17 December 1916 25/50
Lloyd George, Prime Minister to VM

When we come to the organisation of women for industrial purposes I hope you will lend us a hand.

1 February 1917 4/4
Constance Smith, Factory Inspector, to VM

Writes to congratulate Markham on her appointment as Deputy Director of the newly created Women's Service Department.

If only the feminine organisations do not sweep over you like a flood before your scheme is even plotted out.... they are an impatient crowd, I fear.

Our 'hierarchy' goes on in its old way, &, though every man of capacity has been taken from the Department, seems determined not to give the most experienced of the women a shred of power.

1 February 1917 4/4

J.A. Spender to VM

....I will certainly do my best to shield you from the malicious criticism to which everyone is exposed in these days....

10 February 1917 4/4

VM to I.G. Gibbon, Local Government Board

I wish we had been allowed to tackle this problem nine months sooner. It is full late now to try and call any sort of National organisation into existence however simple. Mrs Tennant and I are firmly determined to organise the work before we appeal for workers. As you say so truly, these appeals in vacuo lead to nothing but irritation and disappointment.

16 February 1917 4/14

VM to Alfred Zimmern[24]

....The work here [Women's Section, NSD] is going to be frightfully difficult for a good many reasons. In the first place this organisation of women has come too late. To have done any good we ought to have started a year ago. Then there is the great difficulty of setting up another costly bureaucracy....

6 March 1917 4/4

VM to Sir Robert Fox, Town Clerk, Leeds

Organising war work

One of the very real difficulties of our work is the enormous number of people, leagues, societies, committees, who all roll up clamouring to do things for us. But of course, as you know, a Government Department cannot delegate its work to voluntary societies. It is most perplexing to know how to fit in all these amateurs who are proffering service....

---

[24] Alfred Zimmern (1879–1957), Oxford historian, who in 1917 was in between working as an Inspector at the Board of Education and working in the Political Intelligence Department of the Foreign Office. Worked for Foreign Office during Second World War and then became the Executive Director of UNESCO before returning to academic life.

11 April 1917   4/5

VM to Neville Chamberlain, Minister, National Service Department — not in Cabinet

The Employment Department [of the Ministry of Labour] was created in haste, largely staffed by political jobbery, and the faults of the Exchanges have been glaring in many cases ....I appreciate fully the very difficult and unfriendly spirit shown by the Employment Department and the great provocation you have received from their officials....

4/5

VM — unsigned & undated memo on relations between the Women's Section of the National Service Department and the employment department.

....disastrous lack of cooperation between the National Service Department and the Employment Department is contrary to the public interest, and is creating an indefensible position departmentally....

7 June 1917   4/5

VM to May Tennant

....a situation has arisen at St. Ermin's[25] about the W.A.A.C. which brings us really to the parting of the ways....Mr. Chamberlain has made a complete and entire surrender to the War Office in the matter of the W.A.A.C. All recruiting and publicity is to be removed from us, and we are to have no lot or share of any kind in future in the recruiting or management of the Army. [There is] a definite intrigue on foot to oust our Department from any share in the work....As a result of [a conference with the War Office]....I felt it very important to bring the circumstances to Mr Chamberlain's notice, and not allow him to drift through lack of knowledge once again into a thoroughly undignified and humiliating position. Recruiting for the Women's Army has proved very unsatisfactory during the last few weeks. The terms are not sufficiently attractive, and as you know, the conditions of service are hampered by a large number of stupid and irritating restrictions.

....I was particularly anxious to avoid being manoeuvred....into a position of having failed to produce the right number of women when they[26] could turn round and say they were obliged to remove recruiting from us because we had made a mess of it. It seemed to me essential, therefore, to put our position and our difficulties on record and to press that certain changes should be made which would facilitate better recruiting....I was determined he [Chamberlain] should face the position and appreciate the

---

[25] Headquarters of the National Service Department
[26] The War Office.

other side of the issues involved.... He put me off several times, and finally in the evening I got a message from his secretary that the letter could not go in its present form. I had an interview with him and Stephen Walsh[27] yesterday morning. He then informed me he had seen both Geddes[28] and Scovell[29] and that there was to be a clean cut in the future between ourselves and the War Office about the Women's Army. He seemed to think it quite a desirable arrangement; said a dual responsibility was very unsatisfactory, generally speaking that the War Office had better go to the devil in its own way. None of the issues which I had urged upon him seemed to have the smallest weight with him, and in his usual blind fashion he does not in the least appreciate the infinite discredit which will attach to our Department to be ignominiously kicked out as the War Office propose to do, and as he without a struggle proposes to acquiesce in.

I am bound to say I greatly resented Mr Chamberlain's attitude yesterday. In the first place he has no business to be consulting with Geddes and Scovell about matters concerning the Women's Section without any consultation with the heads of that Section. His attitude to me was that of champion of the War Office, I being the enemy — the same attitude with which we have been familiar on the occasion of other struggles.... He swept aside as quite impracticable the suggestion made... that you should be asked to go to France and inspect the conditions there. I pointed out the way we were being out-manoeuvred by the War Office, the discredit which would fall upon the Department, the abandonment of the cause of the women, the irritation of the National Service Committees who we were dragging in daily to assist with recruiting and who would find themselves abandoned. In all of this I might as well have talked to a stone wall.... He does not seem in the least to appreciate the added disadvantage of our Department becoming daily more deeply involved in recruiting if the whole organization we are building up is suddenly to be scrapped by the War Office.... I am anxious to resign at the first possible moment. I have been increasingly dissatisfied and unhappy about the whole policy of the Department and the position of impotence in which the Women's Section has in particular been drifting. This is due I think to two causes, first, the fundamental error of setting up a new Department without thinking out carefully beforehand its relations with the other Departments: secondly, Chamberlain's series of surrenders

---

[27] Stephen Walsh (1859–1929), Labour MP for Ince 1906–1929. 1917 Parliamentary Secretary Ministry of National Service, 1917–1919 Local Government Board, 1924 Secretary of State for War.

[28] Sir Auckland Geddes (1879–1954), Conservative MP for Basingstoke 1917–1920. 1917–1918 Minister for National Service and Director of Recruiting, 1918–1919 President of the Local Government Board, 1919 Minister of Reconstruction, 1919–1920 President of the Board of Trade.

[29] Head of one of four branches, Recruiting Dept., Ministry of National Service.

which seem to me to have cut the ground absolutely away from beneath our feet. We are not in any true sense a Department of National Service. We are simply an inferior Employment Department kicked in turn by all the others....

I think you and I must face the position that all the high aims and hopes with which we set out on this adventure have fallen to the ground, and personally I am not disposed to give time and strength much longer to building on shifting sands with a Chief who lets you down at every turn and corner....

It is a very humiliating and unsatisfactory for you and me to feel we should be left in a position in which the elements of usefulness are daily reduced....

I do not want you to think the views I have expressed in this letter are merely the result of yesterday's interview with Chamberlain and the irritation and contempt with which his attitude filled me. Unfortunately I have been losing hope about the National Service for a long time past, and this latest surrender is only another illustration of the attitude of mind on the part of our Chief which renders all constructive work practically impossible.

30 June 1917 4/5

VM to Mr John Jeffrey, Edinburgh[30]

Matters with the Employment Department have gone from bad to worse .... I feel that the National Service Department lives on the brink of a chronic volcano and that we may blow up at any time....

Markham told May Tennant on 17 July about a meeting the previous day between the NSD, War Office and Ministry of Labour. Markham wanted the NSD to deal with recruitment and publicity, and the Ministry of Labour to deal with women once recruited. The Ministry of Labour's officials rejected this. Markham spoke privately to Derby after the formal meeting had ended.

17 July 1917 4/5

VM to May Tennant?

He was extraordinarily nice, said he hated going back on his word but that he had been let down by Chamberlain and what was he to do.... I could only tell him that if he had to choose between us and the Employment Department he had better take the latter. They had the machinery, we had not.... I let Miss Stevenson know what had taken place so that she might tell Lloyd George, and I also wrote to Milner....

---

[30] Previously the only man working in the Women's Section of the NSD and now on sick leave.

17 July 1917

VM to Frances Stevenson, the Prime Minister's secretary

You asked me to let you know about the new position which has arisen here. Mr Chamberlain told Lord Derby in a letter some days ago that he would require a little time to perfect his machinery for recruiting for the Women's Army Auxiliary Corps.

Yesterday Lord Derby called a Conference at the War Office, at which Mr Hodge[31], Sir David Shackleton, Mr Rey[32] and Miss Durham[33] were present in addition to the War Office representatives, Mr Chamberlain, Miss Wilson and myself.

Mr. Hodge and Sir David Shackleton urged in the strongest terms that the whole of the recruiting should be taken over by the Employment Department, and emphasised the undesirability of two Departments dealing with the recruiting of labour.

I stated that Mrs Tennant and I entirely agreed as to the undesirability of two competing agencies, and that we had always much regretted the lack of cooperation with the Employment Department, that the failure in cooperation did not lie at our door, as we had always sought it.

I proposed that a satisfactory solution might be arrived at on the lines of recruiting and publicity for the Women's Army Auxiliary Corps being undertaken by the National Service Department, the Employment Department to deal with all the handling and packaging of recruits, the local Exchanges being reinforced by Selection Committees. This proposal Mr Hodge and Sir David Shackleton refused to entertain — they claimed the entire control of recruiting as well as of placing.

Lord Derby is to give his decision to-day, and I think he will give it rightly, under the circumstances, to the Employment Department. They have local machinery, we have none. It is out of the question we should create a new and costly machine. Co-operation on the lines I suggested would, I think, have been the best plan, but as it is refused I do not feel the Prime Minister's time or Lord Derby's should be wasted in arguing with either side over such an issue, a very trifling one as compared with the problems they have to face. If the Employment Department takes over the work the Women's Section will do everything to facilitate and help the transfer.

In informing the Prime Minister of the situation, will you, however, say I hope that the disappearance of the Women's Section here may not in any sense hinder or retard the more fundamental reforms connected with the general situation between this Department and the Ministry of Labour,

---

[31] John Hodge (1855–1937), Labour MP for Gorton, later Manchester Gorton 1906–1923. 1916–1917 Minister of Labour, 1917–1919 Minister of Pensions.

[32] Assistant Secretary, Employment Department.

[33] Woman Inspector, Employment Department.

which he discussed with Mrs Tennant. In view of these new and important duties, the reforms become more than ever necessary.

23 July 1917 4/5

VM to Lord Milner

I think our poor Department had its coup de grace by the refusal of the Treasury to grant any more railway fares. It now transpires that part of Mr Rey's amiable efforts has been directed to wrecking all our communications with the Treasury, and we have to thank him for the unconscionable delays and obstruction which have arisen over financial matters....

24 July 1917 4/5

VM to Lord Derby

....I think it would be very undesirable to keep a remnant of the Women's Section of the National Service Department alive to undertake recruiting ....Fundamental reforms of the Employment Department are necessary for the Labour Exchanges to be equal to the work they are now called upon to do....

27 July 1917 4/9

Lord Milner to VM

At present I have not recovered from the shock of Derby's announcement. I had not heard one single word about it before it was suddenly fired at us, and I have not the dimmest notion what it means. The whole business is now in absolute chaos....The greatest difficulty will be when Lloyd George returns from Paris, with his head full of other things, to get him to attend to it.

P.S. May I make you a personal confession, which I think you will understand. I sometimes sigh for the old South African days of reconstruction, where there was only one *directing* brain. It made many mistakes but it did make something. Forgive this egotism.

10 August 1917 4/6

VM to John Jeffrey

You were at St Ermin's long enough to realise how entirely unfitted Mr Chamberlain was for his work. He is a good man, thoroughly honest and disinterested, but I think I have had to do with no one so devoid of quick wits or lacking in the power of grasping a situation....Mrs Tennant has practically been away all the time I have had the whole Section on my shoulders....

19 August 1917   4/6

VM to C.P. Scott[34]

Mr Chamberlain... utterly devoid of administrative instinct or experience and through weakness he allowed his Department to be driven on to ground where success was impossible. A stronger man would have refused to carry on for forty eight hours under such conditions....

Mr. Chamberlain never realised that so long as the Employment Department was left at large to intrigue against him, his own position was impossible. Chaos can only result from two Departments in the State supplying labour on competitive lines. So strongly do I feel this that in the end I withdrew from the competition.... I feel very strongly that the intrigues carried on by both Mr Rey and Miss Durham against Mr Chamberlain and the species of guerilla warfare waged by the Officials of the Ministry of Labour against the National Service Department. This kind of split is, alas, too common, but it ought in my opinion to be put down with a strong hand....

It was of course the business of Mr Chamberlain to see that he was not treated in such a way, and the business of the Cabinet to ensure that he had adequate powers to carry on his work....

20 August 1917   4/6

VM to A. Tracey, Senior Lady Factory Inspector

....I was not able to go on the Billeting Board Pilgrimage to Barrow. How grotesque these incessant Government enquiries are — all enquiry and no doing. I think the officials arrange them in order to have a little gossip and joy-riding at the public expense.

25 August 1917   NLS 6027 ff 76

VM to Elizabeth Haldane

Dear Fellow Companion I should say!.... One has always some searchings of heart about honours. Much of the best work is of a character which can never be rewarded. But I know you will be glad as I am to see womens' labours officially recognised....

---

[34] C.P. Scott (1846–1932), Editor, *Manchester Guardian* 1872–1929. Liberal MP for Leigh 1895–1905.

21 November 1917   4/12

Katharine Furse to VM

I am very disturbed by symptoms of intrigue and opposition to practical organization of women.

18 December 1917   4/6

VM to John Buchan

.... I was talking to May Tennant last night. We both feel that steps must be taken to rally the morale of the nation. I am really shocked to find how much Lansdownism is abroad....

18 December 1917   4/6

VM to S. [? Coupland, Commissioner at Board of Control]

I am a good deal concerned by the wave of pacifism and pessimism which is sweeping over London especially among the intellectuals.

2 January 1918   25/78

VM to Philippa Strachey[35]

.... When I left the National Service Ministry in August I confess I nearly touched the bottom of disgust and despair, so odious were the intrigues with which we had been surrounded, so useless the inefficiency with which a great piece of national work had been conducted....

The special object of my letter today is, however, to ask you whether some organization of public opinion should not be attempted to stem the prevalent war weariness and depression. I am a good deal concerned by the extent of this evil among our own class. Opinion always filters down from the top, and if the well-to-do classes and the intellectuals throw in their hand most certainly the workers will do the same. I was amazed by the response Lord Lansdowne's mischievous letter received in the most unexpected quarters....

7 January or February? 1918   24/4

Sir Robert Morant to VM

.... for three weeks past the Cabinet have been gravely concerned at the state of things which they believe to exist inside the Food Ministry. They

---

[35] Philippa Strachey (1872–1968), feminist campaigner. With Ray Strachey had set up the Women's Service Bureau to help place women in jobs previously held by men.

have begun to find that Rhondda[36] himself does not know one single word of his job, and makes no decisions on his own knowledge or judgment; that the office is a congeries of disconnected sections with no top grip of it as a whole anywhere.

Wintour, the Head of it, is frankly unable to decide between rival policies within various Departments of the Ministry. Beveridge[37] and Tallents[38] are committing the Ministry to certain lines that are incompatible with the Vivian National Plan.... the Cabinet's grave concern at the Rhondda ignorance and the office lack of cohesion, is causing them to think seriously of superseding Rhondda.... There was a push in some quarters ten days ago to get *me* to go there as Head of one Half, Wintour remaining Head of another Half of the Department. I have definitely said no. Nothing will induce me to go to the Food Department....

Further, the real position of the Consumers' Council has never been properly considered and settled. At first Clynes[39] was in the Chair. On another occasion Hyndman[40] was put in the Chair, no Minister being present, and 'decisions' were adopted by the Council thus left to itself, and subsequently *published* as the *decisions* of the Council, that became virtually imposed on some Food Committees as orders from the Ministry of Food.

Of course that clash of 'responsibility' between the Minister and the Council will not do. Had it not been for the political crisis which is still in a limited sense seething, the Cabinet would this last week have settled as to Rhondda, Wintour, and the rest....

My War Cabinet Secretariat friend this afternoon told me he thought the decisions would *have* to be reached (as to Rhondda, Wintour, etc) within four or five days because B. Law is panic struck at what he sees of the mess....[41]

---

[36] Lord Rhondda (1856–1918), Liberal MP for Merthyr Tydfil 1888–January 1910, Cardiff January–December 1910. 1916–1917 President of the Local Government Board, 1917–1918 Minister of Food Control.

[37] Sir William Beveridge (1879–1963), 1909–1916 Dir. of Labour Exchanges, 1915–1916 Assistant General Secretary, Munitions, 1916–1919 Second Secretary, later Permanent Secretary, Ministry of Food. 1919–1937 Director LSE, 1937–1945 Master, University College, Oxford. Liberal MP for Berwick on Tweed 1944–1945. 1941–1942 Chairman of Interdepartmental Committee on Social Insurance and Allied Services.

[38] Assistant Secretary, Ministry of Food.

[39] J.R. Clynes (1869–1949), Labour MP for Manchester NE 1906–1918, Manchester Platting 1918–1931, 1935–1945. 1917–1918 Parliamentary Secretary, Ministry of Food, 1918–1919 Food Controller, 1924 Lord Privy Seal, 1929–1931 Home Secretary.

[40] Labour representative on Consumers' Council, Ministry of Food.

[41] For a sweeter taste of Rhondda and the Food Ministry see José Harris 'Bureaucrats and businessmen in British food control, 1916–19' in K. Burk (ed), *War and the state: the transformation of British government, 1914–1919* (Allen & Unwin, London, 1982), pp 135–156, 140–146.

30 January 1918 25/76
Lord Derby to VM

.... I cannot understand Northcliffe and I think at times he must be mad. I saw him not a week before the attack on some business and he was most friendly in every way and very complimentary about the way the War Office was being run. I had again to see him on the Friday before the article appeared and he was exactly the reverse. I hate all this newspaper intrigue because one always feels that there may be somebody else at the back of it. By that I do not mean Lloyd George because I do not think he is but I think there are some of his friends who feel that I should be well out of the way if I was turned out. The worst part of Lloyd George is he never believes people in authority. He always believes the last person he sees and the opinion of a subaltern returned from France would weigh more with him than that of any General. All this makes it very difficult to carry on and I confess I am heartily sick of the work. But one has to stick to it because it would never do to be driven out at such a moment as this unless it is by Lloyd George himself....

13 February 1918 2/3
VM to Elizabeth Macadam, Liverpool social worker

Markham was involved in discussions over the future training of social workers

I am very sorry if I gave you the impression that I did not want the voluntary worker to exist, or that I picture the future of the state as one crowded with paid officials. Voluntary service will probably be more necessary to the State in the future than it has ever been in the past. The whole question is the platform on which you get these people together and the point of view from which you present their work to the public.

She argued for an organisation called Social Students Union rather than Union of Voluntary Workers as she feared the latter would rouse the ire of the labour movement. The former

presents our work on a basis of training in citizenship and study. You will be dealing with exactly the same people who will in the main be well-to-do folk of leisure and means.... The more widely we can spread true ideals of citizenship the better....

18 February 1918

VM to Sir Cooper Perry[42]

.... The term 'voluntary worker' is weighted with associations of philanthropy and charity which are not at all in line with modern social expression.... the presentment which is given to the work.... should take the form of citizenship and social study, not that of voluntary work in the old charitable sense. It seems to me quite essential if reconstruction is to be more than an idle name that we should endeavour by every means to raise the general standard of citizenship, education, and intelligence in the country, and the middle and upper classes for whom this particular form of training is desired in practise if not in theory present a very wide field for missionary effort.

20 February 1918

VM to Elizabeth Macadam

.... There is no question in my mind to try and camouflage voluntary work. I do feel strongly, however, the more one can impress upon voluntary workers that they are all part of a big social organism with duties and obligations towards other workers and to the State the broader will be the point of view from which they regard their work as citizens....

28 February 1918

VM to J.A. Spender

Markham doubts that the rumours about the behaviour of WAACs is true, but thinks the rumours might have got abroad as a result of the organisation of the corps and its method of discipline.

.... this Commission suggests to me a concertina turn while England is burning. Grave and heavy as one's anxieties are these days about the military and shipping position, these trials are as nothing compared with the sense of indignity and humiliation one suffers at the recent performance of the Government.

Local Derbyshire Liberals are looking to her to carry on brother's work but

I am very much at a loss at the moment how to orient myself. I feel in the future my sympathies may rest far more with the Labour Party than with the old fashioned Liberals.

---

[42] Sir Cooper Perry (1856–1938), medical doctor. 1892–1920 Superintendent of Guy's Hospital, 1917–1919 Vice-Chancellor of London University, 1920–1926 Principal London University.

22 March 1918 1/11

To The Right Hon. Lord Mayor of Dublin from Dublin cooked food depots central committee

.... Employment is poor at the best of times in Dublin. At the present, it is very seriously curtailed. The Port of Dublin is frequently closed for three or even four days in a week, even when it is open the amount of shipping is much less than the average; hence the Quay labourers are having much less employment than usual. The ordinary Dublin industries are necessarily hindered by these restrictions on the trade of the Port, and many of them have had to dismiss a considerable proportion of their employees because of the shortage of material arising from this and other causes....

In England industries have been interfered with as seriously but there has been no curtailment but rather an increase of employment because of the enormous demand for munition work and allied industries.... In Dublin there is very little munition work to take the place of the local industries which have suffered, and the demand for labour has in consequence fallen off.... In Dublin the rise in wages has been very much less, and is not commensurate with the rise in the cost of living.

.... there are large numbers of families in Dublin who are not paupers, but who are earning a wage totally insufficient for a livelihood.

.... those of us who have personal experience of still poorer classes are emphatic that the diet of many thousands in Dublin consists mainly of bread and tea, supplemented by potatoes, and dripping when it can be got.

The health of a community fed in this manner is of necessity low. If proof of this were necessary it could be supplied by the appalling figures of infant mortality in Dublin.... The present abnormal distress and semi-starvation press more heavily on a population which was already living at or below the Poverty line....

26 March 1918 4/16
VM to Lord Milner

Duplication of facilities for WAACs and VAD in France

.... each body was provided with separate administration, kitchen, and household,—a more glaring example of wastefulness and bad organization one could not wish to see.... I am a great believer in the value of Women's work, and returned full of enthusiasm for the WAACs in France. But I do not think anything can justify the waste and duplication of the present system.

4 April 1918   4/16

VM to Frances Stevenson

[The WAAC commission of enquiry] has brought me into close touch again with the various women's Corps of which I am a great admirer.... the organization of the Penguins[43] is causing a good deal of anxiety among people who are interested in women's work.... all questions connected with their recruitment, welfare, and discipline out of work hours should be entirely in the hands of responsible women....

The chief Superintendent of the Penguins has no Executive power, and questions concerned with the housing and clothing of the women, and the selection of administrators for the Corps are all being dealt with by Air Board officers....

The solution of the work and the relative youth of the officers in command makes the presence of experienced women administrators in positions of real authority essential for good morale and discipline.

6 April 1918   4/13

VM to Julia Varley[44]

Report on morals of women in the services

The War Office actually proposed to leave out all references to cases of venereal disease.

Ministry of Labour and Markham protested against this.

The Ministry of Labour pointed out the extraordinary ostrich-like proceedings of this attitude, that to omit any reference to these cases would be at once to excite public suspicion of the gravest character... the most absolute frankness and candour are essential in dealing with such cases of immoral conduct which came to our notice.

10 April 1918   4/16

VM to Cecil Harmsworth[45]

....I am greatly concerned at the moment about the whole question of woman power. It is deplorable that this grave crisis should find us without proper organization of any kind, for drawing in large numbers of additional

---

[43] Women's Auxiliary Air Force.

[44] Julia Varley (1871–1952), trade unionist and social reformer.

[45] Cecil Harmsworth (1869–1948), Liberal MP for Droitwich 1906–January 1910, Luton 1911–1912. 1915 Parliamentary Under-Secretary at the Home Office, 1917–1919 member of Prime Minister's Secretariat, 1919–1922 Parliamentary Secretary at the Foreign Office, 1919 Acting Minister of Blockade.

women who will be required to fill the places of men.... I feel very strongly about the intrigues and obstructiveness of the Ministry of Labour who I hold very largely responsible for the present unsatisfactory position.... I feel even the over-driven War Cabinet should find time to consider the women's aspect of this question....

10 May 1918 25/76
Lord Derby to VM

I was very unhappy in many ways at leaving the War Office but there were wheels within wheels and there is some compensation in having left. The very painful controversy with Robertson,[46] where I took a line which some people think disloyal to him, made my position difficult. If only people knew that in this particular instance of Robertson's the man whose advice I acted on in staying was Sir Douglas Haig's.[47] I think they would have a different opinion as to one's loyalty.

Markham sat on a sub-committee of a Select Committee on Luxury Duty. By the time it reported on 1 August Markham had already resigned from the sub-committee. (There were jibes in the press about those members of the committee, such as Freddy Guest's rich American wife, with experience in the use of luxuries, and the presence of Markham who was by now well-known for her association with the ill-starred Women's Section of the NSD.)[48]

23 May 1918 2/4
VM to Sir Arthur (J.A.R.) Marriott[49]

....I believe that the principle of a Luxury Tax is economically unsound, and that excessive expenditure should be dealt with either through the Income Tax or a new Expenditure tax. The whole business...is a bit of flagrant eye wash on the part of the Government who want to demonstrate their virtue by taxing the wicked rich ....

---

[46] General William Robertson (1860–1933), 1915–1918 Chief of the Imperial General Staff.
[47] Field Marshal Sir Douglas Haig (1861–1928)
[48] *The Queen*, 15 May 1918.
[49] Sir J.A.R. Marriott (1859–1945), Conservative MP for Oxford City 1917–1922, York 1923–1929.

13 September 1918   4/16

VM to Miss Violet Douglas Pennant[50]

Looking at the matter from a purely abstract standpoint it seems to me intolerable that a man in authority can dismiss a woman in authority at a moment's notice and order her out of the office. Against such a precedent all women ought to protest....

5 October 1918   25/16

Henry Clay[51] to VM

I wish you could wake Asquith to a sense of the responsibilities of his position. The real charge against the coalition is that by destroying the Opposition, it removes the possibility of an alternative Government & so leaves us in the hands of LG. The essence of constitutional freedom lies in the existence of an available alternative Government, because a Government that knows there is an alternative on the other side of the House will take good care to do nothing that it thinks the people really object to. Asquith *ought* to offer that alternative Government, but he is taking no steps to demarcate his following, by framing a consistent & positive programme, from LG's on the one hand & Henderson's[52] on the other.

---

[50] National Insurance Commissioner for Wales and very briefly Commander in Chief WAAF.

[51] Sir Henry Clay (1883–1954), economist, temporary Chief of Section, Ministry of Labour.

[52] Arthur Henderson (1863–1935), Labour MP for Barnard Castle 1903–1918, Widnes 1919–1922, Newcastle East 1923, Burnley 1924–1931, Clay Cross 1933–1935. 1915–1916 President of the Board of Education, 1916 Paymaster-General, 1916–1917 Minister without Portfolio, 1924 Home Secretary, 1921–1931 Foreign Secretary.

3
Women without Work
1918–1939

After the First World War, Markham's interests continued to be wide-ranging. Living in Germany stimulated her interest in foreign affairs; she maintained links with Chesterfield, acting as Mayor from 1927 to 1928, but as her letter of 22 February 1920 shows, she was careful only to take on work which carried with it a degree of prestige. Her main governmental work was overseeing training schemes for unemployed women, which was a continuation of her war-time work, and fitted in well with the Liberal Party's concern about high levels of unemployment. Markham's interest in the problem of unemployment was typical of a number of Liberals, most notably Lloyd George, who from the late 1920s, campaigned around the issue of unemployment, and periodically produced schemes for solving the problem.

Contemporary writings and historical analyses of unemployment focus on unemployed men. Markham's correspondence in the 1920s shows the kinds of schemes governments ran for unemployed women, and the attitudes of Markham, and other officials, to women without paid work.

In January 1920, largely at the instigation of Mary Macarthur, the wartime Central Committee on Women's Training and Employment (CCWTE) was revived to devise and oversee schemes for unemployed women. Initially, the committee, with funds left over from the Queen's Work for Women Fund and the National Relief Fund, was fairly independent of the Ministry of Labour, but as the Treasury took over more and more of the funding, governmental control increased. Between the wars roughly 90,000 women passed through CCWTE schemes. At first, from 1920 to 1922, the committee provided commercial and industrial training, but in 1921 it switched to domestic service training schemes for unemployed working-class women in industrial areas. Centres developed from temporary courses held in schools and halls and organised with local education authorities to more permanent institutions, both residential and non-residential. From time to time courses were arranged for hotel workers and older women. From 1927 to 1930 the CCWTE administered, on behalf of the Australian government and Overseas Settlement Department, a domestic training residential centre for women before they emigrated to Australia.

Markham was also involved in promoting middle-class women's work. She sat on a Home Office committee which recommended the amalgamation of the men's and women's sections of the Factory Inspectorate, she pressed for the employment of women in senior civil service posts, and she sat on a committee, set up after the passage of the 1919 Sex Disqualification (Removal) Act, which advised the Lord Chancellor about the appointment of women JPs. Markham herself was to become a JP.

14 November 1918 UCT BC 643 B18. 17
VM to Cyril 'Tommy' Newton Thompson[1]

.... I have been persuaded *most reluctantly* to stand as an independent Liberal for Mansfield. My brother's old friends appealed to me on grounds I couldn't resist. I hate it all badly but I am quite sure I shan't win so it will be just an election campaign & I am accustomed to them. I have only taken it on for a year in any case—Parliament is no job for a married woman. But here & now it seemed a bit like shirking to hang back....

3 January 1919 25/16
Henry Clay to VM

It is rather curious that the Labour Party taking the place of the Liberals as the Opposition is not only far more 'Lib-Lab' than Socialist, but really more Liberal than either the Labour Party in the late Parliament or the Liberal Party in the late Parliament....

4 January 1919 25/60
VM to Nancy Nettleford

Markham had recently discussed her ideas about the future of industry with Henry Clay

.... the State should not except in the case of monopolies concern itself with the management of industry but with the control of the conditions under which industry takes place.... It is the business of the State to see that the citizen is born under proper conditions, grows up under proper conditions of health, is properly housed, properly educated. The State must ensure proper standards of life and wages for all its citizens, proper conditions of work, reasonable hours, adequate leisure. The nightmare of unemployment

[1] Husband of Joyce Newton Thompson, a friend of Markham's, living in South Africa.

must be removed, and pensions for mothers, widows, and families must be secured on a scale little contemplated at present....

The State must insist upon measures being taken in the management of industry which will counteract the present dehumanising effects of large scale production.... It is here that I part company definitely with the collectivists. Industry in the long run must be conducted on lines which make it profitable, and the very conditions of State ownership and management by State officials would paralyse a large range of industries in which capacity and power to take risks is often a determining factor

Markham goes on to discuss the League of Nations.

The interference of the League in economic matters might be as dangerous as I feel the interference of the State in trade matters is likely to be....

There are other matters of the first importance with which the League should concern itself. There is the question of appointing Trustee Powers under carefully laid down Trusts for all the derelict countries with which the world is strewn at present; there are questions of communication and waterways; a new body of international law and practice has to be worked out as regards the air ways; there is the standardisation of labour laws; there are currency problems and... the conservation of the world's resources. Above all, there is the inestimable moral and political advantage of a development in Government which brings the heads of all the States together once or twice a year....

12 January 1919 25/24

Sir Malcolm Delevingne[2] to VM

....The war has done those of us who work in Government Offices the service of bringing us into closer relations, and creating new ties of acquaintance and understanding with those who are doing public work outside; and of all those who have come in and shared in our work at the Home Office I would most gladly have your good opinion....

---

[2] Sir Malcolm Delevingne (1868–1950), civil servant and reformer. 1913–1922 Assistant Under-Secretary Home Office, 1922–1932 Deputy Under-Secretary Home Office. 1936 Chairman of interdepartmental committee on rehabilitation of persons injured by accidents. Heavily involved in improving health and safety at the workplace and with drug regulation. Worked closely with ILO. Interested in charitable work. In 1939 became chairman of Dr Barnardo's Homes.

15 January 1919 25/12

VM to Hilda Cashmore

I have [been] thinking a great deal about women and Parliamentary life, and feel satisfied that the key to the situation lies in the Local Government position and in organising women for Municipal elections. This would familiarise women with the procedure of elections and familiarise the electorate with the idea of women standing. Also, the great social questions Health, Housing, Education, etc., are all carried out at present through local bodies, and there is a great deal of work crying out to be done for which women have special gifts. I am really keen to get women organised on these lines, but I do not feel inclined to embark on the adventure unless we could be sure of the support of younger women. The Women's Local Government Society is mainly composed of the dull females of the N[ational] U[nion of] W[omen] W[orkers], aged ladies bowed down with years and general stuffiness....

I am pondering deeply the whole problem of Equal Pay for Equal Work and the question of the Endowment of Motherhood,[3] and I want very badly to know your views. I am absolutely opposed to a dual standard in industry. On the industrial side equal pay for equal work is the only safeguard for the standard of life for the working classes. Clearly work should be paid for according to its value and the advantageousness to the employer without regard to the sex of the worker. I see the force of all this, but I am pulled up short by the fact that as society is at present constituted the burthen of bringing up the next generation is mainly thrown upon the man's wage, and you have this social factor cutting across the industrial position in a very distracting manner. Endowment of motherhood may be a way out, but if Miss Rathbone's scheme were to be adopted the effect on wages would I fear be disastrous all round.

23 April 1919 NLS 6028 ff34-36

VM to Elizabeth Haldane

....I went to France to lecture to the Army under the auspices of the Y.M.C.A. I formed a very poor impression of the efforts of the latter to dabble with education. I have never run up against anything so muddle headed & inefficient as they were & I didn't bless them for the way they wasted my time. Fancy a lecture on the Whitley Report being backed on to a Lena Ashwell concert....

In the summer of 1919 Markham was asked to look into the living conditions and behaviour of 30–40 women clerks working for the British High Commission in Coblenz. During her visit she found no evidence of any se-

---

[3] Family allowances, for which Eleanor Rathbone was now heading a campaign

rious trouble or bad behaviour, but nevertheless she suggested that better care should be taken in the selection of women to work in Germany, that they should all have to live in hostels and that various regulations should be introduced for the women. If they did not like the regulations, they should leave. She also suggested that the women should wear a uniform, because it would encourage the growth of a 'corporate sense and would be a check on flighty behaviour'.[4]

In July 1919 Markham had been asked to sit on a committee of inquiry into the organisation of the Factory Inspectorate and, in particular, into the fusion of the men's and women's sections. Women Factory Inspectors had first been appointed in the 1890s, specifically to investigate the working conditions of women.

13 January 1920 5/1

Constance Smith, Factory Inspector, to VM

All the events of the last two or three months — the new doors opened to women, women in the [Forces], and on the Magistrates' bench, and in Parliament — make the argument for defining and strengthening their position in the Factory Department more evident and constraining than it was before. I have been trying hard to clear my own mind (and, incidentally the minds of some colleagues who seem to me far too much inclined to view the question from a personal point of view, coloured by recollections of past friction) on the points at issue....

18 January 1920 5/1

Constance Smith to VM

[Sir Malcolm Delevingne] is definitely prepared to put the man under the woman as well as the woman under the man....

No, Adelaide [Anderson] doesn't like the ... scheme, but she wants a kind of feminist modification of it which would still keep the women Inspectors in a side current—this is where I think her fundamentally wrong.

Constance Smith held a meeting with the younger women Factory Inspectors.

---

[4] 2/7 Report on women clerical staff at Coblenz, Violet Markham, August 1919.

27 January 1920 5/1

Constance Smith to VM

One said 'it is we who would have to work under men, not the seniors—and if we are willing, for the sake of the future and of women in general, then why not?'

22 February 1920 2/6

VM to Mr Robson

.... It would be very unacceptable to me to serve on the Chesterfield Borough Bench which is a body of small repute or standing locally—I hope therefore I may be allowed to serve on the County Bench....

29 March 1920 NLS 6028 ff84

VM to Elizabeth Haldane

On women JPs

....I hope we shall avoid getting the list too aristocratic. I get dreadfully bored with the type of woman who 'presides' just because she is her husband's wife....

26 July 1920 5/1

Malcolm Delevingne to VM

We have got the Treasury reply at last. The scheme of fusion [between the men's and women's sections of the Factory Department] is sanctioned but they have reduced most of the women's scales on the grounds that the Government have decided that there must be a 'certain differentiation' between the scales of men and women as recommended by the report of the Civil Service National Whitley Council....

26 August 1920 NLS 6028 ff 107-108

VM to Elizabeth Haldane

.... We leave Cologne tonight & I have nothing but regret in doing so. The year I have spent here has been so worth while in every way. If anybody had told me two years ago I should be leaving Germany & a variety of humble German friends with something perilously like a lump in my throat—how mad I should have thought such a person! But oh the tragedy of the war—the great & horrible tragedy that it ever happened. And I come home horribly baffled about the Germans. I can't understand how these decent self respecting people for whom one has such real liking & regard can have these sinister & brutal sides.... The whole European situation makes one almost despair. What will the Poles do with their victory & in what further folly will they engage? And here in Germany the feeling between the Germans & the French grows more bitter daily. There is little feeling against us. The Occupation is run on just fair lines & we don't irritate the people. But as for the French their attitude is impossible. I want to stir up the League of Nations people in England about the position of the Saar where all manner of abuses are going on in the name of the League. There has been a General Strike & the whole place topsy turvy....

14 June 1921 3/14
VM to May Tennant, vice-chair CCWTE

I went with Gertrude [Tuckwell][5] and Miss Barker[6] to have an interview with Sir Robert Blair[7] about the cost of training schemes. I can assure you it was one of the most painful and humiliating half hours I have ever sat through. Blair was extraodinarily disagreeable and did not spare Miss Barker.

He showed them that costs had risen while the amount of training had decreased.

.... Dr [Marion] Phillips[8] showed great hostility to the suggestion of having another Civil Servant in; declared those we had at the beginning of the war were quite useless. This amazed me much because my mind went back to the struggles of those early days. I remember how it was part of the disagreeable duties of Bunbury, Salter & Co, to amend her letters and check wartime ambitious and quite unsuitable schemes she was bent on developing. She agrees another good business head is wanted in the office, but would like to get a person outside the Government ranks.

---

[5] Gertrude Tuckwell (1861–1951), President of Women's Trade Union League 1904–1921, member of CCWTE.

[6] Lilian Barker (1874–1955), during First World War organised training of cooks for the army, 1915 appointed woman supervisor at Woolwich Arsenal, CCWTE executive officer and Hon.sec.

[7] LCC education officer.

[8] Marion Phillips (1881–1932), suffragist, Fabian. Appointed to CCWE, Reconstruction Committee, and Consumer's Council of Ministry of Food during the First World War. 1918 appointed Chief Woman Organiser of the Labour Party. Also a JP and member of CCWTE. Labour MP for Sunderland 1929–1931.

1 July 1921 3/14

VM to Laurie Brock

....As you know, I think the administrative side of the Central Committee is weak at present.... At the same time I can assure you it is my honest conviction that nothing very bad has happened, neither do I think a lot of unsuitable cases have been given grants. A few doubtful cases may have slipped through, but a great deal of trouble has been taken with the applications ....

As for the three disgruntled women, I think I have composed the row on the Committee and there are to be no resignations. Mrs Chamberlain never attends a meeting so any view she may hold is picked up second hand from the others. Lady Askwith is a quarrelsome, incompetent woman filled with a sense of her own importance, radically sloppy minded and has never realised that any fool can make trouble, but it takes a certain amount of brain to keep the peace and get business along. Lady Midleton is quite a good soul, but also amateurish and sloppy minded. By this I mean they have never put their objections on paper, that they could not I think at the moment raise a single concrete case, and as I told you, Lady Askwith was Chairman of the Sub-Committee which drew up the revised Eligibility Rules, accepted the recommendations, made no protest or reservation, and then came to the main Committee and said she would resign if the Report of the Sub-Committee of which she was Chairman was accepted. When her somewhat curious position was put to her she said she had had no time to read the papers ....

I am very anxious, as you know, to get the work of the Committee on to sound lines, and your help from the outside will be quite invaluable to me in doing this because you can put pressure in certain directions which it would be difficult to apply from within.

19 November 1921 3/14

George Murray to Laurie Brock

....I wish we could persuade the Committee to do more for domestic service.

....On every side you hear of the difficulty of getting domestic servants, especially in the lower grades; and yet thousands of them are getting unemployment pay.

22 January 1922 NLS 6028 ff 199-201

VM to Elizabeth Haldane

....The Liberal attitude towards education is deplorably negative. Yet I cling, like yourself, to the party for great though its weakness at the moment

& deplorable though the lack of vision in our unsatisfactory leaders, Liberalism as a *faith* & a *principle* is what I cannot give up.... [Lloyd George] is at once too clever & too dishonest. He hates organisation or organised bodies. Parliament, the Cabinet the Civil Service — he seeks to destroy them utterly & turn them into bodies he can manipulate. Manipulation is the key note of his character.... He has too much genius & in many ways too much soul not to see rightly & bigly at times. But you can't rely on him....

27 March 1922 3/15
Lilian Barker to VM

.... at the last Main Committee meeting, in real simpleness of heart, I suggested that we should wipe out entirely all applications, except those of real war detriment, on the professional side. This would have meant eliminating all cases where there was the slightest doubt as to eligibility. I knew that Margaret Bondfield[9] agreed, and the whole of those present at the meeting were with me, with the exception of Miss Durham, and she raised the point that it was too big an issue to put before the Committee without notice.

There was a fearful lot of discussion, and in the end Lady Askwith entered the arena, saying that she was outraged that there was still any question of doubtful cases going through.

I must tell you that previously she had been very angry, and in my opinion justly so—because during my absence in the North, the daughter of a conscientious objector had been given a grant.

....I have a letter from Lady Askwith stating that if the Committee do not agree to rule out cost of living cases entirely—she will resign, and I think she means it this time ....

Dr Marion Phillips objects to these cases being ruled out, because she thinks that we cannot, at the eleventh hour, alter our terms of reference.

....We had a deputation of unemployed women, representing all the Women's Unions, to [Thomas] Macnamara,[10] Minister of Labour asking that our Committee should be given a further grant for training. Another deputation from Lady Astor's[11] Consultative Committee, urging the same

---

[9] Margaret Bondfield (1873–1953), Labour MP for Northampton 1923–1924, Wallsend 1926–1931. 1924 Parliamentary Secretary Ministry of Labour, 1929–1931 Minister of Labour. Labour Party Women's Organiser.

[10] Thomas Macnamara (1861–1931), Liberal MP for Camberwell North 1900–1918, Coalition Liberal Camberwell North West 1918–1924. 1907–1908 Parliamentary Secretary Local Government Board, 1908–1920 Parliamentary and Financial Secretary to the Admiralty, 1920–1922 Minister of Labour.

[11] Nancy Astor (1879–1964), Conservative MP for Plymouth Sutton 1919–1945.

thing, was to have been received last Thursday, but owing to the Engineering strike it did not come off; Lady Astor is attacking Macnamara privately, however.

I do not think it is the least likely that the Government will give us a grant, but it is rather nice to know that our work is so appreciated that warring factors like Lady Astor's Committee can unite in asking for a further grant in recognition of the good work we have done.

13 October 1922   3/15
VM to T.J. Macnamara

Macnamara had suggested deleting singing from the curriculum in homecraft centres.

.... When the Committee first organised training in Homecraft the subjects of the curriculum engaged their attention very closely, and singing was included advisedly in the course. The difficulties of converting factory workers into domestic servants were considerable from many points of view. Those difficulties could only be met, in the opinion of the Committee, both from the side of the employer and that of the girl, by the introduction of a certain physical and cultural element into the curriculum. After much reflection it was decided, as you are aware, to devote 25 hours weekly to vocational training, and 5 hours weekly to physical exercises, singing, and general education. In this view the Committee had behind them the support of a large body of expert opinion — educational experts, and social workers familiar with the problems of training girls of the industrial type. The reports from the Homecraft Centres during the last eighteen months have amply confirmed this general opinion. The inclusion of singing has proved of special value in the stimulation of esprit de corps and in the maintenance of good discipline and morale.

In view of these facts you will understand that the Committee feel considerable difficulty about deleting singing from the curriculum. In considering the nature of the charges levelled against the Ministry of Labour in this matter, and also the ill considered and even malicious tone of the correspondence to which the Committee themselves have been subjected, they cannot regard these attacks in the light of genuine criticism or in any light save that of calculated political hostility.

.... concession to an attack of this character, confined as it is to a small and hostile section of the Press, would encourage further ignorant attacks on the whole scheme. The Committee feel that criticism of this type is directed, not against any given detail of the curriculum, but against the general principle of training courses for unemployed women .... a desertion of principle at the present time would undoubtedly arouse merited criticism from another section of the public which believes in the training of working class women....

30 December 1923 25/24
Sir Malcolm Delevingne to VM

....By the way, the men inspectors or some of them are growsing again about the new organisation on the grounds that some women are getting much quicker promotion verdicts than the men and they want to bring the matter up at the Departmental Whitley Council. Under the Whitley Council system and the organisation of the different classes of civil servants which it implies, there is certainly a tendency for sectional interests to be emphasised which is going to make difficulties.

8 January 1924 NLS 6030 ff 8
VM to Elizabeth Haldane

....I feel there are few joys in life like the joy of *creation*. And I think book writing is a special consolation to us childless women who haven't fulfilled ourselves in the normal way....

At the end of 1924 Margaret Bondfield wrote to Markham to suggest that she join the Labour party, because their goals in the field of education were so close. Markham remained a Liberal.

9 January 1924 NLS 6029 ff 120
VM to Elizabeth Haldane

....Oh my dear—my path has been so encumbered by odious servant worries & a procession of damsels through this house who arrive with wonderful testimonials & reveal the standards of a lodging house....

20 April 1925 UCT BC643 B18.28
VM to Joyce Newton Thompson

....I am in the thick of my municipal contest & it is a hard fight. This is a very anti feminist place. I suppose it's only fair that I who once 'persecuted the church' should be up against the unfair prejudices about women. It riles me when vulgar & degraded men say women are no good & they dont want a woman on the Council....

April 1925 UCT BC643

Markham's election address

.... as women now share the privileges of equal citizenship with men, they should not shirk the responsibilities of that new status, but be prepared to pull their full weight in the boat. Municipal affairs, it should be remembered, fall very largely within a woman's special province. A woman's first job is homemaking, and the great activities of a Municipality, Health, Housing, Education, are concerned with the nation's homemaking on a public scale. The day is long past when men and women could be cooped up in separate pens; a few ladylike, philanthropic duties being left to the women, while men do the rest....

I look on a sound education as the master key to citizenship....

15 July 1925 UCT BC 643 B 18. 31

VM to Joyce Newton Thompson

....I am perpetually bombarded by Birth Control enthusiasts who want me to join their committees. This I will never do because I make it an absolute rule never to give my name to any committee for which I am not working & I *can't* take on a difficult & controversial subject like Birth Control; not from any lack of sympathy with the aims but because I literally haven't the time to devote to it.... I am enjoying my municipal work & feel it really worth while. After the futility of political life in recent years I feel the dustbin splendidly concrete. However small the scale *something* happens....

During the coal strike Markham told Cynthia Colville, Lady-in-Waiting to Queen Mary, that she found the owners stupid and lacking vision, and that the mines should be nationalised, but she also thought that the miners should take a pay cut, and 'Every comfort I possess in life is bound up with their work'.[12]

7 December 1926 3/15

VM to Dame Meriel Talbot, Overseas Settlement Department

....I do hope we shall be able to come to an arrangement at once satisafactory and amicable with Australia House about the question of selection. Obviously the responsibility and final choice is theirs. On the other hand you will understand that our Committee would be unwilling to admit girls to the hostel whom our own people were convinced would be unsuitable for training... we have a good deal of experience of what sort of stuff is trainable and what is not.

[12] 26/14 VM to Cynthia Colville, 1 June 1926.

.... May Tennant .... told me what serious complaints she had heard when she was in Australia and New Zealand about some of the girls who had been sent out. She said that some of them had got thoroughly demoralised on the journey and had refused to do a hand's turn of work when they arrived. Nothing would destroy the success of the Centre more certainly than any large proportion of failures among the girls either as trainees or on arrival in Australia.... [13]

4 February 1928 2/6
VM to Laurie Brock

VM had just refused an invitation to serve on a committee of inquiry into a VD hospital.

Of course on a job like this you do not want one of those rampant feminists, the type of woman who exasperates me more and more each day....

14 December 1928 5/8
VM to Sir Arthur Steel-Maitland[14]

At a meeting of the Central Committee yesterday great concern was expressed at the state of affairs in the distressed mining areas.

.... we would ask you to consider establishing in the distressed areas a certain number of workrooms for unemployed women of the kind that were successfully organised by the Committee in the early days of the war.

2 April 1930 3/16
VM to G.T. Reid, Acting Assistant Secretary, Employment and Training Department, Ministry of Labour

.... As you know, the Committee generally and the office bearers in particular have got very restive about the delays with schemes, and the fact that discussion apparently went on about our work with the Treasury, of which we had only vague second-hand information.

---

[13] The scheme was wound up in 1930.
[14] Sir Arthur Steel-Maitland (1876–1935), Conservative MP for Birmingham East January 1910–1918, Birmingham Erdington 1918–1929, Tamworth 1929–1935. 1915–1917 Parliamentary Under-Secretary Colonial Office, 1917–1919 Joint Parliamentary Under-Secretary Foreign Office and Parliamentary Secretary Board of Trade, 1924–1929 Minister of Labour.

28 October 1930
VM to Tom Jones 26/48

Markham wrote to TJ about ways of spending Pilgrim Trust money; she suggested prizes for essays on political science.

The democratic system, to work properly, requires an educated poeple and an honest press. We unfortunately, have neither the one nor the other. We have gone on mechanically extending the franchise without any regard to the quality of the voters who are called upon to decide vast national and international issues. We have collected a mob, a mob liable to be swayed by the crudest appeals to prejudice and self-interest, and then we are surprised we have not got good government....

29 January 1931 3/13
VM to J.A.N. Barlow, Principal Assistant Secretary, (Acting Deputy Secretary), Ministry of Labour

A year earlier Markham had gone on a tour of Lancashire to discover why, with rising unemployment, CCWTE centres were so unpopular.

....It is a paradox that we have to scrape and struggle in some areas to keep a group of 40 girls going at a Training Centre when there are thousands of women on the Live Register.

Markham suggests reasons for this

1. Timidity and reluctance about leaving home. 2. Uncertainty about conditions of domestic employment. 3. Long hours and lack of personal freedom in the evenings (Time off may be given in the afternoon and work is not continuous but the day straggles out at both ends). 4. A servile tradition which has brought domestic work into contempt. 5. The questions of the Insurance Act. Great reluctance on the part of genuine workers to leave an insured for an uninsured trade apart from the supposed loss of status. The temptation to loaf indefinitely (thanks to the 30 stamps in 2 years provision of the Act) among the less worthy type of girl who can secure benefit with so much ease.

[The individual Training Schemes]

Miss Tomlinson [Ministry of Labour] would explain to you the mental or physical weaknesses which lead to so many applicants being turned down. Girls of the poorest unskilled labour type want to be clerical workers for no better reason than class snobbery.

....I am perfectly clear in my own mind that the average worker nowadays in England interprets the Insurance Act not as a protection against

Unemployment but as laying on the State the obligation to provide an exact type of work at a given wage and in a given place, and failing this the right to an indefinite pension.

Markham had a longstanding interest in unemployment, especially women's unemployment and in the early 1930s she, like many others at the time, toyed with various ideas for job creation schemes. Little resulted from the range of proposals until 1934 when the government decided to take the problem more seriously. Four special investigators were dispatched to the regions to report. Markham was an obvious candidate for the statutory female appointment to the Unemployment Assistance Board (UAB), which was created by the 1934 Unemployment Act. The UAB was charged with drawing up and putting into practice a system of standardised means-tested benefits for claimants who were not covered by unemployment insurance, and which would replace the old public assistance committees (smeared with Poor Law connections). Although some of Markham's papers on the subject of unemploymemt in the 1930s are rather formal, particularly extracts from memoranda, they have been included because they reveal the attitudes and assumptions of one of the most central, and most influential woman participants in government policies towards the unemployed. They show her attempts to find out about the conditions of the unemployed for herself and the extent to which this actually altered her assumptions.

27-30 January 1933   5/8

Notes VM made for a conference on Welsh distressed (high unemployment) areas

The scale of unemployment among women is substantially lower than that among men, the figures being respectively 25 and 12 per cent. But in addition to women normally in industry we have to consider the needs of the wives and daughters of the unemployed men. These women suffer cruelly from the anxieties and uncertainties which oppress family life in an area of severe unemployment. Women, like men, pass through a well recognised cycle of apathy, demoralisation and despair. No attempt, therefore, to deal with the consequences of unemployment can be satisfactory which ignores this side of the question. We have to consider the family as a whole, not the sections of which it is made up....

Work among unemployed women and girls falls mainly under four heads. Occupation, Recreation, Physical Training and Education. As an opposite number to the men's Occupation Centres, Make-and-Mend Centres can be started with advantage to the women. The need of clothes in many distressed areas is urgent and when women come together in a spirit of neighbourliness to make clothes not only for themselves but for their friends, such a Centre goes a long way to dispel apathy and that sense of uselessness which is one of the most cruel consequences of unemployment. The provision of material is often difficult in areas long hard hit and such areas are forced to rely on outside supplies in money or material. Mass organisation here as elsewhere should be avoided, but if it were possible to link up units of women in districts still prosperous with clubs and centres in a distressed area, such contacts would have a human, as well as a practical, value.

From an occupation centre many useful activities can spring. Women who come together for work may find it worth while subsequently to explore other possibilities.... New interest taken in opportunities provided for further education, music, physical training, handicraft, dancing, may help to dispel some of the prevailing gloom. In any scheme two principles should be kept in mind; first that a successful Club or Centre must always carry the confidence and good will of its members or give expression to their ideas; secondly that as far as possible efficient bodies already on the ground should be helped to develop their work.... Generally speaking all large scale schemes should be avoided. Work among unemployed people involves much care and sympathetic personal handling.... A whole-time leader is necessary for working up the general activities, but voluntary helpers who give regular service can play an important part on the social and recreative side.

Cookery talks and talks on domestic management can be of great value to the women and help them to improve the efficiency of the home. Talks on health and hygiene are no less desirable .... Joint activities for men and women together should always be kept in view. Where a men's centre exists a weekly social evening for the wives is a good plan. If a canteen is started women can help in the preparation of meals and in so doing may learn a whole range of new facts about food values and economical cookery. In some areas where distress is acute, the provision of nourishing food for purchase at a low figure offers many advantages to the family.

.... Local schemes are real schemes and variety is a sign of vigour and vitality. One principle, however, should be kept in view wherever this movement spreads—the principle of work for and with one another, not work autocratically directed from above.

19 December 1933 3/19

V M to Sir Henry Betterton[15]

I forward you at the request of the Central Committee the following resolution that was passed unanimously at their meeting on December 14th last: 'In view of the separate interests of women involved in the Unemployment

---

[15] Henry Betterton (1872–1949), Conservative MP for Rushcliffe 1918–1924. 1923–1924 and 1924–1929 Parliamentary Secretary Ministry of Labour, 1931–1934 Minister of Labour.

Bill, that in any machinery set up under Part I or Part II, place should be made for a representative woman with special knowledge of industrial conditions.' In forwarding this resolution may I add that it was not inspired by any feminist spirit or in accordance with the mechanical principle that exacts the presence of a woman on every occasion irrespective of her qualifications.... We feel that in many respects the interests of the unemployed women differ from those of the men and that their special needs may very easily be overlooked unless it is someone's business to keep them in view.

On a small administrative body a woman can hardly hope to find a place unless special provision is made for her.... We feel sure that the machinery to be set up under the Bill will benefit by the cooperation of a woman with experience in industrial matters and that her presence will gratify working class opinion.

18 April 1934 5/9

VM to Geoffrey Dawson

....I know that there is everything to be said normally against Emergency Loans and Relief Works. But no-one can view Jarrow where 90% of the insured population have been out of work for some years without feeling that it would be far better for the Government to take over Palmers Yard and build a cruiser — even if they found it necessary subsequently to take it out into the Atlantic and sink it — rather than allow the present rot to go on indefinitely.

14 May 1934 5/9

Neville Chamberlain, Chancellor of the Exchequer to VM

Thank you for your letter received this morning about the derelict areas.

I don't quite know why you pick me out as the Minister specially concerned, as I should have thought that this description should rather have applied to the Minister of Labour or the Minister of Health. If, however, you mean that I am personally specially interested in this problem, you are quite right, and I have indeed given a great deal of thought to it for a long time past.

....I shall be delighted to discuss things with you.

I will only say this now, that I am convinced there is no easy or short way of solving the problem. Every district has its own features, and it is only by study of them that one can find the appropriate means of dealing with them.

23 May 1934

VM to Neville Chamberlain

To clear the ground before we meet and to avoid any undue waste of your time, I am putting on paper the ideas I have in mind so that you may be able to judge whether any further discussion would be profitable.

.... So long as the wave of an unparalleled trade depression submerged the whole country, it was impossible to set special measures on foot even for the areas most affected.... To-day, though we are still far removed from normal conditions, the outlook is brighter and there is a greater background of hope ....

It is important I think to distinguish between areas that are distressed and those that are derelict. The first may recover any way some measure of prosperity; the second cannot.... In such places, where the unemployment figures have reached a fantastic total, human beings are sinking day by day ever deeper into misery and despair. The steady loss of craftsmanship is a national peril. And as time goes by, the months carry away with them hope, heart, and skill from the elder generation and cleanliness of mind and body from the younger people.... But goodwill is frustrated by the sense of being caught in a barbed wire entanglement of convention and of objection. We fall back on the dole because any constructive proposal, judged by orthodox standards, seems impossible. I submit that abnormal circumstances call for abnormal remedies even though the remedies involve the temporary scrapping of principles sound as a general rule .... If men are to be saved morally and physically from the abyss into which they have fallen, the provision of work has become far more important than that of dole money even were it possible to double the existing amount. This need has become so overwhelming that other considerations must yield to it....

First of all I would schedule a few special areas for experimental measures and draw a line round them....

First, in each area it will be necessary to appoint a Director with an adequate staff and give him practically autocratic powers; second, it will be necessary to raise an Emergency Loan at a low rate of interest to provide the funds required....

The Director .... must be directed ultimately to getting as many people as possible out of the district.

.... In a scheduled area the Director would set men to work on a variety of small amenity schemes of a kind that will be of permanent benefit even to a shrunken population. A playing field for the children, a recreation ground for the adult population, a public bath, a swimming pool, a community hall to act as a social service head-quarters, are activities that would involve a minimum of interference with ordinary economic employment. In a mining area the clearing away of tips and rubbish would employ a large number of men and be a boon to the men and women whose lives are encompassed by this dismal wreckage.

.... The machinery used by the Director should, wherever possible, be that of the Local Authority.... It is essential to get away from the demoralising atmosphere of relief works.

.... It is of the first importance that the Director should keep his finger on the pulse of local opinion and goodwill and carry the community with him in his plans. Equally important will it be to secure the goodwill and co-operation of the Labour and Trade Union leaders.

.... His primary aim in a stricken area will be to set a proportion of the population to work again; to get some measure of normalcy restored to life.... Grandiose land schemes are out of the question for an industrial population, but young men, when suitable, should be encouraged to train for work on the land and fit themselves to become small-holders.

... Meanwhile the Director would promote transference among the younger people by training suitable girls for domestic work and by industrial training for boys and young men.

.... If I could, as a start, get between 30 and 40 per cent of the insured men into regular occupation, personally I should be satisfied. It is difficult in a derelict area to over-estimate the psychological effect of a resumption of work. After years of idleness the new fact of work and wages for even a proportion of the population will create a new position. Money will begin to circulate, hope to revive. With employment will come the revival of self-respect, of courage, of physical vigour.

.... The dole is a heavy burthen on the taxpayer; yet when through stress of circumstance it has become the normal not abnormal income of the family, it provides but a miserable pittance for the family needs and one incapable of supporting life at a decent level.

.... The Personal Service League with its efficient distribution of clothes, the National Council of Social Service with its occupation centres and other schemes for leisure activities (to name two organisations out of many others), deserve our warmest thanks for the work they have done and the candles of hope they have lit in districts where but for their efforts complete darkness would have reigned.... But they are powerless to touch more than the fringe of the problem. They can only alleviate some bye-products of the evil; they cannot attack or cure its root. In the nature of things they can only deal with a fraction of the numbers concerned. It is an auxiliary not a primary force but in so far as charitable appeals for the unemployed lead the unthinking public to believe that something substantial and constructive is being done, they may serve as a dangerous narcotic to the national conscience.

7 June 1934   5/9

VM to Henry Brooke, working for Political and Economic Planning (PEP)[16]

.... My interview with the Chancellor and Sir Henry Betterton took place last week, and nothing of any sort or kind resulted from it. Mr. Chamberlain's attitude was that he could say nothing and do nothing until his investigators had reported. He told me that some of the ideas in the memorandum I put forward were very present in his mind but that it was idle to discuss policy in any form until the Commissioners had sent in their reports. He was quite friendly, but I left the hall of audience wondering why he had wasted half-an-hour talking to me and could only conclude it was from kindness of heart and the memory of old days when I worked under him.

17 July 1934   9/3

VM to Philippa Strachey

.... I wonder if your Society[17] has any particulars of the number of women engaged in the Local Government Service? As you know, there will have to be a readjustment of staff between the Public Assistance Committees and the Board, and I am very anxious to lay my hand on any intelligent women that are in official positions in the provinces. Investigating posts under the Poor Law Authorities are nearly always filled by men, and this, I am sure, is quite wrong. Very often, it is the roughness and rudeness of these people that has raised such bitter resentment among the unemployed over the inquiries that are necessary in assessing the needs of a family. The experience of the women rent collectors shows that the properly qualified women are much better at this type of work than men, I have an impression, however, that there are, in fact, a very small proportion of women in the Public Assistance services, and I should be very grateful for any facts about this that you can place at my disposal.

19 July 1934   9/3

Philippa Strachey to VM

The conviction that the help of women of ability is a real essential in the work of Local Government has become almost an obsession with me. As you say, the number of such women in official positions is very very

---

[16] Henry Brooke (1903–) Conservative MP for Lewisham West 1938–1945, Hampstead 1950–1966. 1954–1957 Financial Secretary to the Treasury, 1957–1961 Minister of Housing and Local Government and Minister for Welsh Affairs, 1961–1962 Chief Secretary to the Treasury and Paymaster General, 1962–1964 Home Secretary.

[17] National and London Society for Women's Service.

small except in the Public Health services (where however they get very little chance of showing initiative) and latterly in the growing occupation of Estate Management. There are, however, some women who have done first-rate work as Relieving Officers and I will see if I can locate any of these.

Roughly speaking, I believe that about 17 per cent of the Local Government employees over the whole country are women, but the large majority of these will be clerical workers of the least responsible type.

As regards the staffing of the new Department the most important point seems to be to try and get the right women put in at the start. In the administrative class to share in the working out of policy and in the executive class where their attention to the detailed carrying out of the work would be of the utmost value.

The initial traumas of the UAB had by now died down, and the UAB committee was working to the satisfaction of Tom Jones at least. He found Markham 'keen and quick if a trifle voluble'.[18]

1 September 1934   9/1

VM to W. Eady, Secretary UAB

.... I leave for Glasgow tomorrow night, and during the next ten days am making a tour of some of the big towns in the north where the unemployment question is pressing. I feel that it will be helpful to inform myself first-hand about some of the appalling questions we shall be up against in the next few weeks.

11 September 1934   7/4

VM's Notes of a tour of Glasgow, Liverpool, Manchester, Stockton and Sheffield 4–11 September 1934

So far as malnutrition is concerned I could find no evidence among medical officers and social workers of any marked deterioration in the health of the community.

In Glasgow, Liverpool and Manchester the reports of the Medical Officers are satisfactory so far as the children are concerned.... Dr M'Gonigle of Stockton was the only Medical Offiicer who asserted the contrary view with great emphasis.[19] But though the nutrition question may be considered

---

[18] Thomas Jones *A diary with letters 1931–50* (Oxford University Press, London, 1954) 30 July 1934
[19] G.C.M. M'Gonigle, Medical Officer of Health for Stockton-on-Tees was well-known for highlighting the relationship between ill-health and poverty. In 1936 he was to publish *Poverty and public health* with J Kirby [G.C.M. M'Gonigle & J. Kirby *Poverty and public*

satisfactory as far as it goes, I gathered that the argument could not be pushed too far. Some doctors to whom I talked were clearly uneasy about the existence of a large volume of low standard health above the malnutrition lines but not high enough to have much resistance power. Such people collapse easily when an epidemic is abroad. A more generous and varied diet (if a family living on relief were in a position to provide it) would certainly lead to better physical stamina. Much depends of course on the presence or absence of house-keeping capacity in the housewife. Here it was satisfactory to gather in the different towns I visited that there was agreement as to a rise in standard of house-keeping capacity among the women. Also that the opinion was held that in the large majority of cases more money would go on the provision of better food, not on beer and betting. Some of the working-class homes on Transitional Payment that I visited in my tour of Glasgow tenements.... were models of what a home can be.

I found some medical authorities, however, concerned with another aspect of the health question. Anxiety was expressed in more than one place as to the piling up of considerable if ill-defined nervous strains among the unemployed and their families. On the one hand, you have the growing dejection and unhappiness of the man out of work and on the other the growing exasperation and irritation in a Means Test family of the supporting children or members of the household. This state of affairs is leading to an increase of nervous disorder. And here I might mention that between 1928 and 1932 the suicide rate in Liverpool has increased 40% as compared with the previous triennial period.

As to grievances concerned with the Means Test, I was astonished to find wherever I went complete unanimity of opinion as to their nature, the consequences to which they give rise, and the legitimate grounds for complaint. The two chief grievances are concerned, (a) with the unemployed man himself, and (b) with the family that has to support him.... Take the case of a respectable artizan who has been in regular work all his life, till caught by the recent economic blast. He has a good home and has brought up his children well. His family—often thanks to his past sacrifices—are in work. The wage they bring in lifts the household above the scale of any public relief. The position of the father is humiliating in the extreme. He has not one penny in his pocket except what he owes to the alms of his family. He can't buy a stamp or a paper nor a cigarette or pay for a tram fare unless he begs the money from his children. That is a situation that leads to extreme bitterness in the heart of the man....

Wherever I went there was but one opinion that this evil called for redress

health (Gollancz, London, 1936).] which argued that people who were transferred from slums to better housing suffered from worse health than those who did not enjoy the better accommodation, because the former group paid higher rents, and therefore had less money for food; their diets suffered, and as a result their health was impaired.

and that some small pocket money allowance should be paid the unemployed man living in a household apart from Means Test or Needs Test....

Turning now to the grievances of the family, with one exception (the Mayor of Stockton-on-Tees), I did not find any challenge to the general principle of a Means Test. Family responsibility is an axiom accepted probably more fully by the working classes than by any other class in England.... But a burthen cheerfully accepted by a family during a temporary period — however long — of unemployment becomes intolerable as a permanent factor in family life....

The bitterness and resentment to which it gives rise are concerned not so much with its principle as with its indefinite application. The wage earning members of a Means Test family feel caught in a trap from which there is no escape save the drastic one of leaving home and breaking up family life.... The point was well put to me by one experienced social worker — the reasons of the man's unemployment is a failure in the economic structure of the State: why should the burthen of that failure be saddled indefinitely on the shoulders of his family? Granted that the principle of family responsibility is still accepted, I ask the Board to consider whether that responsibility should not be assessed on a sliding scale, and that as time goes on the burthen on the family should diminish automatically and that of the State increase.

Again, opinion was unanimous that some provision of this kind would go a very long way to meet the exasperation and discontent widespread at the moment — an exasperation the social consequences of which may be incalculable.

.... It has been put to me strongly that Means Test Regulations are harsher and press more rigorously on the family than the Poor Law Regulations....

Though scales have varied in different localities there is general agreement that there is no margin for replacing clothes, blankets, etc.... The question of replacements is getting cumulatively serious.... Also it is hard for the unemployed to be dressed in perpetuity by charity.

The difficulty of applying a national scale to the immensely varied conditions even of the industrial centres was forceably impressed on me during this tour. Without some power to make discretionary allowances over and above the normal scale, I fear serious discontent will arise especially in places like Manchester where public assistance, thanks to vote catching of an unblushing type, is on lavish lines....

I was rather concerned to find a vague but widespread idea that the Board was about to inaugurate a social millenium and that its scales were 'bound' to be much higher than either insurance rates or public assistance.... in view of the great expectations which unfortunately are rife, the future clearly holds much disillusion for certain localities and considerable abuse for the Board.

.... no feature of my tour was more encouraging than the testimony borne by the officials to the good behaviour of the unemployed and the good-will shown to the general administration of relief. Both at Liverpool and Manchester I was present at the Exchanges during rush hours of payment when hundreds of men and women were pressing through the buildings.... complete order and good discipline prevailed.... At the Liverpool Exchange it was only perhaps once a month that a policeman had to be brought in to deal with an unruly member.

24 October 1934 19/30
VM to Geraldine Hole, her sister

Markham had expressed concern that her sister had to manage with only day-servants.

The servant question becomes more & more acute & there is no prospect of it being any better so far as I can see while the present trade boom continues & the rearmament programme lasts.... The Government training centres for which I am responsible are half empty & we are having great difficulty with them. I am having a training centre started in London for elderly women in the hope of training them as cooks but the bad health among these women is incredible — bad eyes, bad teeth, rheumatism & general debility. Our experience at the Board is quite definite that the percentage of real slackers among the unemployed is quite small. But the volume of *feeble* folk in mind & body is appalling. I sometimes wonder how the country carries on at all with such a dead load at its base....

21 November 1934 7/7
VM to Miss M.L. Harford, Sheffield Council of Social Services

Personally, I think a lot of nonsense was talked about the Unemployment Assistance Board and the new social era it was to inaugurate. Fine words butter no parsnips, and as far as I can see all that we are engaged in is the elaboration of a new Poor Law.

However, it is very important to link up the voluntary agencies with the machinery of the Board in the way you indicate. That we have entirely in mind so far as we have been in a position to think about it. Just at the moment the pressure continues enormous and first things have to come first.

You ask me what is the position in regard to the appointment of women to the higher posts. I am afraid, for the time being, all the appointments are made and so far only officers from the Local Authorities and Civil Servants have been eligible to apply. Again, this is a matter to which I hope to devote a substantial amount of attention in the future. Speaking strictly between ourselves, I am not altogether satisfied with the present position, but until the immediate pressure is removed, one cannot expect harrassed officials to sit down and consider adjustments in the women staff.

29 December 1934 25/4
Henry Betterton to VM

It is quite absurd of you to *thank me* for suggesting your name as a member of the Board — I made up my mind from the moment the Board was set up, that you alone of your sex, if you could be induced to take it were the right and proper person....

When the UAB's new standardised payment scales were introduced on 7 January 1935 they provoked a spontaneous outcry both among the unemployed and in Parliament. Under a national scale of payments many claimants were to be worse off than under the old system. The Cabinet decided to introduce a transitional payment, so that claimants could receive the same amount of money as under the old system, if it was to their financial advantage to do so.

2 January 1935 VM 7/5
VM to Strohmenger[20]

Copy of this letter sent to Tom Jones.

This is just to follow up our conversation a few days ago, lest what I said then should [seem] too complacent. During the past few days, I have heard from several quarters that there are *now* fears of real trouble blowing up. Merthyr, Rhondda and Pontypridd are bad patches, but the discontent is not confined by any means to those areas. The immediate objective appears to be the Conference to be held on January 26. There are rumours of organised marches on that occasion, and a large number of preliminary meetings of protest against the Regulations are being organised. People on whose judgement we can rely tell me that the 'temper' is uglier than anything they have seen for years, and these people are strongly urging that something ought to be done to give the decent minded folk a chance of refusing to be stampeded into a general rising. They suggest for instance that something should be done, (if possible through the new Special Areas Commissioner) to provide work on a reasonably large scale. They suggest that the effect of this would be to split up the malcontents. There is a feeling of the greatest

---

[20] Deputy Director of UAB from 1934 until 1937 when he was replaced by VM.

disappointment that the new Special Areas Act seems to make it impossible for the Commissioner to start paid work of any kind. They laugh at his *only* pronouncement so far, which relates to the addition of a large number of allotments.

The Lloyd George campaign simply adds fuel[21] .... the preparation of all this campaign has been going on quietly during the recess in the innumberable meetings with their constituents held by the M.P.'s. I told you something of these meetings, but when I saw you I had no idea of the intensity of the feelings that are being expressed during the past few days.

The *main* objection of the Regulations, so far as I can sense the position, appears to be the steep cut made in the allowances where a member of an unemployed man's family happens to be in work and in receipt of wages. The drop in the family budget where this occurs often amounts to something in the region of 12s. a week, and there is great resentment at this. They say this cut is *too severe*, not that no cut at all should be made....

The net result is that I have to revise very much the general report to you as to the situation down here. It is *not* now all quiet on the Western Front.

Lloyd George had suggested to Markham that she might like to visit him at Churt.

8 January 1935   5/9

VM to Lloyd George

.... I should like very much to talk to you about unemployment. Long before I found myself, to my great surprise, on the Unemployment Assistance Board I have felt the deepest concern about this tragic question....

16 January 1935   5/9

Sir Malcolm Stewart[22] to VM

I have been reading with interest the memorandum you forwarded to Mr Chamberlain last spring after your tour in the North-East.

I see that you suggested the appointment of a Director in each area. I suppose in a way that I hold the kind of office you contemplated though the Act hardly gives me 'practically autocratic powers'.

Your labour policy is very akin to that which I am hoping to put into force, but I have not yet got it finally agreed with the Government.

---

[21] In 1935 Lloyd George launched one of his many campaigns to reduce unemployment, with a Council of Action to get his (hardly novel) proposals — to reorganise the staple export industries and develop basic services — across to the public.

[22] Sir Malcolm Stewart (1872–1951), industrialist. 1934–1936 Commissioner for the Special Areas.

1 February 1935 7/13

Minute of meeting

The Chairman [of the UAB, Henry Betterton] and Mr Eady reported the extreme anxiety and disquiet of the Minister [of Labour] at the agitation that had arisen over the Regulations. Two suggestions reported by the Chairman to the Board last night which were communicated to him by the sub-committee of the Cabinet [which had met at 5.30 p.m. on 31 January]
(a) the 'stand still' plan;
(b) a general cash increase of the allowances were reviewed at the meeting between the Minister of Labour, the Chairman and Mr Eady. The insuperable difficulties felt by the Board as to accepting either alternative were conveyed to the Minister by the Chairman.

The unofficial members of the Board told the Chairman that they had met the previous evening at 8.30 p.m. to consider their position in view of the situation that had arisen. They recognised that the Regulations had in various respects worked out more harshly than they had anticipated. They were prepared on their own initiative and without pressure from the Cabinet to take immediate steps to ease the situation.... But they refused to entertain either of the suggestions made by the Minister to the Board as to a stand still or an all round increase of allowances. Such a step, they held, would be disastrous in the public interest. They laid stress on their appointment as a non-political body and protested against the severe political pressure to which they were being subjected.... they also informed the Chairman that in any deadlock with the Cabinet they would not resign.

4 February 1935 7/13

VM

A personal appeal was made by the Chairman to the Members present to come to the assistance of the Government in the grave crisis that had arisen. According to the figures supplied by the Ministry of Labour, there had been some miscalculation about the effect of the Regulations. Instead of an increase of £3 millions in the money spent on the unemployed, it was now estimated that the result would be a decrease of £3 ½ millions. In view of the forthcoming [silver] Jubilee celebrations.[23] and also of the widespread expectation that more money should be provided for the unemployed, the Sub-Committee of the Cabinet held that afternoon, with the Chancellor in the Chair, had decided unanimously that the proposals of the Board.... were quite inadequate to meet the situation. The Sub-Committee were of opinion that the proposals made by the Board would fail to satisfy the House of Commons....

[23] Of King George V and Queen Mary.

The proposals contained in the Minister's letter amounted to an immediate stand-still order in respect of all cases where there had been cuts until such cases had been reviewed by the Tribunals. Meanwhile the Board were to prepare new Regulations. The Chairman pointed out that the Board were pledged to Parliament in matters of policy and urged that the Board should assent without delay to the proposals.

5 February 1935 7/13

VM

He [the Chairman, Henry Betterton] wished to explain the constitutional position. The Board are in effect officials of the Government and cannot act in the last resort contrary to the policy of the Government. The question of the independent administrative position of the Board was raised frequently in Parliament during the passage of the Unemployment Bill. When Minister of Labour in charge of that Bill he had assured the House repeatedly that the administration of the Board was not and could not be removed from the criticism and ultimate control of Parliament. In the end the Government must have its way.

6 February 1935 7/13

Meeting of UAB with H.M. Hallsworth, member of UAB

Mr Hallsworth said that the impression uppermost in his mind was the way in which the Labour Party realised the Government's complete confession of failure and gigantic retreat....

Miss Markham added her impressions of the Debate. It was on a totally different level of sincerity and dignity from that which took place when the Regulations were introduced. Many members showed an almost complete ignorance of the Regulations. On the other hand some genuine cases were adduced where Investigating Officers had erred, e.g. in the case of failing to allow for travelling expenses. So far as the Government were concerned the Board was simply 'thrown to the wolves.'

The Chairman agreed that the Board had been monstrously treated....

12 March 1935 9/3

VM to Geoffrey Dawson

.... Of course, our Rent Rule must be revised. So far as the Means Test is concerned, I am racking my brains to find a formula which will let the little fish through the net and catch the big ones....

... one of the main problems of the whole situation — namely that we have two different types of people in the unemployed pool, the permanently and the temporarily unemployed. Now as I see it, regulations that are on the generous side when applied to a family temporarily unemployed, become meagre when unemployment is chronic. Similarly, the Means Test, which the earning members of the family ought to shoulder cheerfully when unemployment is temporary, becomes a very onerous charge on the younger generation when it is prolonged *indefinitely* ....

The 'reconciliation' tea-party took place last Tuesday. Neville gave us a beautiful tea in the Treasury room, and the unofficial members of the Board exhausted themselves in civilities to Mr Stanley![24] I hope the gathering managed to break some of the ice that had formed between Thames House[25] and the Ministry of Labour, but I became very conscious, during the afternoon, that there was a very hostile personality present in the shape of Mr Hudson[26] who made a most unfavourable impresson on me. I have a shrewd suspicion that he has been responsible for a great deal of the trouble that has arisen between the two Departments.

30 March 1935 9/13

Philippa Strachey to VM and other members of the UAB

.... The administration of relief is a matter in which women have for generations played an important part. At a time when the education and training of women was in general neglected and their opportunities limited in the highest degree, their keen interest in philanthropy enabled them to surmount obstacles of almost incredible difficulty and to make proof of constructive intelligence and organising ability .... thousands of women of capacity .... who down to the present day have given devotion and gained experience in bringing help to the unfortunate on lines of understanding and good sense.

When the Unemployment Assistance Board was set up under the Act of 1934 it seemed therefore to my Society unquestionable that the services of women should be enlisted in its work. We believe this to be the view of most persons experienced in these matters and it was shown to be the view

---

[24] Oliver Stanley (1896–1950), Conservative MP for Westmorland 1924–1945, Bristol West 1945–1950), 1931–1933 Parliamentary Secretary Home Office, 1933-1934 Minister of Transport, 1934–1935 Minister of Labour, 1935–1937 President of the Board of Education, 1937–1940 Board of Trade, 1940 Secretary of State for War, 1942–1945 for Colonial Affairs.

[25] UAB Headquarters.

[26] Robert, Viscount Hudson (1886–1957), Conservative MP for Whitehaven 1924–1929, Southport 1931–1952. 1931–1935 Parliamentary Secretary Ministry of Labour, 1935–1936 Minister of Pensions, 1936–1937 Parliamentary Secretary Ministry of Health, 1937–1940 Department of Overseas Trade Board of Trade, 1940 Minister of Shipping, 1940–1945 Minister of Agriculture and Fisheries.

taken by Parliament by the clause laying down that there must be a woman member on the Board.

....The Board saw fit nevertheless to fill every one of the controlling positions on the Head Quarters Staff without exception with men....

It is clearly impossible for outsiders to criticise individual appointments and it is far from the desire of my Society to advocate the appointment of a less well qualified woman in the place of a better qualified man. It is our belief however that the problems to be dealt with by the Board are viewed from somewhat different angles by men and women and we hold that the solution of these problems will soonest be found by the participation of both sexes in the endeavour.

Further, if real advantage is to be taken of the special contribution that women can bring to this task they must take part in its general planning and lay-out and in the higher branches of its administration and execution. Without women officers of sufficient status in the hierarchy, experience has shown the extreme difficulty of obtaining attention in the departments to aspects of a question which do not immediately strike the eye of the male official and no multiplication of women in subordinate positions will alter this....

It is a matter of surprise to my Committee that in the state of Society which exists in this country at the present day it should have been possible to set up a fresh government department for the assistance of unemployed men and women in which women were placed in the position in which they have been placed by the Unemployment Assistance Board, where but for the appointment of Miss Markham by parliamentary action, not one woman has a voice in the administration. My Committee's surprise, they are assured, is widely shared.

3 April 1935? 9/2

VM to Ronald Davison, PEP

First of all about the general condemnation of the Board's organisation in P.E.P.[27] Is it possible, with any fairness, to pronounce judgement on a system that was only allowed to function for three weeks? The Board's plan may have been right or wrong. But I maintain that no one is in a position to form a reasoned opinion one way or another after so brief a term of life. A vast centralized system can hardly get into its stride in the first fortnight of its existence. The discretion which was provided for at every turn could not attain its maximum flexibility in the first few days. The scheme wanted a little time to become supple. 'The board is not spending enough money',

---

[27] Political and Economic Planning was a non-party 'think-tank'. Committed to 'planning' and critical of the National Government, it drew support from MPs of both parties.

said the Minister, and you repeat his words. But week by week he is finding out his error in that as in other matters.

Certainly we made some mistakes — the rent rule was one; the earnings rule, after the lax administration of the Local Authorities, proved a hardship. We were as fully alive to these defects as any of our critics. They were all in process of being eased and relieved when the standstill was forced on us. Had the Minister made the least attempt to hold the House instead of surrendering at once to clamour, the difficulties might have been all resolved within the existing machine.

.... The Board remember is only concerned with the primary needs of life. The great variations in rent have been provided for separately. Apart from rent, stomachs, I might remark, are just the same (and ache just as much when they are empty) in London as in Merthyr. In London, as in Merthyr, people want the same minimum amount of heat and light and clothing.

.... Regional administration only means a reflection of varying political and social theories which are not directly related to stomachs except that some political theories fill stomachs more generously than others.

In saying this I am not for a moment disputing the necessity for local help and counsel in the affairs of the Board. Curiously enough, we have not been attacked at a point where I feel we are most vulnerable — the failure to set up advisory committees when the Regulations came into force. This was due to shortness of time — the four months period allowed by the Act was wholly inadequate for carrying out the colossal job which lay before the Board. And it was better to do nothing than to set up Committees in haste....

You and others talk of the breakdown of the Board. But the Board hasn't broken down!.... Let me say I agree with you entirely as to the relations of the Board and the Minister being more clearly defined. At the moment, we have the worst of all worlds. I agree that it is impossible to take unemployment out of politics.

.... the recent storm. To me it was one of the most ominous incidents in latter day public life. The Government had put their hand to an unpopular plough. They had been warned by us and others that the tangled administration of the Local Authorities could not be cleared up without large numbers of people having their knuckles rapped. Yet, what happens? At the first symptoms of trouble, they made no effort to stand firm. They flung in their hand and ran like hares — ran from every principle they had themselves advocated and set up the Board to implement. They did this, of course, because there is a General Election on the horizon and they were concerned not with principles but votes.... I do suggest to you that democratic government can never survive unless rulers are prepared to say and do unpopular things and stand up when necessary to the electorate. Every failure of democratic government plays straight into the hands of dictatorship, and to me the tragedy of recent events lies in the sinister weakening of what I hold to be the props of the only political system under which men and women can live with self-respect.

25 July 1935 9/1

VM to Lady Cynthia Colville, Lady in Waiting to Queen Mary

.... the whole situation betwen the Board and the [Personal Service] League has been greatly eased. We have had several conferences with Lady Reading[28] who, I think, is now satisfied that we wish to co-operate with her on friendly terms.... The Board and the League will keep in touch centrally and locally over practical administrative matters as may arise.

First it may be thought that the Board is taking a long time to develop its permanent policy. I submit that in the circumstances delay is not only inevitable but necessary. A voluntary organisation has a flexibility and power of choice in dealing with its subject matters that are impossible for a Government department. The voluntary body is not compelled to follow a rule of national application; it can discard, develop and experiment as it goes along. On the other hand any step taken by the Board involves national consequences with widespread social repercussions.... I must draw attention to a further circumstance which complicates our task and makes it the more imperative that we should go slowly.... the very poor conditions that exist not only among a section of the unemployed but among many low paid wage-earners who do not come within the scope of the Board. This is a grave matter for if the unemployed are not to be made in fact a privileged class better off in some respects than families who are in work, the Board is bound to have regard to the circumstances of the low paid wage-earners.

Secondly, the Board have always realised that the true welfare of an unemployed family exacts services of a kind that cannot be supplied merely by a grant of money from a State machine. The needs of a family may call even more than for money for the help of a sympathetic and experienced visitor who will be a friend to the household.... the 1934 Unemployment Act laid down that Advisory Committees should be set up throughout the country consisting of people with local knowledge and experience in matters affecting the functions of the Board. In the circumstances that have arisen there has inevitably been delay in setting up the Advisory Committees but when established we hope that they will form a valuable link between the Board and the various social agencies in the country.

.... there are a large number of voluntary organisations, mostly local,

[28] Marchioness of Reading (1894–1971), 1932–1938 Chair of the Personal Service League. In 1938 she founded the WVS (Later WRVS).

but including some large ones, such as the Personal Service League, who for some time past have been helping people in this condition by giving them clothes, blankets, etc. Behind these distributing bodies there is a very large body of people in more fortunate circumstances who feel that they would like to make a personal contribution to the unemployed by providing money for clothes or working up material into clothes. Voluntary help for people in distress is a widespread and distinctive feature of our national life.... where it exists it would be disastrous if the Board did anything to damage the spirit of good will it represents. We want, therefore, to make working arrangements with various responsible volunatry bodies who command public confidence and are in a position to help a family.... By degrees we shall build up these contacts in each town through the Advisory Committees and the arrangements will naturally vary.

First come the catastrophic cases. For example, a fire may have occurred and destroyed or damaged the furniture, or a member of the household may have an infectious disease which has compelled the destruction of the bedding in the household, or some other crisis, for which the household obviously could not have made provision, has turned up. In such cases it is necessary to move quickly and to deal adequately with the need. In principle, therefore, the Board have agreed that such catastrophic cases are our business.

Second, the cases of households where clothing is rapidly being worn out by normal wear and tear. This sort of case is not really the business of the Board but falls within the sphere of charitable effort. We have agreed in principle with the Personal Service League that these are the cases that they and other voluntary bodies should continue to help in the future....

There remains the third class. To this class belong the persons who have been unemployed for a long time and have been in receipt of a small allowance, very often much smaller than the one we are now paying.... Here we are prepared to help as soon as we are satisfied that the household is making plans for the future to avoid getting into these difficulties again. As you will understand, nothing so quickly saps the independent outlook of a household which is in distress as the knowledge that clothes and bedding are to be had for the asking....

Naturally people with small incomes require both persuasion and inducement to develop the habit of saving.

16 November 1935   9/2
Dorothy Keeling[29] to VM

I am becoming more and more troubled about the inelasticity of the Un-

---

[29] Founder, Liverpool Personal Service Society (and Citizens Advice Bureaux).

employment Assistance regulations and by the fact that whereas under the old Public Assistance system, money was available for extras such as high rent and clothing, it is very difficult indeed to find loopholes in the Unemployment Assistance Act for extras of this kind.

4 December 1935 9/2
Dorothy Keeling to VM

.... I felt rather disappointed with my interview with Mr Reid[30] and the other officer of the Board, and much regretted Mr Eady's absence. I was amazed at Mr Reid's statement that the Board recognised the British Medical Association's scale as the minimum on which a family could manage, although, as you will remember, he afterwards qualified his statement by saying that this only applied to 'a normal family of three children'. It is, of course, the large families who are so short, but alas a great number of these find their way into this office.

22 January 1936 7/10
W. Eady to VM

.... Once one starts on the moral ground it is not exactly easy to see why the girl who has been seduced and has a baby should be compelled to go to the Poor Law, while the wife who has driven her husband away because of her bad temper should be an honoured recipient of the Board's benevolence.

By 1936 Markham was fed up with the way the Board operated; she thought it was a costly scandal. She told Tom Jones that if there were any further delays with the Board they should 'put the shutters up'.[31]

4 April 1936 7/10
W. Eady to VM

.... When we have had a holiday I would like to have a chance of talking to you about the conduct of the Board's business because I know that two or three of you are not satisfied about it, and the officials also are a bit disturbed, but I am sure we all need a rest from each other first.

I am bound to say that I think we are rather in a pickle now.

---

[30] Principal Assistant Secretary, UAB.
[31] Thomas Jones *A diary with letters 1931–50* (1954) VM to TJ, 30 January 1936.

26 June 1936   19/24
VM to James Carruthers, her husband

Writing about the UAB, Markham refers to the Cabinet as
   a set of craven jelly-fishes

No day or month 1936   25/54
VM to Cynthia Colville

.... two years ago I (and others) were urging on the Chancellor of the Exchequer the immense demoralisation that was being created by doles instead of work, and the pressing need for new measures however unorthodox.

But the conditions in Durham and in S. Wales have not changed in essentials since that time and there is no prospect of any such change.

The provision of doles and social services has gone steadily ahead of late years. There is no stint from the Treasury when it is a question of providing millions for keeping people in idleness. I can speak of this from my own experience on the Unemployment Assistance Board where for political reasons and because votes are at stake money is poured out like water in a sort of Dutch auction between rival parties.

But the one vital thing, the *provision of work* so that men and women may live not on State charity but in decency and self-respect, has been neglected. Here the action, or rather non-action, of the Government has been most culpable. Money is provided for doles but not for industry. Special Commissioners are set up for the distressed areas and then strangled by red tape. In 'The Times' of July 29th, Sir Arthur Rose, Commissioner for Scotland, calls attention to the limitation of his powers and the inevitable delays caused by the control and influence exercised by various permanent Departments. Certain palliatives have been provided in the Special Areas but fundamentally the problem position remains unchanged. There is only one cure for unemployment — namely *work* and that cure the Government seem incapable of providing in the Special Areas except in the smallest doses.

I happen to know privately that very strong representations on this subject have been made both to the Prime Minister and the Chancellor of the Exchequer. They have been urged to bring pressure to bear on leaders of industry to establish works and factories in the Special Areas, and no doubt they have tried but nothing like hard enough. Even if subsidies were necessary to this end, would not a few of the many millions provided for doles be better spent on giving people work instead of subsistence allowances? But very little has happened as a result of all the pressure brought to bear upon officialdom ....

Again it has been known for months past that there is to be a large development of the munition services. But action under this head has been incredibly slow. So far as South Wales is concerned the naval and mercantile shipping programme affords it no help. The coal trade is in a worse position than ever and though the blame is thrown on sanctions, the position viz a viz Italy was equally bad before sanctions were imposed as she was defaulting in her payments. Some of the new munition factories should certainly be placed in South Wales, but compared with the need of the area the steps have been negligible.

The improvement in industry has of course reduced the numbers of the unemployed. But we are left with the problem of nearly 2 million workless men and women, many of whom, as I have seen with my own eyes, are living under conditions of misery and hopelessness that are terrible to contemplate. The Unemployment Assistance Board, in spite of its troubles, is trying to carry out its relief work with sympathy and humanity.... But we are only a relief organisation whose function it is to deal with the consequences of unemployment. We do not touch the root of the evil.

Along side the misapplication of public money on doles there has been a great reluctance on the part of the Government to enforce discipline and training. There is a very serious problem of the young men who will neither train nor transfer, and who prefer to live in idleness on the dole. You speak of the training camps abroad and the enthusiasm they inspire. I saw some admirable camps of this type recently in Poland. But there is such deep seated prejudice in this country against semi-military organisations of this kind that it would be hopeless to try and introduce them here. Even transfer meets with much opposition and in South Wales the transfer of young men is opposed as strongly from the right as from the left as leading to the destruction of Welsh national life.

What, therefore, can be done? The Queen is, I know, profoundly moved and concerned about the whole problem. Any lead from her is of course of capital importance. But there are difficulties in Her Majesty's path owing to the deplorable element of political bias which runs like a corroding threat through this lamentable situation. The unemployed are deliberately exploited by the Communist party and the extreme Socialists for political ends. Many useful measures are opposed by people who have a veiled interest in discontent. The Occupation Centres, the Councils of Social Services and the Settlements have provided valuable safety valves in the distressed areas. We might have had revolution without them. But apart from individuals, the Labour Party and the Trade Union Council have given no official support to these movements. Personally I think we cannot do too much for these agencies, and I also think that the Queen can safely make any gesture of sympathy and support in this direction to organisations of approved merit. Reports by the National Council and by the South Wales Council have been published in the last fortnight and you have doubtless seen them. But for all its value, this work is palliative. It cannot cure the fundamental evil.

But there is another channel where Her Majesty might exercise a profound influence. She will pardon my boldness I hope for making the suggestion. It is well known that the King has not only a special concern for the unemployed but special knowledge of the problem. Would it be possible for the Queen when discussing this question with His Majesty to consider with him:-

(a) What proper constitutional pressure he can bring to bear on his Ministers to speed up their action and fire them with some measure of his own vision and enthusiasm. Is it not possible for more of the 'munitions industries' to be forced into South Wales?

(b) What personal persuasion His Majesty could exercise so that owners of prosperous and expanding concerns would be willing to establish factories and works in or near the Special Areas? I say in or near because so far as South Wales is concerned it was very unfortunate that Cardiff, Barry & Newport were excluded from the Special Areas Act. The narrow Welsh valleys present very difficult problems geographically and employers would be more willing to consider schemes for factories at the points where they emerge near the coast than higher up among the hills.

I believe that the King is the one hope of the country if the paralysis of the Government is to be brought to an end and transformed into energy and action. Employers who turn a deaf ear to Whitehall would listen to the King.

One Sunday evening in March 1937 Henry Betterton, chair of the UAB, telephoned Markham to ask her if she would become deputy-chair of the UAB. At first Markham thought it was a joke, but when she realised he was serious, she accepted.[32]

6 April 1937 UB 7/4
W. Eady to VM

There really is no catch about it at all! The Chairman did not want to have a stranger foisted upon the Board. This view was also held by other members of the Board. Stroh[menger, Deputy chair, 1934-37] had his own ideas, which in my judgment were unsound. He has not really understood 'the Board' as an institution! If a member of the Board was to be Deputy I think it is is clear that, internally in Thames House—you would be the most acceptable to the other members—and externally, the most significant choice.

[32] Thomas Jones *A diary with letters 1931–50* (1954) VM to TJ, 21 March 1937.

.... internally, neither you nor anyone else expects (or indeed wants!) you to be another Stroh[menger]. The 'Board' ought now to run for a time with its official staff, and there ought not to be a continuance of these equivocal arrangements where a member of the Board is also an 'official'. The situation during the past two years has not been free from difficulty, & S. & I only succeeded in making his arrangements work by keeping our 'scrapping' in private!

26 April 1937 25/23

VM to Ronald Davison

Thank you very much for your kind words about the U.A.B. job. It is really rather a domestic rearrangement within the office and is not nearly so pompous or important as it sounds. We have all learnt to feel great affection and regard for our dear Stro[hmenger] but the truth is that none of us were very anxious to have another Civil Servant of his eminence and character introduced among us at this particular point in our history. The Board is really in much calmer waters and I hope that now the earlier alarums and excursions are over we may be able to settle down to some decent administrative work....

I am painfully impressed by the way in which industry is being run by juveniles. Apparently adults, both men and women, are being thrown out between the ages of 25 and 30 and replaced by the cheaper young people.

.... I met Jimmy Mallon[33] two days ago and poured out my anxieties on this subject to him. To my great surprise he told me that I was exaggerating the whole problem. It was nothing like so serious as I feared. This view is in direct contradiction to what I have found for myself in the sample of women I have been seeing in the London Area Offices of the Board.

31 May 1937 7/21

UAB memo on training for older women in London, by VM

.... My investigation revealed a distressing amount of low grade existence among the women applicants to the Board living in London.

.... The largest age group was betwen 51 and 60 (29 percent). The second largest age group is between 41 and 50 (27 percent).

.... The women interviewed varied considerably in type. They included at one end superior applicants who had held responsible posts as cashiers, hotel managers, saleswomen in shops, clerical workers, telephonists, etc. Some had been in business on their own and had been left stranded by the collapse of the undertaking. The samples also included singers, actresses and

---

[33] James Mallon (1875–1961), Warden of Toynbee Hall.

dancers of the minor grades in their respective professions. At the other end there were industrial women engaged in a variety of unskilled jobs. Taken as a whole they were a very decent, respectable set of applicants. Many bore signs of obvious poverty. Some were very rough. But I was struck by the small proportion of women obviously of a degraded or disreputable type. The barwomen, of whom there were a certain number, were invariably solid and respectable in appearance with no trace of either peroxide or flashiness....

The women who have seen better days are often anchored with their bits of furniture salved from the wreck of past prosperity in a room the rent of which is proportionately high. Women of this type who come on to the Board after a spell of Unemployment Benefit have often had a hard struggle to live. I was uneasy more than once about the allowance paid to single women living in a high rented room when presumably it was not reasonable in the special circumstances of the case to ask her to find cheaper accommodation....

Among the older age groups the health of the women interviewed was very poor. A large number of our applicants suffer from rheumatism, bronchitis, nerves, bad eyes, bad teeth and a host of minor ailments. Some have severe operations from which owing to the absence of after care there has been no complete recovery. It is the exception, not the rule, to hear a woman say her health is good. Nervous strain is common, due to unemployment, unsatisfactory home conditions and insufficient food. Anxiety about the future preys on their minds and as the weeks and months pass by the futile task of registering at the Exchange and seeking illusory jobs takes the heart out of them.

The medical aspect of these women is most unsatisfactory. The majority have long since exhausted their health benefit and do not know where to turn for medical aid. In theory they should be dealt with by the Local Authority but either through the ignorance of the applicant or failure of the local Medical Service, a mass of illness remains untouched and unrelieved.

The Board is responsible for the welfare of its applicants and cannot allow this state of affairs to continue indefinitely.... The help of voluntary societies and the interest of Advisory Committees should be secured so that holiday and convalescent treatment may be brought within the reach of some of these women....

The occasional younger women thrown up by the sample were of poor type. A young woman (apart from special circumstances such as sickness, protracted illness or the care of an illegitimate child) who cannot hold down a job sufficiently to qualify for Unemployment Benefit is presumably of low grade.... When unemployment is practically chronic, life touches an ebb so low that recovery from it becomes impossible without special measures. It is the desirability of such special measures in selected cases that I have to suggest to the Board....

Many who have lost all social contacts and are incredibly lonely could with advantage be put in touch with a club. The investigation made in London brought home to me the importance of co-operation between the Board and voluntary agencies of varied type....

Though industry rejects the elderly worker and, whatever her record, is ruthless in throwing her out on grounds of age, there is one field, domestic service, which presents an unsatisfied demand for women's labour. The present supply is wholly inadequate.... The shortage adds materially to the burthen of life for the professional and commercial classes.... Age does not present the same handicap in domestic work as in industry.

8 June 1937 9/2

VM to J. Mallon

I was interested in your views and those of Mr Balaam[34] about the absorption of juveniles, but am still not satisfied that the position is healthy. Obviously London at the present time is prosperous enough for young people thrown out at 16 or 18 years of age, or even later, to be re-absorbed, even where they have not acquired much skill or knowledge. The same is true of Birmingham. It does not, however, appear to me to hold good in the case of less prosperous places such as Liverpool.... Nearly all of these say when questioned that they have been displaced by younger workers.... Some are employed on a casual basis by firms and weeded out after a stoppage. Others have lost their work through sickness and find a younger girl taken on in their place, while yet others have found that wages did not increase as they approached adult age, and, leaving to better themselves, have secured work which proved to be only temporary. We find the same phenomena in Glasgow, and I believe that they must be universal when prosperity flags.

The difficulties I feel about factory workers are more than multiplied when the question arises of unemployment among shop assistants and clerical workers....

In the course of the investigation I have made among the Board's women applicants in London I have come across many cases of senior women who have been on the staff of one firm for 15 or 20 years and then are ruthlessly scrapped on the ground of age ....I doubt whether adequate efforts are being made by a large number of employers to equip young workers against unemployment by giving them a reasonable variety of experience ....It seems doubly unreasonable to let workers reach adult age without any range of experience and then refuse to train them afterwards; I do feel from the many cases I have interviewed that with the increasing pace of industry, the

---

[34] C.J. Balaam, London divisional controller, Ministry of Labour.

high cost of modern plant and its rapid obsolescence, there is a tendency to get the most out of the vigorous years.... I need not remind you of the anxiety expressed in the last report of the Chief Inspector of Factories about the excessive amount of overtime worked by juveniles in some places and the higher accident-rate prevailing amongst them.

12 October 1937   7/21

VM

Report on an analysis made in 1,056 cases of the circumstances of umemployed women over the age of 15 in households of applicants of the Board

The upshot of this investigation is surprising. It will be remarked that out of 1,056 cases only 27 emerge as showing unoccupied girls or women living at home without any valid reason being forthcoming....

Certainly the prima facie case is overwhelming against the theory of large numbers of young women living at home in idleness on the dole.

Markham, who had a life-long interest in attracting women into domestic service had been asked for her views on a charter to be signed by an employer and a domestic service employee.

29 October 1937   9/2

VM to Mrs Wintringham

I do not wish to take up any sort of defeatist attitude about domestic service but I am convinced that it is neither a general problem nor capable of any general solution. Some of the most difficult factors that enter into this form of employment are psychological and very individual. One of the great drawbacks is the stigma that seems to attach to this form of employment in working class families.... Then I am sure that in households of more than one maid the difficulty arises of their all being cooped up together under one person's roof.... Girls complain very much of the restriction on their personal liberty in the evening.... girls complain that the opportunity of marriage arises less frequently for women in domestic employment than for those in other forms of employment.

Finally I am sure the whole question is weighted by the remnants of the slave tradition, since personal service lasted longer in old days among men and women who were not free than among the classes that were emancipated.... the really big factor is the one of status.... the supply of servants is likely to go from bad to worse

8 December 1937   25/4

Sir Henry Betterton to VM

Of course Lary's[35] departure is a real blow for us all — but I have no fears for the future. The Board is I believe now fully established both in its administrative side and in public esteem — T[om] J[ones] I sent for yesterday and told him the story: he fully agreed that the course I had taken was the only possible one.

No day or month 1937   7/21

Dora Ibberson, UAB, special enquiry officer to VM

I classified 320 cases in London, Manchester and Liverpool into good, fair and poor health. The number of women who appeared to be in less than good health was London — two-thirds Manchester — one-half Liverpool — one-third.

The general state of health of the women interviewed generally varies in direct ratio to their average age, Liverpool owing its better health not by any means to a better population but to a much younger age distribution....

The causes of a poor condition of health are most frequently: – Operation or serious illness in the past from which the patient has never made a complete recovery, owing, no doubt, in many cases to inadequate facilities. Protracted unemployment with the consequent worry and scanty and monotonous feeding, producing lack of appetite and general debility. Overstrain due to nursing sick or aged relatives while in work. Arduous working conditions, sometimes combined with low wages. A frequent instance of this is the long hours worked by hotel and restaurant workers. The most frequent manifestations of ill-health are a poor nervous condition, rheumatism, chronic bronchitis and general debility. There is a great deal of deplorably bad dentition but this has not led to an inferior health classification unless accompanied by Pyorrhoea. Sight requires attention in a certain number of cases. In other cases the applicant suffers from some definite disability — deafness, loss of sight, mutilation of a limb, valvular disease of the heart and, very frequently, rheumatism or chronic bronchitis. Some are low-grade mental defectives, but neither this nor deafness has caused me to classify them as in less than good health. In some cases applicants in receipt of N[ational] H[ealth] I[nsurance] allowances have found that they could not live on them and induced the doctor to give them a certificate as fit for light work only. In two cases, an applicant had been advised to retire from industry on disablement benefit but her parents had declared the amount inadequate to support her and had obtained medical permission for her to take light work. The proportion of applicants fit for light work is substantial.

---

[35] Strohmenger.

Some of the cases described as in fair or poor health are almost unemployable in their present condition and fall for treatment by hospitals, clinics or convalescent homes. Others need a holiday pure and simple.... There remain a substantial number of women whose health, self-confidence and general employability would be much improved by a stay in a reconditioning centre for a period of from one to three months.... There should be a strong recreational and cultural side, a rest-room and, if possible, a garden.... Apart from reconditioning I have been struck by the need to provide Social Centres for these older women in various parts of London.... It would be specially advantageous if such centres contained a small amount of living accommodation where a few of the older women, such as those coming out of institutions, could be housed but this will necessitate the appointment of a resident Warden. The over 30 Association is beginning to think of expansion and it might be possible to provide grant aid for the opening of further Clubs....

5 April 1938 8/16
VM to R.L. West, UAB, Dundee

....I was never more completely defeated than I was in Dundee by a situation which left me without even the most feeble and futile suggestions for dealing with it. No problem is insoluble but I had the impression that very heroic measures would be necessary to deal with housing so awful and a standard of life so low....

In September 1938 international tensions increased with fears of an imminent invasion by Hitler of Czechoslovakia. Neville Chamberlain flew to Germany to try and reach a compromise with Hitler, but the latter raised the stakes and war seemed more and more likely. Air Raid Precautions were set in motion, including the evacuation of children from the cities. Chamberlain again flew to Germany and an uneasy and temporary peace was achieved with the Munich agreement between Germany, France, Italy and UK.

6 October 1938 25/10
VM to John Buchan

....Last Wednesday — Black Wednesday as it's called — war seemed inevitable. I was busy with the evacuation of our old friend the Central Committee [on Women's Training and Employment], but when within 48 hours we all expected death to be rained on us from the air, who could say whether after the first raid any of us would be there to carry on and make the necessary arrangements. The [Unemployment Assistance] Board had in prospect the care of about 3 million refugees from London alone — the office was to move out of London but the future seemed to lie on the very uncertain lap of very grim gods....

14 October 1938 9/2

VM to Elsie Jones, Borough Welfare Office, Chesterfield

To say that our allowances barely provide enough for food when rent is met is a very serious indictment of the Board. And apart from the accuracy of your statement it's an old rule that dog doesn't eat dog!

I can't of course admit your contention that 'it is common knowledge' that the Board's allowances are insufficient to provide clothing. The answer to that contention lies in the fact that the large majority of our applicants do in fact make such provision without any further demands on us. I have discussed this question of clothes very often with our District Officers and some of them hold strong views on the subject. The more you give and the more you may give where clothes are concerned. These are men not only of experience but who bring real sympathy and humanity to their work and I know they would disagree entirely with your generalisations about the Board's allowances....

29 November 1938 8/16

VM to R.L. West

....I am sorry to find that there is no change in the circumstances of the Peter Murrays. It was a dreadful house — nine people in one room and there was certainly a very definite suspicion of tuberculosis in the family. I see from my notes that there was no bedding in the house, that the squalor was terrible and that there was an outside W.C. used by 23 people! I am sure you will feel with me that it is not in the public interest that public money should continue indefinitely to provide some unknown landlord with the rent of such premises....

Mrs Dunn, is still I see living in the same condemned property. I hope she is allowed to see her grand-children. In spite of the bug-ridden room in which they were living the children were well cared for and there was a decent meal on the table. I have no doubt the children are best out of that room but it would have been preferable if the grandmother had been able to keep them with her under proper housing conditions.

I hope that your Advisory Committee in Dundee is alive to this state of affairs, of which these applicants are only typical, and they do not propose to acquiesce in such conditions being perpetuated indefinitely.

10 January 1939 25/23

VM to Ronald Davison

.... I sometimes despair of any effort being successful which aims at getting a move on in a Government Department. They are dug in to such a point that an earthquake would not move them, and of course it is far easier to make broad their phylacteries and go on minuting to the last decimal point than to take the risk of doing something adventurous and novel!

The Civil Service machine is over-complicated and too rigid to meet a situation like the present one. You cannot go on minuting about the possibilities of a given proposal when the Gaul is at the gate!

When can we meet and talk? I want to do a memorandum for the Board about idleness of the young men and women, and should be greatly helped if I could have your views to reinforce my arguments....

I am sometimes overwhelmed by a great feeling of depression over official inertia and the apparent impossibility for getting anything done. I was philosophizing in my garden last Sunday when I saw how the tiny spikes of the snowdrops had managed to push up heaps of most unpromising looking heavy soil. May this be a good omen for our case.

17 January 1939 25/10

VM to John Buchan

.... The sense of dilatoriness and congestion is exasperating; nothing much seems to happen. And the official complacency is hard to bear.

I can't help feeling that the machine has collapsed on the top of us, and you may be surprised to hear I have arrived at the conclusion that the Civil Service has become the dead hand paralyzing the country. The Civil Service, as a body, are men of the highest character, intelligence, and integrity. The system of check and balance through which they work may have suited the spacious times of the 19th century when public business was a fraction of its present volume, but it is perfectly hopeless for an emergency situation like the present which calls for rapid decision and action. The delays are inconceivable. Any proposition, big or small, is examined and re-examined, then examined again and once more re-examined by about a dozen people before anything happens. I know what it is like in my own office, and the state of despair and fury to which official inertia and delays reduce me.

The amount of time and money wasted on this meticulous control, the verbiage and the delays are beyond belief. Occasional error would be a hundred-fold better and less costly. But no one is allowed to get on with a job—the pea is always being pushed beneath a superior thimble. Little wonder that there is chaos in the departments which are concerned with A[ir] R[aid] P[recautions] and war preparations, and in the end nothing happens. The Treasury is the tiny neck of a huge bottle and things just don't get through. And the autocracy of the Treasury is pretty serious.

I am deeply concerned about all this, and T[om] J[ones], is the same. He would agree, I think with all I have written. But very few people seem alive to the situation. You have to be inside an office, as I am, to realise the coils of the system.

.... Then again if there was a big man in public life, one might look to him for reform. Except Chamberlain himself, and Herbert Morrison, who is there?....

It's the deplorable absence of men of real character and capacity which, as I see it, is our great national peril at the moment. For there is no constructive control of the machine and no one to insist upon the necessary changes in administration....

T[om] J[ones] organised two conferences recently at Blickling on unemployment and national service. But it is extraordinarily difficult to fit any national service scheme into a democratic peace frame-work, and though there were some first rate brains present, we entirely failed in the attempt.

.... I hope something may come of the triangle at which a few of us are working—unemployed, evacuation camps and holiday camps.

P.S. If you could dress up some sort of job for me in Canada and requesting my presence, I could get away earlier perhaps!! But I can't go off joy-riding in theory though it wouldn't matter two straws if I were away. It's part of the job of the Civil Servants to see that members of the Board are immobilised into positions where they are not troublesome, and the work I do is mainly work into which I insist on thrusting my nose.

2 February 1939 7/17

VM to C.W.K. MacMullan, Assistant Secretary, Training Branch, Ministry of Labour

These women [Unemployed under-30s in Liverpool and Glasgow] have been terribly on my mind for a long time and as you know I have made repeated efforts to raise the question and get something done....

Markham then goes on to discuss older women

I felt a little doubtful on closer enquiry whether the numbers of over 40's in Glasgow and Liverpool would justify rather a doubtful experiment. I should, however, be thankful to have the money with which to start another centre or centres for the older women in London where both the supply and the demand are very high.

14 February 1939

24/13

VM to Max Nicholson, PEP

.... Board is to sit for three days to evolve its annual report, and T[om] J[ones] and I are bent on dragging some unpleasant facts to light and radically altering the milk and water draft circulated by the office. The Board, if it goes on as at present, will soon entirely eclipse Speenhamland! But to get a move on with the Ministry is a colossal task — the Minister's complacency and the prospect of a General Election in the autumn will make them disinclined for any radical measures.

I am very excited about the Camps, and of course, we ought to jump in at once and secure a percentage of the work. But the deadly lethargy and complacency of the Civil Service overshadows the Board like every other department, and though I stick to my rather dreary job of yapping like a terrier at their heels, you know the semi-pitying contempt with which an outsider like myself is regarded by the hierarchy.

.... If Labour would come in and help and not hinder all the time, it would be so much easier to get a move on. A degree of compulsion there must be in any solution of this question. Personally I should like to see a Labour Corps in which the slackers and inefficients were enrolled at a learner's wage until they are fit to earn an economic wage.

16 February 1939

7/28

Sir Ronald Davison to VM

.... I think friend Radcliffe with his National Service Battalion (unpaid) is a jump or two ahead of practical politics. For the present I prefer the plan of say 50,000 specially created offers of graded employment (paid for & insured) for the 100,000 chronic cases on our registers. But this must be backed by an unpleasant alternative involving, I think, segregation of some kind....

3 May 1939

9/1

VM to Henry Carver, London Secretary of the National Men's Defence League

My views have entirely changed since the Albert Hall speech.... and I should certainly not make it today.... There are a majority of women in this country. Many of them have to rely entirely on their own exertions and large numbers have in addition dependent relatives....

This was in response to a leaflet complaining about the 'feminine invasion' of men's jobs, and a demand for women to be removed from these jobs.

No day or month 1939   7/21

VM

.... the principle of money for nothing is certainly in the air and may spread with very undesirable results. The very fact of the Board being a universal machine makes evident eleemosynary principles which were less evident in former days owing to the divergent practices of the social authority.

.... I feel... it is necessary to discriminate very sharply between allowances paid to unemployed men and women who have earned their position among the Board's applicants and idle young people who are deliberately sitting back, content to remain at a low level of life provided by public funds and making no effort to raise themselves above it.

.... when every reservation has been made there remains an unsatisfactory and disquieting case so far as the young women are concerned.

There is a striking difference in the character and worth of the older unemployed women who have worked at a regular task as compared with the irresponsibility of the girls who have had little or no industrial discipline.

I was concerned from my limited interviewing to realise how far that degree of irresponsibility had gone among some of these girls....

Many of these girls are of a very poor type and have little value, either as home-makers or industrial workers. Their lack of intelligence or lack of skill are reflected in the low wages they earn.... The girls are useful at home and the parents often regard the money as a housekeeping allowance to which they have a right. Rights not duties is in fact the normal attitude I have met during my tour about the receipt of public money....

Girls in Glasgow seem to display an almost unreasoning hatred of domestic work and refuse absolutely to consider it as a career. They are however most sadly ill equipped themselves to perform elementary duties as wives or mothers.

Undated, presumably 1939   7/22

VM Unemployed girls in Glasgow and Liverpool

Many of them are of low grade and low intelligence with a background of casual work and unemployment in their homes....

The homes from which they come are almost invariably very poor and sometimes shockingly overcrowded. Many girls of this type are growing up without any discipline, training or experience to fit them as citizens, workers and housewives....

Some effort should be made to check this present manufacture of human wreckage ... it is essential to try and rouse them to a greater sense of responsibility and to stimulate some spirit of adventure which would encourage them to push out and fit themselves for a better type of employment.

1939 7/22

Dora Ibberson to VM, on Unemployed Girls

We have I think always agreed that what these younger Liverpool women needed primarily was an improvement in their personal appearance, hygiene, and manner....

The first necessity seems, therefore, to be the provision of premises where these girls can turn themselves into 'ladies'.

4
The Home Front
1939–1945

While Markham's papers for the Second World War period reflect common prejudices of the time and show that her derogatory view of civil servants remained unaltered, they also throw light on the working of the Assistance Board in wartime, a subject which has received scant attention from historians.

In the 1930s it was widely assumed that a future war would rain bombs on the country, leading to widespread death, disease and destruction. Evacuation plans concentrated on an orderly exodus from the cities, in particular, London, rather than on what would happen to people once they reached a safe rural haven. Although discussions had been under way since the 1920s, much of the detailed planning was carried out in the last year of peace; it was never completed, and anyway some of it was out of date by the time war broke out. It was assumed that it would not be possible to evacuate everyone who wanted to leave the cities, so certain groups were given priority: school children removed with the entire school under the control of their teachers, young children with their mothers, pregnant women, and disabled adults.

The traditional view of evacuation is that it exposed the middle classes for the first time to the poverty of many working-class people. As a result of this, and the spirit of comradeship created by the evacuation of Dunkirk, class barriers were broken down and plans for a welfare state, with the support of the entire community, were laid. In recent years a rather different view of the impact of evacuation has emerged. The stories (much exaggerated in the telling) of dirty and and ill-mannered working-class children provoked a condemnation of working-class mothers, and class prejudices were reinforced.[1] *The Unemployment Assistance Board, later renamed the Assistance Board, could give immediate cash help to evacuees as well as the victims of bombing; help in kind was the responsibilty of local authorities.*

---

[1] John Macnicol, 'The evacuation of schoolchildren', in Harold Smith (ed), *War and social change: British society in the Second World War* (Manchester University Press, Manchester, 1986).

10 September 1939

VM on billeting of school children and adults at Sutton at Hone

.... Generally speaking the billeting here has gone well.... Members of the Women's Voluntary Services — mainly drawn from the Mothers Union and Women's Institutes — have worked with an energy and kindness beyond praise in placing the children in their new homes.

A good many difficulties and problems are however becoming apparent which call for solution if this novel experiment is to prove a success. Enthusiasm and good will in face of a national emergency tend to evaporate if the presence of the new comers results as time goes on in a variety of minor frictions and irritations in daily life. It is no small matter to have transferred one and a half million people to homes among strangers.

The billeting of children proved far more easy than that of adults or of mothers with babies. Families who willingly received two girls or two boys refused absolutely to house adults....

Great efforts were made when a whole family had been evacuated with a mother to house them as a unit....

Generally speaking evacuated children in small numbers can be absorbed more easily by working-class families than by middle class or upper class households. In one or two families of a different social status some serious strains have already appeared. This is apparent where the house is large but the owners are not well off and live with a minimum of staff.

One old lady of great public spirit aged nearly 80 with a large house, small means, and one maid, took in ten children. She and the maid collapsed within four days and the bulk of the children had to be transferred. Similarly the vicar also with a large house, a modest income and one old housekeeper is finding the position daily more difficult. Six children and a mother are billeted at the Vicarage....

A matter which calls urgently for elucidation by higher authority is the question of payment. Considerable doubt exists on this point. There is much divergence of opinion and confusion about 5s. and 3s. rate and that of 8s. 6d. I had gathered from what I heard at Thames House that when a mother and family were evacuated the 5s. and 3s. were in respect of housing and that the absent husband was supposed to pay for their food. If unable to do so then the U.A.B. was to step in with its P[revention of] R[elief and] D[istress] scheme.

Not one word of this has got across to the public. The women and the householders alike are under the impression that they are to be kept by someone or something. The question of payment by the husbands so far as I know has not been raised....

Children are destructive. If furniture and equipment suffer, to whom must the occupier look for redress? Blankets and mattresses will very often be ruined beyond possibility of cleaning.

The beautiful weather of the last week has greatly simplified the billeting problem. But a certain number of people (I cannot give exact figures at the moment) have thrown up their billets and gone home. In other cases parents have come and removed children.

.... The question of a communal meal should be considered in the near future. The provision of a mid day meal would lessen the strain on many householders and the removal of the children from 9 a.m. to 4 p.m. would equally deal with the complaints about noise.

.... Many of the children have come poorly clad with only summer clothes and plimsolls instead of shoes....

It has caused me a good deal of irritation to realise the skill with which some large establishments in this neighbourhood have successfully evaded their responsibilities about evacuation. Over averages I have the impression that the rich have been more reluctant than the poor to shoulder their fair share of the burthen. At the same time I am bound to say that evacuated children fit much less well into the economy of a large house than they do into that of a working-class home. Servants are often snobbish and difficult, and when hostile to the incursion of strange children may create a very difficult problem for the mistress. Further, children are happier in surroundings of a type with which they are familiar. A large house with its large rooms seems to them an unfriendly place.

.... More use, in my opinion, should be made of large empty houses converted into hostels for mothers with babies and families and for other adults.

Undated

5/14

Second report by VM on evacuation

After three weeks experience I am confirmed in the view that the Billeting of evacuated children at Sutton at Hone has generally speaking been a success.... the young visitors, so far as I know, have not been guilty of any of the outrages of which stories are told in other districts.... The average child obviously came from a decent working-class home and we had no experience of the slum child whose manners and customs have shocked and dismayed many districts.

.... Nearly all the mothers have gone home (thereby solving a major problem)....

Both in working-class and middle-class homes the presence of the children throws much extra work and responsibility on the housewife. In small middle-class houses the strain is I think the greater since the standard of living is higher, and normally the householders are accustomed to privacy

22 September 1939   *Home Front*

which disappears with the presence of strange children....

    I am satisfied that available accommodation in many reception areas is not as yet fully occupied. I only know that in Sutton some of the large houses escaped altogether and were not on the original lists.

    ....A house left by an evacuated mother or family almost invariably refuses to receive fresh inmates. Housewives plead illness, strain, the arrival of relatives and other domestic causes or beg to be relieved of the children they have taken in as boarders. These excuses are sometimes legitimate, sometimes they are not.

    ....Evacuation has proved a fierce search light turned on to the social services of the country and the nation has realised with a shock the very low level of life which still persists in certain urban areas.

18 September 1939   5/14

Mary Sutherland, Chief Woman Officer, the Labour Party, to VM

I was afraid you would not find the Ministry of Health sympathetic to the idea of hostels for evacuated mothers. I found them disappointingly stubborn on this point and I am afraid until they are prepared to tackle the question on these lines there will be quite considerable failures so far as the evacuation of mothers is concerned.

    ....I think your suggestion of having one of our centres in use to train institutional cooks and ward maids is valuable....

    I think it is ridiculous that the Central Committee on Women's Training should have to win the approval of Lady Reading's organisation [The Women's Voluntary Service] before any scheme we put forward is likely to be sanctioned.

22 September 1939   5/14

VM to Charles Vickery[2]

I was greatly interested to hear your account of the evacuees at Barnard Castle.... We have been lucky in my particular area because we have had children from a decent school, but evacuation has been a fierce searchlight on our health and education services in many areas. The disgraceful and disgusting conditions of which you write have their parallel elsewhere. The evacuation of Liverpool and Glasgow revealed a shocking state of affairs, and the reception areas which received children from those two cities are in a state of revolt. I am afraid from what you say that the standard in Newcastle is little better. In view of the millions we spend annually on

---

[2] Former army officer, JP and later High Sheriff of Durham.

education and health, it is intolerable that such numbers of families living at a sub-human level have come to light.

16 October 1939 5/15

VM to George Reid, Secretary of the UAB

Any general provision of clothes by the Government for evacuated children would I feel sure be a great mistake.

Apart from the curious demoralisation which in the experience of all social workers attaches to any wholesale distribution of clothes, such action would certainly lead to friction in the reception areas.

.... Parents.... who are quite able to provide what is necessary should not be relieved of their responsibilities by any general clothing scheme. Further, what impression will be made on self respecting families in rural areas who are bringing up their children on a small wage, if clothes are to be provided as a matter of course for the billeted town child, while the country child is left to carry on poorly clad?

Undoubtedly there is a situation to be dealt with when the needs of the evacuated child of the low-paid wage earner have to be met, but I feel it should be approached with great circumspection.

It seems to me the problem should be dealt with as need arises through the local machinery of the welfare committees supplemented by voluntary action and voluntary funds. If evacuation is prolonged such local funds may require help from a central grant.

These local committees understand the local conditions and to them the visiting teachers who know a good deal about the home background of the children can report cases of need.

Local effort, local funds, local make and mend parties will go a long way towards meeting need in many areas.

But admittedly there are areas where the welfare committee is either non-existent or owing to lack of personality and funds is not a competent body and the local Council is in much the same position.

In such areas the initiative must come from some outside agency.

I agree with you that our experience at the Board points to the Personal Service League as a responsible society whom the Ministry of Health might appoint as its agent to administer a supplementary grant in areas where voluntary effort cannot deal with undoubted need among the children. The Personal Service League did their work with great efficiency in the Distressed Areas and they have considerable experience of wholesale buying and distribution of boots and materials.

I do not know however how relations stand today between the Personal Service League and Women's Voluntary Service or whether Women's Voluntary Service is preparing to take executive action itself in this field. Various voluntary bodies to my knowledge are at this moment turning their eyes on the evacuation areas. It is essential whatever is set up that it should avoid multiplicity of competing agencies with consequent friction and confusion.

The Local Authority, the Welfare Committee and the Billeting Officer remain the channels through which organised effort should flow. Many different societies can contribute to the common end if their efforts are thus directed.

23 October 1939   25/10
VM to John Buchan

.... And now the war. It is all so extraordinarily different from the last time. We have at least learnt something in the last 25 years, namely that war is a hideous business which excites neither emotion nor enthusiasm. The absence of war fever and excitement is remarkable, — no songs, no nothing. Just a grim dreary business which has to be gone through grimly — great determination, but everyone hating the whole horrible business. Of course the black-out (and London is inconceivably dark) restricts all activities, and as the winter advances the long nights will weight still more heavily on us all.

I find myself on the shelf; one of the veterans of the Great War whose main occupation is to complain about this one.... Every war job is in a state of suspended animation. Nothing has happened according to plan. The Board, for instance, anticipating panic refugees from bombing all over the country started about 400 emergency offices. We have had to shut them down to all intents and purposes. The time and money lost on every side have been incredible. If it was a calculated policy on Hitler's part, it was extremely clever.

About the Home Front, what am I to say? After six weeks of war, there is profound discontent and, more than discontent, profound anxiety about the conduct of affairs. The impression of muddle, confusion, and incompetence in every direction goes beyond anything I remember in 1914. At least we had a Cabinet then containing outstanding personalities. To-day, apart from Winston (whom pressure of public opinion forced Chamberlain to appoint to the Admiralty), the front bench is a sorry sight. I know you admire Chamberlain and he has many fine qualities, but he is a very poor judge of character and he is in no way a leader. He is tired and obstinate and in his appointments he has a genius for the third rate. As someone said to me bitterly, he has men about him who have wish-bones rather than back-bones. The Ministers put in for Shipping, Supply, and Economic Warfare—three key points—are regarded as public scandals — Gilmour[3] who was the

---

[3] Sir John Gilmour (1876–1940), Conservative MP for Renfrewshire East January

despair of the Scottish Office 20 years ago; Burgin[4] who is regarded as a crook lawyer; Cross[5] an amiable and insignificant individual of whom I had never heard a month ago. The scandals of the Ministry of Information have, I am sure, reached you across the Atlantic, and I need not dwell on them.

Irritation at the Government's handling of the war focused on the Ministry of Information. Its work was characterised by muddle and confusion, and although this was not always the Ministry's fault, Chamberlain contemplated disbanding it altogether.[6]

There is profound discontent in the House of Commons, but, until the Conservative rank and file revolt, nothing can be done and party discipline is as yet too strong for rebellion. So we drag on and the muddles grow.

Also the waste! I cannot describe the gross extravagance and the way money is being poured out like water. My old enemy, the Office of Works, has spread itself nobly in the commandeering of schools, hotels, and private houses on the most wasteful and extravagant lines. A.R.P. is my pet King Charles' Head. Millions have gone down the gutter over that organisation, and people carrying gas masks in country lanes and digging trenches in remote villages are to me objects of public ridicule.

.... This war has brought many discomforts unknown last time. Railway travelling has become a real trial. Not only do the trains take incredible hours to go anywhere, but the entire absence of light in the carriages makes a journey after dark pure misery....

.... Chatsworth is a girls' school! I cannot describe the horror with which I saw those glorious rooms filled with iron beds and cheap furniture. The State rooms and the corridors were all dormitories.

This letter, or rather this chronicle, has been written in bits over several days. Since I began it, the prolonged leisure I foresaw for myself has been broken into. A queer and novel job has come my way as Sam Hoare[7] has invited me to serve on the Aliens Committee at the Home Office.

1910–1918, Glasgow Pollok 1918–1940. 1924–1929 Secretary of State for Scotland, 1931–1932 Minister of Agriculture of Fisheries, 1932–1935 Home Secretary, 1939–1940 Minister of Shipping.

[4] Edward Burgin (1887–1945), Liberal MP for Luton 1929–1945. 1932–1937 Parliamentary Secretary Board of Trade, 1937–1939 Minister of Transport, 1939–1940 Minister of Supply.

[5] Sir Ronald Cross (1896–1968), Conservative MP for Rossendale 1931–1945, Ormskirk 1950–1951. 1938–1939 Parliamentary Secretary Board of Trade, 1939–1940 Minister of Economic Warfare, 1940–1941 Minister of Shipping.

[6] Ian McLaine, *Ministry of morale: Home front morale and the Ministry of Information in World War Two* (Allen & Unwin, London, 1979), pp 36, 38–41; Paul Addison, *The road to 1945* (Quartet, London, 1977), p 64.

[7] Sir Samuel Hoare, Lord Templewood (1880–1959), Conservative MP for Chelsea January 1910–1944. 1922–1924 1924–1929 and 1940 Secretary of State for Air, 1931–1935 India, 1935 Foreign Secretary, 1936–1937 First Lord of the Admiralty, 1937–1939

In September a large number of Nazi sympathisers and some refugees from Germany and Austria, 'enemy aliens', were rounded up. Most of the remaining enemy aliens came before tribunals conducted by the 18B committee which decided whether to intern them, restrict their movement or set them free. Markham was the first woman to sit on the 18B committee.

It will be almost a full time job up to Xmas for there are several hundreds of these people to be interviewed. I have always thoroughly disliked everything I have heard of M.I.5. — I have bristled with Magna Carta and Habeas Corpus when their name is mentioned. Now I am to be mixed up with them. Jimmy Mallon will be a colleague with Walter Monckton[8] and Norman Birkett[9] as joint Chairmen. It ought to be interesting and though I had made up my mind I should be merely an onlooker in this war and had bought three new pieces of needlework to occupy my leisure, I didn't feel I could refuse when asked.

....I dined with the Hutchinsons last night....He seemed quite happy about the Government and even Gilmour! — an appointment which has made most people hysterical with wrath. Do you see the New Statesman? It's a querulous rag, but it's comment about Gilmour made me roll with laughter — namely that it was the most surprising appointment since Caligula had made his horse a Consul!

23 November 1939 19/31

VM to her sister, Geraldine Hole

Markham refers to her work with aliens on the 18B committee

....the majority are inoffensive creatures who ought never to have seen the inside of a prison....

Home Secretary, 1939–1940 Lord Privy Seal and member of War Cabinet. 1940–1944 Ambassador to Spain.

[8] Sir Walter Monckton (1891–1965), 1939–1940 Director-General, Press and Censorship Bureau, 1940–1941 Ministry of Information, 1941–1942 British propaganda and information services, Cairo. 1945 Solicitor-General. 1945 United Kingdom Delegate, Allied Reparation Committee, Moscow. Conservative MP for Bristol West 1951–1957. 1951–1955 Minister of Labour and National Service, 1955–1956 Minister of Defence, 1956–1957 Paymaster-General.

[9] Norman Birkett (1883–1962), barrister and judge, Liberal MP for Nottingham East 1923–1924, 1929–1931. 1939 chairman of 18B Advisory Committee; 1941 knighted; judge at post-war Nuremburg trials. 1950–1957 Lord Justice of Appeal.

26 November 1939 28/45(1)

VM to Nan Carruthers, her sister-in-law, living in the USA

I sit all day and every day on the Court who investigate doubtful aliens who have been locked up. The Court has Norman Birkett, a very famous lawyer, as Chairman, and its most exciting work — like living in a perpetual Edgar Wallace thriller....

19 January 1940 28/45(1)

VM to Nan Carruthers

I am finding my Aliens Court very depressing.... Our clients are like a cross-section of Germany from people in Hitler's entourage to humble domestic servants. Some of them, indeed the majority, are very decent people, but with few exceptions they follow the Nazi theory of life like sheep and admire it....

22 February 1940 25/49

VM to Marquis of Lothian (Philip Kerr)[10]

I have been sitting for the last four months on the Aliens Appeal Court over which Norman Birkett presides.... It has angered us all to find what a complete and tyrannical organisation the Germans had in this country. The Nazis kept tabs on everyone and everyone who came here from Germany, and compelled their nationals to join the Labour Front or the Nazi Party under threats either of personal hardship or of persecuting their families in Germany....

The Court sits all day and every day, and I always say that to work in a Government Department is the modern equivalent of entering the Cloister....

11 March 1940 28/45(1)

VM to Nan Carruthers

The Aliens Appeal Court is still working at high pressure, and the Unemployment Assistance Board, which was just ticking over normally when I was 'lent' to the Home Office, has burst into activity again. There's a new Old Age Pensions Bill before Parliament and we are to be charged with its administration which means another three-quarters of a million people are to become our care....

---

[10] Philip Kerr, (1882–1940), journalist, 1910–1916 Editor *Round Table*, 1916–1921 Secretary to Prime Minister, 1931 Chancellor of the Duchy of Lancaster, 1931–1932 Parliamentary Under-Secretary India, 1939–1940 British Ambassador in Washington.

The following month the UAB was to drop 'Unemployment' from its title and become 'Assistance Board' as it took over responsibility for supplementary pensions, which it paid out from 3 August.

4 April 1940   3/21
VM to Ernest Bevin[11]

You and I are old friends who have battled together in many fields....

The Central Committee [on Women's Training and Employment] met yesterday and we are very much concerned at the position in which we find ourselves. To all intents and purposes we are ham-strung. Our old training work has come to an end and we receive no encouragement to undertake new duties. The question I want to ask is this — do you pundits want to wind us up?

We realise that the Committee has been established for many years, that it is now an odd, even superfluous adjunct to your Ministry, and that its membership is largely composed of a troup of aged pre-war follies whom your bright young things at Montagu House may feel should long since have been consigned to the property box. I write official letters — I get no reply and between delays and red-tape our work is reduced to a grotesque minimum.

Now we are not prepared to continue on these lines. If your officials think it is time for us to come to an end, why do they not say so frankly?....

The Central Committee on Women's Training and Employment had been trying to get the Ministry to allow them to develop canteen cookery courses, but without success and on 28 June 1940 it was wound up.

13 May 1940   28/45(1)
Nan Carruthers to VM

.... [The President's speech] has definitely put the country as a whole on the side of the Allies — if it wasn't there already. I still doubt that the country would agree to the sending of men across, but the feeling is increasing that we should send as much material help as possible. The Red Cross is having an emergency drive and there are British Relief Association Chapters all over where we go to knit and sew. There are just as many women who have no British affiliations attending these meetings as others....

---

[11] Ernest Bevin (1881–1951), Labour MP for Wandsworth Central 1940–1950, Woolwich East 1950–1951. 1940–1945 Minister of Labour and National Service, 1945–1951 Foreign Secretary, 1951 Lord Privy Seal.

14 July 1940 28/45(1)

VM to Nan Carruthers

Materially we are quite all right. I hardly know rationing is in existence. But the working classes will feel the small tea allowance.

11 August 1940 28/45(1)

VM to Nan Carrruthers

....I often feel life is far too comfortable....It's the governing class at the top which is all wrong, and we have all got slack and easy in consequence....

21 August 1940 3/21

Laurie Brock to VM

He regrets the folding of the CCWTE

....I honestly feel that there are so many questions relating to women's employment which the Civil Service is not really competent to handle, without the advice of someone from outside who will look at the job from an altogether different angle. For example, there is the problem of attracting young women into domestic service, and training them for it, an important problem, not merely because of the demand, but because, given a good mistress, domestic service is the best training for married life that a young working-class girl can have. Then there is the problem of finding some remedy for what I would call the blind-alley type of shop. What can you do with the badly educated and bad mannered type of girl attracted into shops of the Woolworth type, and then thrown out a few years later when she is beginning to lose her 'pep', and can no longer stand the racket....I feel so strongly, in spite of a great faith in the capacity of the Civil Servant, that these are the sort of questions which the professional administrator, with a succession of files to do every day, can never give the time to tackle them properly.

22 September 1940 28/45(1)

VM to Nan Carruthers

I am busy with homeless people, and am trying to get a canteen started to feed women and children who have spent the night in a shelter and emerge tired and hungry in the morning. And to feed ARP firemen and other workers through the night....

13 October 1940

28/45(1)

VM to Nan Carruthers

My Canteen[12] is going like hot cakes. We serve gallons of tea and food to the poorest of the poor, many of whom have lost their homes.... There is a disused tube where *seven thousand* people sleep — it's dreadful, on bits of papers and rugs and any old thing. They come in so tired with their bundles, and as I hand out mugs of tea at $1\frac{1}{2}$ d (I don't give free food but at cost price)....

I am up to my eyes in work for the homeless people and people who have to spend their nights in shelters.... Why am I doing all this as a private person? Because I am trying to *shame* the Ministry of Food and the London County Council into doing a job which wants doing all over London and the need for which they deny — blast their smug official minds. Even the firemen and demolition squads can't get food in the night....

I foresee that soon I shall have no servants here....

11 November 1940

5/87

VM to Irene Ward[13]

....We know, of course that delays, niggardly payments, and discourtesy are incidents wholly contrary to the instructions of the Board and the spirit in which they wish those instructions to be carried out. Among a staff of 12,000 people, however, there are bound to be personal failures though I am glad to say we have had many testimonies of the kindness and sympathy of officers....

Members of the Board are scattering over London next week to make personal investigations....

Of course, the imponderabilia of failure in courtesy to applicants are very difficult to assess. Pressure is great, the waiting-room may be full, and some of these poor people, as you know, are very long winded and it is difficult to keep them to the point. I suspect that what has happened in certain cases is that the officer has cut short many of the rather irrelevant appeals that are made to an investigator in the course of his duties.

....As to the quality of the investigators, you must remember that they belong to the lowest Treasury grade and are the worst paid class in the Government service. I protested about this on the first day that the Board met, and I have protested about it during the last six years, but the situation remains unchanged. If I am not mistaken, you spoke to me about women on the Professional Register, but none of them, of course would look at the

---

[12] In Southwark.
[13] Dame Irene Ward (1895–1980), Conservative MP for Wallsend-on-Tyne 1931–1945, Tynemouth 1950–February 1974.

salary paid to the Investigators who include the temporary clerks.

Local offices were now instructed to treat people with sympathy and courtesy.

21 November 1940   25/87
VM to Irene Ward

The Assistance Board was swept up [to Southport] for the week-end and was sitting in continuous session for three days in order to devise new Regulations and to get rid of the Means Test. Many millions, of course, are involved, but money seems of no consideration to anyone these days!

....All the members now have visited a certain number of offices. I am bound to say we are entirely non-plussed to account for the complaints that have reached us. So far as we can judge, officers are doing their work well under very difficult conditions....

I understand that no less than 1,000 'casuals' as they are called, were taken on for this work, 300 of whom were dismissed almost immediately. I must make it clear, however, that no assessments are done by these people. Their duties consist solely in taking down full particulars on a sheet of paper, and the actual money grant is made subsequently by one of the Board's officers.

In each office, I sat with a case from the first to the last, and the average time taken from the beginning of the interview to the moment the money is paid is about 20 minutes. This, of course, does not include the time spent in the waiting room, and when there has been heavy bombing in a district and some hundreds of applicants flood in during the day, I cannot see how waiting can be avoided. Many of our offices too are pokey places for, whatever criticism can be made about the Board, that of spreading themselves in lordly premises is certainly not among them. As it happened, the week of our visits did not coincide with heavy bombing and so there was no pressure on these particular days.

The taking down of the particulars is not an expert job, and there is no reason why a saleswoman, who knows how to sell stockings or ribbons in a pleasant or a competent manner, should not do this part of the job properly....

I quite realise that the presence of a member of the Board has naturally the effect of making the whole office pull up its socks so to speak, and since personality is everything in a matter of this kind, I do not deny for a moment that there are probably cases where the manner of address has been brusque and unsatisfactory.

....no less than 70 of the London offices have been bombed, many of the staff injured or their homes destroyed....

Curiously enough, in more than one district, we have had difficulties with social workers in the area whose views of what ought to be done differ considerably from that of the Area Officer, or indeed from what the instructions permit. In more than once instance, these good people have protested vigorously against their ideas not being carried out to the full....

31 December 1940   3/21

VM to Norman Birkett

The Assistance Board is closely concerned with war damage, and since bombing began[14] I have had to visit many of our offices in London and in the provinces. Since we were all overworked and no less than 80 of our offices had been damaged in a greater or less degree, Bevin thought the moment appropriate to abolish the Means Test. That means new legislation and new regulations, and we have had somehow to find time to squeeze in a horribly technical and difficult job in the midst of other immediate and urgent matters. The unfortunate Board consequently had to retire for some days to Southport to consider these problems at leisure. It has been a difficult time for us all....

From January 1941 there was no family means test, but the personal means test remained.

2 February 1941   28/45(ii)

VM to Nan Carruthers

Markham writes to thank her sister-in-law for sending oil stoves. Markham had had an acrimonious correspondence with Herbert Morrison[15] on the subject.

There's a lot of talk about a New World after the war. God forbid it should be run by Departments and Civil Servants!

27 May 1941   9/2

VM to Lloyd George

Could you spare one day in London to let me call on you? My work at the Assistance Board has brought me into intimate contact with several of the bombed towns. Like many other people I am greatly concerned about the Government apathy in insisting on effective arrangements beforehand

---

[14] In the summer of 1940.

[15] Herbert Morrison, Baron Morrison of Lambeth (1888–1965), Labour MP for Hackney South 1923–1924, 1929–1931 and 1935–1945, Lewisham East 1945–1950, Lewisham South 1950–1959. 1929–1931 Minister of Transport, 1940 Minister of Supply, 1940–1945 Home Secretary, 1945–1951 Lord President of the Council, 1951 Foreign Secretary.

to meet the effects of a blitz, and the consequent local breakdowns which repeat themselves with painful and monotonous regularity.

The Times had an article by a Special Correspondent on this subject on May 16th which was in fact written by myself....

The following extract is typical of Markham's comments about the French.

13 July 1941   28/45(ii)

VM to Nan Carruthers

Thank heaven that miserable Syrian campaign is over. Its made the English more furious than ever with the Vichy French. If Vichy had shown as much energy in fighting the Germans as she has shown in fighting us, France might still be a going concern....

17 July 1941   28/45(ii)

Nan Carruthers to VM

We had a very fine trip to Canada, and saw a great deal. We met some very nice people both English and Canadians. The English were mostly refugees.... There is universal dissatisfaction regarding [money]. I heard it on all sides. These people are almost destitute, and just having to be 'kept' by their longsuffering friends and relatives.

29 July 1941   28/45(ii)

VM to Nan Carruthers

The new Chairman of the Assistance Board has been appointed, and we are all greatly relieved. Ramsbottom[16] who comes from the Board of Education, is a nice man and highly cultivated. We were menaced by some dreadful possibilities — one who would have gone about with a perpetual brass trumpet and another who would have strewn the office with empty bottles!

---

[16] Sir Herwald Ramsbottom, Viscount Soulbury (1887–1971), Conservative MP for Lancaster 1929–1941. 1931–1935 Parliamentary Secretary Board of Education, 1935–1936 Minister of Agriculture and Fisheries, 1936–1939 Minister of Pensions, 1939–1940 First Commissioner of Works, 1940–1941 President of the Board of Education, 1941–1948 Chairman of the UAB, 1942–1949 Burnham Committees, 1949–1954 Governor-General Ceylon.

21 August 1941
VM

A lunch was given by the American ambassador on 21 August to discuss the possibility of Americans coming to work in UK government departments and with voluntary organisations, whose staff had been depleted by the war

.... Mr. Reid pointed out to me that the Assistance Board, which is an administrative, not a technical body, would find it very difficult to introduce American staff with no previous experience of the work into its higher ranks....

The luncheon was a very interesting experience.... The significance of the gathering, however, lay in the demonstration it afforded of the growing sense of Anglo-American co-operation and the urge of the two nations to pool their resources.

7 September 1941
VM to Nan Carruthers

.... The Assistance Board have started mobile units—vans to act as offices with sleeping accommodation for the staff. So when a town is blitzed we can send in our people without any delay to do their work. There is to be a Women's Unit and I am busily engaged selecting personnel and discussing uniforms—are collars to be light or dark? Can the women wear battledress and what will the Treasury do next?....

Labour statistics have never been collected by socio-economic group, so it is impossible to know the relative participation rates of middle- and working-class women in the labour force during the second world war. As regulations tightened up it is unlikely that middle-class women would have done less work outside the home, with the exception of some older middle-class women who, like older working-class women, had domestic commitments, but did not have the financial need to work. Despite claims that class barriers were broken down at the workplace during the war, middle- and working-class women tended to go into different types of work. So, for instance, few middle-class women would have found themselves on the factory floor, while a number of them took up voluntary rather than paid work. The women's services also had a definite class pecking order, with the 'Free' SOE FANYS at the top, followed by the WRENS and the ATS at the bottom. Markham may have been more conscious of middle-class women who were apparently not working because middle-class women may have had more flexible working hours and Markham possibly visited more frequently middle, rather than working, class areas.

10 September 1941   25/47

VM to The Dowager Marchioness of Reading

I hear on many sides a good deal of uneasiness expressed about the sluggish response of many women to take up war work especially among the upper and upper-middle classes. The women who are working work like blacks but others, I am told, are not pulling their weight and it is disconcerting to read these constant appeals and exhortations to our sex to come forward.

I do not come across these people personally and can only speak of them second-hand, but I am bound to say the shops in Oxford Street crowded out by well-to-do women of all ages have filled me with speculation. You, as head of your great organisation and as a member of the Welfare Committee of the Ministry of Labour have unique experience and unique knowledge both of the needs of industry and the women's services and whether or not the response is adequate.

A special point made to me and which I want to pass on to you concerns young women recently married. I know personally of two or three cases where a girl, on being called up for interview at the Exchange, has point blank refused to take up war work either in munitions or the services. In this attitude she has been strongly backed up by the husband. The reason is intelligible. Life is short and precarious, and if the husband is serving, his leave seems more important than the national needs. These young people won't contemplate work for the girl which would prevent their being together when he is free .... Would it involve too much dislocation of industry and discipline if, when a husband comes home, the woman were also given leave?

.... One would hate to think any large number of women are not giving of their best, especially in view of the splendid work other women are doing. But in war time one is very conscious of the double stream running side by side through the national life, selfishness and sacrifice; service and shirking; courage and faint-heartedness, jostling each other.

16 September 1941   28/45(ii)

VM to Nan Carruthers

.... Frankly I feel one has to reverse one's views about Russia .... this heroic resistance, this power of sacrificing *everything* for your country moves me deeply. And its Russia not Bolshevism they are fighting for. Just compare Russia's sacrifices with the perfidy and cowardice of France where two million men laid down their arms because they wouldn't fight. Also the efficiency of the Russian army and their public services have amazed everyone here ....

As in the First World War, there were alarmist claims and unsubstantiated innuendoes about the country's, and especially women's, declining moral standards. VD rates doubled for men in the first two years of war, peaking in 1942, while women's rates continued to rise throughout the war. Divorce rates rose during the war, although a liberalisation of the divorce laws in 1937 would have led to a rise anyway. Illegitimate births doubled during the war, but this is not necessarily an indication of changing patterns of sexual relations: one in three babies was conceived out of wedlock before the war, but 70% of the pregnant women then married; so what probably changed during the war was the number of unmarried pregnant women who were able or willing to marry the baby's father.[17] *Fears about declining moral standards and the breakdown of the family focused opprobrium on women. The war did not see a breakdown in society's (or at least the press's) double standards for men and women; this brings into doubt the notion that the war was a force for change in gender relations.*

10 October 1941 25/47

VM to The Dowager Marchioness of Reading

....I often feel troubled by the extremely injurious stories that reach me frequently about the A.T.S., which I am sure, at the best, are greatly exaggerated. It is very unfortunate that people feel so little moral responsibility about this careless talk and the damage it can do....

26 October 1941 28/45(ii)

VM to Nan Carruthers

Tomorrow I go to Beaconsfield to meet the Queen who is visiting one of the Free French Hospitals. The Free French are giving me a lot of bother and I dislike them cordially, so don't look forward to the trip.

2 November 1941 28/45(ii)

VM to Nan Carruthers

....I must tell you about the Queen's visit to the French Sailors' Convalescent Home. Both General de Gaulle and Admiral Muselier came and stuck to her like leaches! De Gaulle is a fine looking man with a heavy, obstinate face — he has got very much above himself of late and has been troublesome....

[17] Gail Braybon and Penny Summerfield, *Out of the cage: women's experiences in two world wars* (Pandora, London, 1987), pp 210–218.

7 November 1941   25/47

VM to The Dowager Marchioness of Reading

....a very unhappy atmosphere has grown up about [the ATS], thanks to current talk — possibly chatter is the better word, — and I have been told several times that no mother who values the welfare of her girl would allow her to join that particular service....

18 January 1942   28/45(iii)

VM to Nan Carruthers

Markham was sitting on a shelter committee.

I did a shelter crawl in Westminster last Thursday with the Town Clerk, and among them we visited a Club for down and outs run by Conscientious Objectors. It was a remarkable place, and the young men in charge were good fellows and real enthusiasts....

No one is satisifed with the Government. It is too much Winston and third rate men....

I am going to a luncheon for the Soviet women this week. The Soviet delegates have been going round our factories, and are most outspoken when they don't think the standard of work sufficiently high.

4 February 1942   5/20

VM to Kingsley Martin[18]

....I want to write to you to-day about the B.B.C. I don't like what is going on there ....

In war-time it is reasonable and inevitable that the control of foreign broadcasting should be in the hands of the Foreign Office. But are you satisfied that the matter stops there? Is there not ground for apprehension that the independence of the BBC is rapidly disappearing and that the whole broadcasting organisation is passing under Government control? I am sure you will agree that few things could be more disastrous than for the only broadcasting system in the country to become an annexe of the Foreign Office. At any moment (and more and more surely as the war draws to an end) some great question of public policy may arise which will divide the country to the right and left. Should that happen, it is of the first importance that the issues on both sides should be fairly and impartially placed before the public. Will that happen if broadcasting is virtually under the control of a Government Department and a Department, moreover, in which the Catholic element is strong?

[18] Kingsley Martin (1897–1969), 1931–1960 Editor of the *New Statesman*.

17 February 1942 Home Front

This presumably is a reference to Sir Cecil Graves, one of the BBC's joint Director-Generals who was referred to as a 'Papist'. Links between Whitehall and the BBC had increased during the war and two Government 'advisors' had been working at the BBC for the past year.[19]

....The Governors seem to have lost all real authority though the theory of their independence is no doubt a useful camouflage for the group really in power. I could cover sheets with my grievances about the quality of the BBC performances — personally I think that with their ceaseless flow of inferior light music and third-rate entertainments, they are becoming real corruptors of the public taste ....

6 February 1942   5/20
Kingsley Martin to VM

....But how could you hope to keep the B.B.C. independent in war time? Constitutionally it is taken over by the Government for the duration; practically it could only maintain any independence if it had a very remarkable and strong personality at its head. The Governors seem almost to have given up. But I wish you would say your say publicly in the paper....

11 February 1942   5/20
VM to Kingsley Martin

....You say that it is impossible for the B.B.C. to be independent in war time. I agree that a large measure of Government control and a total measure of Government control over the foreign side of the proceedings are both inevitable, but why should there be all this secrecy and the changes made in such a hush-hush manner? Should not the arrangements made for the Corporation be public and above board and so avoid the impression that wirepullers are in charge of whom the public knows nothing?

....A small instance of a trend which I think very undesirable is the displeasure which I understand was incurred by the Archbishop of York when, in a broadcast, he made his distinction between retribution and vengeance.

17 February 1942   28/45(iii)
VM to Nan Carruthers

....What worries me (and many others!) is the number of inefficients in high places and the vested interests of the capitalists and the Tories, which

---

[19] Asa Briggs *The BBC: The first fifty years* (Oxford University Press, Oxford, 1985), pp 201, 146, 203–205.

are a drag on the wheel. I must warn you I am moving more and more to the Left!

8 March 1942 28/45(iii)
Nan Carruthers to VM

.... You have no doubt been reading of our alien problem here on the coast; I think right from the beginning I told you they would be very acute. It is no light thing in a country that has been so hipped on the rights of man to order *United States citizens* to pack up and go to a concentration camp.... When I think of the hours you must have spent on Alien Courts and we just tell them to 'get up and git' and to make it snappy; no court is needed. So everyone is losing his or her Japanese and Italian gardeners, people who have been in the country since birth....

22 March 1942 28/45(iii)
VM to Nan Carruthers

.... Well I have had a busy week, and its all very interesting poking my nose into the Womens Services.... The women on my Committee are excellent, but the men are useless....

17 May 1942 28/45(iii)
VM to Nan Carruthers

.... I am sorry to hear that there is at the moment so much anti-British feeling in America. Everyone who comes back brings the same tale, that the war against Roosevelt and Britain seems more important to some people than the war against Hitler!!....

7 June 1942 28/45(iii)
VM to Nan Carruthers

.... the Cologne raid gave me a bit of a heartache — James and I spent such happy days there during the Occupation — this awful destruction is inevitable, but if one stopped to analyse the horrors of this hideous war one would just go dotty.

2 August 1942   28/45(iii)
VM to CC

Report into Women in Services

.... The women incidentally have done all the work....

23 August 1942   28/45(iii)
VM to Nan Carruthers

.... Sir George Wilkinson — the former Lord Mayor of London, entertained us at dinner last week prior to a tour of inspection [of tube shelters], and I found myself sitting between the Minister of Health, Ernest Brown[20] and Lord Horder[21] — you will know the famous doctor by name. We all agreed what a ticklish problem it was to have this vast number of American soldiers here in a country so utterly different from their own and what tact and care the situation called for. White girls walking out with black men are already creating a problem! We haven't the same strong sense against colour as you have, since normally the clash of races doesn't occur here....

From mid-1942 black and white American soldiers began arriving in the UK. The American segregation of troops according to their colour caused comment. The British government did not wish to give offence to the Empire, but it also wanted to avoid an international incident either by insisting that segregation was not possible in the UK, or by numbers of British women being seen to be friendly with black soldiers as it was feared this would lead to white American soldiers attacking black soldiers and the British women with whom they were seen. The Home Secretary's greatest fear was that mixed race babies would be born; there are no accurate figures, but there were possibly between about 700 and 1000 mixed race babies (out of about 20,000 babies fathered by GIs). A whispering campaign, suggesting that black American soldiers were riddled with VD, aimed at frightening British women into keeping away from the black soldiers.[22]

[20] Ernest Brown (1881–1962), Liberal, later Liberal National MP for Rugby 1923–1924, Leith 1927–1945. 1931–1932 Parliamentary Secretary Ministry of Health, 1932–1935 Parliamentary Secretary Board of Trade Mines Department, 1935–1940 Minister of Labour, 1940–1941 Secretary of State for Scotland, 1941–1943 Minister of Health, 1943–1945 Chancellor of the Duchy of Lancaster, 1945 Minister of Aircraft Production.

[21] Thomas Horder (1871–1955), well-known medical doctor. 1939 honorary consultant physician, Ministry of Pensions, 1940–1955 medical advisor to London Transport, 1935–1939 chairman Ministry of Health advisory committee, 1940 chairman of the commiittee on the use of public air raid shelters, 1941 medical adviser to Lord Woolton at Ministry of Food.

[22] Graham Smith *When Jim Crow met John Bull: Black American soldiers in World War II Britain* (Tauris, London, 1987)

24 August 1942

Cynthia Colville, Lady in Waiting to Queen Mary to VM

I am writing by command of Queen Mary to bring before you a difficult but important matter. Her Majesty has been gravely concerned to hear of the unfortunate results, in many places, of association between American coloured men and English girls. You probably know that there are several negro battalions of U.S.A. Pioneer Corps etc., and these men are to be seen in large numbers in the south and west country, and elsewhere. They are friendly, generous, and have a good deal of money to spend; and there is no reason to think that they are particularly ill-behaved, though I fear there is very little doubt but that many English girls — often about fifteen years of age — do run after these men (and their money!) most persistently, especially in the big seaports, where men of colour are a familiar sight. This is not chiefly a question of morals — however important that aspect may be — but of international complications. American men refuse to allow negroes to associate with white girls, and they are ready (unpunished by their own authorities) to 'beat up', first, the offending blacks, and subsequently the white girls who encourage them. Thus, — apart from the fact that ultimate marriage would in any case be the rarest possibility; (it is unlikely that the Government would welcome an invasion of negro workers after the war, or that they themselves would wish to settle down here, whilst they would certainly not be allowed to return to the U.S.A. with white wives!) — Apart from all this, there is a serious risk of grave ill-feeling between English and Americans, of possible lynchings, with all the disastrous consequences, not to mention the problem of half-caste births on a much bigger scale than heretofore.

The Queen feels strongly that wardens of hostels, factory welfare workers and others who are concerned with social conditions affecting girls, should give them definite instruction and enlightenment in this matter, and that it is an urgent one.

At the same time it is important that colour should *not* be stressed in writing, and that no written or printed word on this subject ever fall into the hands of those who are, after all, our country's guests. These black soldiers have come over with a tremendous sense of patriotism and determination to show that they are proud to work and fight for the U.S.A. The American authorities do not complain of their behaviour, but they do complain of the English girls who hang about the cookhouses etc., and refuse to leave these men alone.

They are determined to crush all association between coloured men and white girls in exactly the same ruthless fashion that they do in their own country, and in one small town alone Americans have shot five negroes who were walking out with white girls. The U.S.A. judicial authorities

6 September 1942   Home Front   171

will certainly not criticise this course, and any English girl who walks out, however harmlessly, with a coloured American soldier should be made to understand that she will very probably cause his death!

.... I might add that Her Majesty does *not* want her name brought into this matter. I believe that the girls in the Services have been warned, and that any who go out with coloured men are at once removed to other areas. It is chiefly shop girls and factory workers who are concerned, and those who live in or near seaport towns. At present, most of the American white troops here are from the *North*, but it is thought that when the Southerners arrive, the difficulties will be greatly intensified, and there will be the further political danger of bad blood between the American North and South, which might be extremely serious.

The coloured troops here are mostly from the *South*, are not used to mixing on equal terms with white women, and are naturally flattered at doing so. It is possible that President Roosevelt, (with a negro vote of 11 million to consider!), has felt obliged to send over these contingents of coloured troops in response to a good deal of pressure, but one theory is that, on the score of their being unable to stand the English winter climate, they will be obliged to return to the U.S.A. about Christmas time!

.... Her Majesty felt that your knowledge & experience might be able to suggest ways & means of tackling this very thorny subject, and, alternatively, that if you had *not* heard anything about it, in the course of your many contacts with people of very varying occupations and interests, you might be able to influence the powers that be to consider the whole matter very seriously.

6 September 1942   28/45(iii)

VM to Nan Carruthers

.... My dear, I do wish your people hadn't sent these negroes over here. Colour is not understood in this country, and since many of the negroes are pleasant people with lots of money and good dancers silly little English girls are walking out with them. That makes your military people see red, and as a *very* reluctant House of Commons has handed over justice in American military areas to the Army things may happen. I am most uneasy about it all, and so are other people. The wretched men are in a very hard position about any sort of social intercourse or leave: it's cruel to be treated as a pariah on one side or as an equal by sentimentalists who say a black man is just as good as a white. *They oughtn't to be here at all*. Please send over some black women auxiliaries as soon as possible!! It's the only alternative....

22 February 1943   28/45(iv)

VM to Nan Carruthers

We have all been on our toes over the Beveridge Report and the lamentable muddle made by the Government over its publication. I was away for the first two days of the Debate, but was present in the House on the third day and heard Herbert Morrison wind up. He was excellent, but the rot had gone too far for him to stop it. I have never known *salesmanship* and *presentment* so deplorable and a failure so complete in psychology. The government gave the impression they hated the whole business and didn't want to do a thing about it. In fact they had conceded a lot, and their reservations were in no way unreasonable. But they managed to convey quite the contrary impression. The House was buzzing like a hive of angry bees....

15 March 1943   25/43

VM to Hector Hetherington[23]

I [am] hovering on the brink of a most unpleasant job. Bevin wants to start a Committee to look into the domestic servant shortage and has marked me down as Chairman. I went to see him and told him I was most reluctant to take on the job as I do not think any satisfaction can come from it either for the proposed Committee or for himself. The shortage, however, is acute and causing very real distress in a good many quarters. I have undertaken for the next fortnight to go and work in the Ministry and, in Civil Service language, 'look into the question' and report to him any suggestions that may seem possible. It will mean an avalanche of correspondence, agitation in the Press and a spate of talk with little or nothing to show for it.

5 May 1943   25/43

VM to Hector Hetherington

I am feeling very depressed about the Ministry of Labour for I fear Ernie [Bevin] will come back at me over this beastly domestic service job which I regard with loathing, but how can one refuse, at a time like this, to take on whatever task one is invited to tackle.

---

[23] Principal of Glasgow University and holder of various governmental appointments.

8 June 1943   12/2

VM to Ernest Bevin

I am venturing to trouble you with another letter about a matter which I know causes you great concern — the hardships to certain classes of private persons, e.g. the old, the young, the sick and women engaged on essential war duties, owing to the shortage of domestic help.

I am fully alive to the acute difficulties surrounding this subject, but so many cases of real suffering have come latterly to my personal notice that the volume throughout the country must be formidable. These people, for the most part, are inarticulate and do not air their grievances either in Parliament or the Press. Probably for that very reason you will be anxious to see if any alleviation of their very hard circumstances is possible.

It is clear that such alleviation can only come through the medium of the Exchanges and, even so, within very narrow limits. The war needs are an urgent priority, and it may be that the old and the sick have to suffer even to the point of death if there is not enough labour to go round. I feel, however, that the existence of a position so extreme calls for very careful examination and in any event where young children and prospective births are concerned, this last category has a claim to protection in the national interest....

I appreciate the great difficulty of checking in any respect the revolution of the wonderful employment machine your Department has created and of putting a few of the wheels into reverse. But since you have already worked miracles, I am confident you could add another to the list if your officials can find time — and it is very largely a question of time — to sort out and deal with these individual cases of hardship.

Again, if I might venture to suggest it, some statement by yourself showing that you are alive to the hardships and are doing what you can to mitigate them would be greatly appreciated. If you see your way to adopting the above suggestion that a small percentage of the call up might be given the option of domestic work in certain hard cases, recognition by yourself of the need would, I think, encourage volunteers to come forward on humanitarian grouds.

When the Corps for Domestic Workers comes into existence I hope it will get busy at once with the creation of the Emergency Orderlies who can be on call to give domestic help in houses where there is illness. Orderlies, however, belong to the future and here and now some steps are needed to deal with a situation which grows more and more aggravated as time goes on. At present certain well-to-do people are using the power of the purse unblushingly to tempt away domestic workers from households less well off where their services are more necessary. Wages are being paid at the moment for a pair of hands which have no relation of any kind to competence or experience. We have indeed reached a paradoxical situation when objection can be taken to high wages, but the selfish rich certainly have all the advantages of reaping at the moment in a limited field....

27 July 1943 12/2
VM to Ernest Bevin

I am very sorry to hear of the difficulties which have arisen about provision of uniform for the proposed Domestic Service Corps.

I realised fully when I urged on you at an earlier stage the importance of uniform that you would probably run up against strenuous opposition on the grounds of supply. I, also, appreciate the objections which have been raised against the proposal....

As Chairman of the Central Committee [on Women's Training and Employment], I had 20 years of bitter experience of the unpopularity of domestic service and the contempt in which unfortunately it is held by the ordinary industrial worker.... Our efforts to make the girls realise that they were learning a skilled trade and one of which a self-respecting worker might be proud were wrecked over and over again by the ridicule and often taunts of friends and relations engaged in shops and factories. We were chronically confronted with a sense of soreness and inferiority among the girls and the question of status (apart from wages and conditions) was a constant pre-occupation to us.

Your idea of a special Corps for service in hospitals and institutions was a new approach which, I felt, offered more hope of success than any of its predecessors. Here, I felt, was an adventure on a new level. Wages, hours, and conditions for domestic workers can be brought into line but the real hard core of the trouble is psychological and unless the present inhibitions can be broken by the whole question being transferred on to a different plane, any new venture will, I fear, be doomed to failure.

Hence the importance of an organised Corps and especially of a uniform which would make the domestic worker feel her status was not one whit inferior to that of girls in the Services. If the uniform goes by the board, then I am satisfied your Corps goes too....

9 August 1943 28/45(iv)
VM to Nan Carruthers

....I don't like the attitude of the king of Italy and Badoglio, and think they should both be sent into retirement. But our Tories here do love a 'gentleman' — just the same arguments that they used to support that little swine, Franco, and they are so terribly afraid of what they call 'revolutionaries' that they would rather support any reactionary deadhead than a popular leader....

20 August 1943 12/2

VM to Mary Smieton, Principal Assistant Secretary, Ministry of Labour

The whole problem of domestic work is engulfed in a sea of dreariness and it is only by something dramatic and picturesque like a Corps and a uniform and a generally attractive set-up that you could persuade people to think about the problem on different lines.

18 October 1943 12/2

VM to Mary Smieton

Markham was worrying about the domestic servant shortage

....to get anything done during war, it must be dramatic and appeal to the imagination....

the 'welfare' carrot has been dangled before the nose of too many donkeys to produce any sort of thrill! It is odious that it is necessary to stimulate people's sensations rather than their sense of duty and kindness to get things done....

12 December 1943 28/45(iv)

VM to Nan Carruthers

....I don't know what you hear about American soldiers and English girls, but some of us are dreadfully worried about the streets of London and other big cities at night. Your men unfortunately have money to burn, and they are assailed by terrible little mosquito girls *quite young* — 15, 16, 17, 18, who skin them in the most unscrupulous way....

30 January 1944 28/45(v)

VM to Nan Carruthers

Hospitals and other institutions are coming to a standstill, hotels are closing down. Individual householders, if they are strong and healthy, can do their own work, but the old, the sick, and the mothers of young children are often in dire straits. The reaction is being felt by many women war workers who can't at one and the same time look after their houses and children and be out all day doing other work....

9 February 1944

VM to Hector Hetherington

We spent Monday going round four industrial establishments. I was shocked to find that little improvement had been made during the 10 years which had elapsed since I first visited these places in Sheffield. It was really like stepping back into the early years of the Industrial Revolution — rickety buildings, very dirty, immense flights of wooden stairs and a general atmosphere of dirt and dust. Some of the work seems very unsuitable for women especially the heavy grinding.

Yesterday we had the [Trade] Board. It was not an easy meeting. The Workers' side had opened their mouths very wide and had raised quite a new point about the women doing men's work being paid on that grade — a real complication. We were all satisfied during our tour that the women were not doing the identical work of the men but that the processes had been broken down. At the same time, they were not being adequately paid for the work they were doing. I think there is a case for the women on production being graded (certainly into skilled and unskilled) not necessarily on the men's grade but on a grade of their own. However, though the workers talked a lot about women doing the same work as the men, we found that this class of work had been done by women for years past, and it was irrelevant to raise it at this particular moment and only complicated the position. I was anxious, however, to get the women's wages up and to shorten the gap between them and the lowest class of male worker....

The employers were absolutely mulish, would not help or do a thing. We all pointed out to them the fact.... that after the war there will be a permanent devaluation of money and that to raise the rates slightly now, as we have done, is a cushion which will help the difficult post-war adjustments. However, the employers were quite impervious to reason, dug their toes in and did nothing so we did the same.

.... We more than halved the Workers' demands especially for the youths, but we improved the position of the women which I was out to do.

15 February 1944

Hector Hetherington to VM

I am afraid a revolution in Cutlery is now overdue. For once, I think the incursion of the Jews into the trade may work some good. The conditions as we saw them 10 or 11 years ago were pretty grim. Perhaps it was not to be expected that during the war any improvement would take place. But I do think that the employers are a little casual in their attitude....

15 March 1944   12/2

VM to Ernest Bevin

The correspondence in The Times about overworked Mothers has brought me a number of personal letters, most of them very acrimonious in tone. Some of these angry ladies apparently bracket me with yourself as a destroyer of the home....

I am very conscious of the growing pressure on the home owing to the lack of domestic help and a steady increase of individual cases of hardship.... some steps should be taken to counteract the ugly spirit which is growing up, and to demonstrate your own good will in this matter.

Markham suggested that the Ministry of Health should extend the home help scheme to all cases of sickness or need.

Action in this direction would do something to alleviate hardship in working-class households and prove a desirable gesture.

She suggests a meeting with voluntary societies.

2 May 1944   12/2

Ernest Bevin to VM

....Dealing with the points made in your letter, we are making progress with the Ministry of Health on the Home Help Scheme and I have written personally to the Minister of Health about it. I agree with you that it would be desirable to have a meeting of voluntary organisations, to tell them the up-to-date position so far as action by this Minstry is concerned and to ask for their help in the working out of local schemes. As I think you know, we have made most exhaustive enquiries into this and come to the conclusion that, as you yourself say, no national and official scheme could be organised; but if the voluntary societies can assist through their own organisations I agree with you they ought not to lack Government support. Such a scheme must, however, work independently of the Local Office machinery of this Department....

25 June 1944   28/45(v)

VM to Nan Carruthers

Lunched with the Churchills

Winston in a boiler suit looking like nothing on earth was in great form .... It's great to hear him talk! 'I am one of the oldfashioned people who believe in democracy', he said, 'Call the nation to duty and not to *booty*, and the nation responds'. He wasn't talking about the war but the general philosophy of political life....

23 August 1944 25/60

VM to Herbert Morrison

I have visited on behalf of the Assistance Board a good many of the areas which have suffered from the flying bombs, especially those of the east and south. I have always made a point of talking to the applicants in our offices and can only marvel generally speaking at the courage and fortitude they show. But I feel more strongly than ever that a very unhappy atmosphere is developing round this phase of the blitz. People feel forlorn and neglected; they suffer and no one seems particularly to know or care. Even when there is no loss of life or physical injury, women see their homes destroyed and their possessions and treasured bits turned into rubble. Others in addition are crushed by the shock and sorrow of seeing their dear ones killed.

It is a terrible ordeal and yet it seems to have become part of the day's work to be treated as such. The monotonous and arid B.B.C. announcements convey little idea of the suffering which lies behind them and tend to exasperate homeless people. Outside London and the Southern counties there seems to be an astonishing lack of appreciation of the daily destruction and all it involves in loss and pain. There is no rush in the provinces to help evacuation problems.

Markham suggests Londoners need a word of encouragement, preferably from the Queen as the brunt was falling on women

....Resentment and bitterness are growing at what is felt to be public indifference to suffering. We don't want the war to end for London on such a note.

14 September 1944 25/19

Rachel Crowdy[24] to VM

I was away in Manchester when a flying-bomb blew our flat to pieces in Sloane Court, and I imagine that my reactions were very typical. Thankfulness for the lives of one's next of kin and one's friends came first, next came the wish to find out as quickly as possible the extent of one's loss and lastly an angry determination developed to save from the hands of looters and fools those things which the Act of God and the King's enemies had left untouched. It is when this last stage is reached that the trouble begins.

One was struck by the want of co-ordination of the different services dealing with people and their possessions on a bombed site. For the first day or so there is an Incident Officer. After that there appears to be no

---

[24] Dame Rachel Crowdy (1884–1964), 1914 appointed Principal Commandant of VADs in France and Belgium. From the First World War until 1931 she was the only woman to head an administrative section of the League of Nations. During the Second World War she was a regions advisor to the Ministry of Information.

co-ordinating authority on the spot to whom one can go, and so one is constantly told: 'You must see the foreman of the gang'; 'Only the District Engineer can tell you that'; 'that is a matter for the Salvage Officer'; 'You must ask the Police'. Thus, in the earliest and most agitating days one finds oneself hunting for different individuals who may or may not be among the group in the street. You may find, for example, that rescue squads or N.F. men are willing and able to get down a few sticks of furniture remaining in a bit of a room inaccessible from the main building but accessible through some back window, yet salvage people are in a position to refuse to remove those 'sticks' from the street. If they are to remain in the street who is to ask for the police to protect them? One's fear of losing the little that remains to one grows, and to one's anxiety is added confusion of mind.

Although in theory only the bomb services and the owners of property are allowed in the bombed area, in fact, other than these people come in and out, unless there is police protection at both ends of the street.

.... After I myself had telephoned to Sir Phillip Game, Chief Commissioner of the Police, the guarding of the street was very much better looked after, but lack of manpower in the Police Service makes it impossible for one to expect adequate protection of property. There could be a system of passes.... After the visit of the Chief Police Commissioner I was on more than one occasion asked for a pass and so were others, but could at no time find anyone who issued such passes!

.... Insufficient manpower also accounts for certain short-comings among the Salvage people....

One cannot speak too highly of the help given by public assistance. When I went for clothing coupons people were being dealt with quickly, kindly and, it seemed to me, adequately, although I was not very clear as to the principle on which, for example, any special number of clothing coupons were given.

The Assistance Board personnel impressed on one that one could go back to them with any further difficulties and obtain further coupons if the necessity for them was proved. They seemed equally courteous to everyone.

15 October 1944   28/45(V)

VM to Nan Carruthers

I got back from Scotland this morning after a busy week. I first went to Windermere, where I harangued the WAAF Officer's Training School, then on to Glasgow and Edinburgh to perform the same kind of office for the ATS. I was lecturing twice and sometimes three times a day.... but though I thoroughly enjoyed the trip I am bound to say I feel profound scepticism as to the value of these twitterings, for they are little more. The Forces are being eternally talked to and lectured at, and I feel must be heartily sick of peripatetics like myself....

3 November 1944   25/91

VM to Eileen Younghusband[25]

I am sorry that the people I work with at Vicarage House are such preposterous idiots, but in some respects Civil Servants are like Jesuits only not always so competent!....

Vicarage House sometimes behaves as though it has a body secreted on the premises and is afraid of it being dug up!

21 January 1945   28/45(V1)

VM to Nan Carruthers

....There is something badly wrong with the whole organisation of society which lands housewives into the dreadful mess which afflicts women both in England and America. The strains are quite intolerable at the moment. In this country with every woman up to fifty conscripted under the National Service Act the difficulties of private service are obvious, but in your country, vast in size and population and with a lot of coloured people, one wouldn't expect the situation to be so acute. I suppose there is no transfer of coloured servants from the South to California? Perhaps inter-State immigration is not encouraged? But I can't help wondering if there isn't a fortune for someone who would organise good domestic bureaux in the Southern States to supply maids for transfer to other parts of the country. Anyway after the experiences of the war the problem must be tackled if women are to have *any* peace and leisure....

29 January 1945   7/17

VM to Lady Rhys Williams (a Liberal)

....for the man who has dropped out of Insurance the only basis for relief is need. And the ascertainment of need inevitably involves asking questions about his circumstances and so you come to the Means Test. Obviously you can't hand out public money without enquiry of any kind to all and sundry who ask for it....

I must put it to you that a good deal of unnecessary prejudice has been worked up over the Means Test. The principal is as old as the Elizabethan Poor Law and it has been operated in a small way by various departments for a long time without outcry of any kind. But it was only when mass

---

[25] Eileen Younghusband (1902–1981), pioneer social worker and LSE lecturer. In 1943 she undertook a survey at the AB's request into the welfare needs of benefit recipients.

unemployment arose and the Means Test became applicable to large bodies of men who were politically important that trouble arose.

As you know, of course, the Means Test can be family or individual. Personally, I am glad that the family Means Test was abolished in 1941 for to make children contribute to the maintenance of their parents was no longer in harmony with modern ideas and at times created both resentment and hardship. But it is difficult to see how a personal means test can be avoided for a person out of insurance or, indeed, what hardship or indignity it entails....

We [the Assistance Board] work on very different lines from those often caricatured in the House of Commons but of course we have made mistakes during our troubled life and are always ready and anxious to learn from our critics.

7 March 1945 12/2

VM to Mary Smieton

....I must return to the question of the long delay in the publication of the Report on Private Domestic Service.

It is 8 months since the Report was presented and I find it a little difficult to believe that its proposals are of such momentous importance or fraught with such revolutionary implication that the Departments concerned are still compelled to go on studying it. Whether or not the Minister decides to adopt the plan proposed is, of course, not for me to say. But what objection is there to the publication of the Report as it stands without in any way committing the Minister to implement its proposals? ....

11 March 1945 28/45 (VI)

VM to Nan Carruthers

....Labour supplies get worse and worse here — the bitter cry of the housewife rises uninterruptedly to heaven. Everything is getting short — clothing in particular. And with all these starving people in Europe I can't see that we can hope to maintain our present rations nor indeed ought we to wish to do so....

The pictures of Cologne burnt out and destroyed give me a real heartache. It was such a beautiful city, and I was so very happy there. Bonn, too, a charming little town is half destroyed. I know its necessary and inevitable, but its a ghastly business all the same....

Every inconvenience and limitation we suffer from is getting steadily worse; trains are more crowded, taxis rarer, shops emptier, and we all realise there will be no letup about these things for ages to come. The goods are simply not there. But unlike the unhappy people in France, Belgium and

Holland we are not dying of hunger, so ought not to complain ....

The British Council rang me up last week to ask if I would go to Paris and lecture to something or someone! Would I not! Of course I jumped at such a chance. It would be a marvellous break after five-and-a-half years.

13 March 1945 12/2

G. Myrrdin-Evans, Deputy Secretary, Ministry of Labour to VM

.... the one thing we wanted to avoid was the publication of a report with recommendations which the Government did not appear to intend to implement. All the post-war policy for which this Ministry has been responsible has been handled the same way — to have the policy thrashed out, discussed confidentially with the appropriate bodies and then put out as a White Paper containing Government proposals. We are most anxious that the problem of private domestic service should be treated in the same way as a problem of equal importance with the others ....

25 March 1945 28/45(VI)

VM to Nan Carruthers

.... What utter brutes the Nazis are! So long as they can still keep some vestige of authority they don't care whether their own people as well as the rest of Europe are involved in common ruin. Personally I would gladly do with less if it would help the situation. The accounts we hear of people dying of starvation really get me down.

5
Creating Good Citizens?
1945–1953

As the war drew to a close Markham was offered the opportunity to expound to French and British audiences on her favourite theme of women's role as citizens. She believed the war had made a positive contribution to the lives of those women who had joined the Forces, by stimulating women who had previously lived 'hum-drum' lives. But, she emphasised, with approval, that women had not been 'brutalised' or 'unsexed' by the work they had done in industry and the Forces. The guns they had fired and the munitions they had made had not killed their interest in pretty clothes, cosmetics and perms.[1]

15 April 1945   28/45(VI)
VM to Nan Carruthers

I have got my lectures for France done, but my plans abroad have got extended. The War Office got wind I was going to France. So they have roped me in after I have finished with the British Council to go on to Belgium and make a report on the Women Auxiliaries serving with the Army. It will be interesting to see the back of the Front, and its a chance that I never dreamt would come my way. Since it never rains but it pours, Army Education (quite a separate show) has asked me to go and lecture to troops in France and Italy!

Markham may have felt some trepidation at the prospect of lecturing to troops, for when she gave similar lectures after the First World War, the audiences had proved to be very tough. Her talks in 1945 were 'mostly concerned with citizenship and rather simple Social history which takes in some simple Beveridge'.[2]

---

[1] 13/6 British Council in Paris lectures 1944–45. Lecture III: 'British women go to war'.
[2] 26/58 VM to Basil Yeaxlee, Central Advisory Council for Education in HM Forces, Overseas Lecture Committee, 11 April 1945 and 28 July 1948.

1 June 1945

28/45(VI)

VM to Nan Carruthers

I reached London last Tuesday, having flown back from Brussels in 1¾ hours with my friend and colleague, Mrs Stocks, after a hectic nearly four weeks on the Continent....

The time spent in Paris was very strenuous. I was lecturing twice a day in French to French audiences of very varied types, and met a host of people. I found myself sometimes in the houses of the great and sometimes (which I much preferred) among working-class gatherings. I addressed an audience one night of seven hundred railway workers. Subsequently I never had a happier meeting than with a group of Christian-Socialists, really poor people, in Montmartre. Class feeling is very strong in France, unfortunately, and I was warned that they were very suspicious of a bourgeois speaker like myself. So I told them straightaway that I was everything in principle that they disapproved of — 'sale bourgeoise', 'capitalistic' and a member of a family which had made its fortune in coal mines! They roared with laughter at this introduction, and we got on admirably after that. At the end the whole audience stood up and sang 'God Save the King', which touched me immensely. I have never worked harder than during this tour, which ended with a cocked-hat lecture in English at the Sorbonne on the theme — 'When England Fought Alone'. It was a large and appreciative audience, who seemed to understand English perfectly and absorbed all the points....

Paris made a very unhappy impression on me, and I felt that France is in a poor way.... The Metro is running. Otherwise there is not a 'bus, not a taxi in the place. Neither is there any food. In a Black Market restaurant you can get a meal at the cost of £8 or £10 per head. Otherwise there is nothing to be bought, not even a scrap of bread since bread is rationed and can only be purchased with bread tickets. There are no travellers in the ordinary sense of the term. There are no strangers in Paris except those sponsored by the Army or official organisations, and they get their food in one of the official Messes supplied with Army rations, generally American.... A superficial crust of life goes on, but below it there are many privations and indeed actual hunger. The rationing system in France is most inefficient, and the whole country is riddled with Black Market. Every class traffics in it from the highest to the lowest. Naturally it is a system that favours the rich at the expense of the poor. People who have no relations in the country and do not get parcels, or who have no bicycles to take them into the country to get food from their friends, fare very badly. Equally serious is the absence of fuel....

The American Army is in full possession of Paris, and there are an enormous number of soldiers about, as it is a leave centre for a very large area. I was heartbroken by four days to miss V-E Day at home. After struggling for so many years with the war in London, I hated being away when the climax came. Of course the scenes in Paris were interesting.... A lot of girls and young men piled up on the American jeeps and cars, drove round the town singing and waving flags, but everyone was most orderly. People danced and kissed each other.... What grieved me was the absence of food — there was not even a crust of bread to be seen among the families walking about or sitting about together during the day and evening. I met a great many people, English as well as French. It is extraordinary what a vast crowd of hangers-on the aftermath of a war always collects in a city. I was often reminded of Paris during the Peace Conference in 1919. Being one of the hangers-on myself I had of course no right to criticise, but it was impossible not to ask oneself what all these people were doing.

My Paris business over I was joined by my friend, Mrs Stocks, and we transferred to the Army. We went first to S.H.A.E.F. at Versailles, where we spent three days. There I met your American W.A.C.'s, who are living on close and very good terms with the English A.T.S. It was strange to see the Army in possession of Louis XIV's stables. We then flew to Brussels and passed under the care of Field-Marshal Montgomery's 21 Army Group. Brussels and Belgium made a better impression on me than France. Though many of the difficulties are the same, they seem to be tackling them with greater energy, and the prospects of a recovery seem brighter.

We found the A.T.S. girls, of whom there are several thousands in the Command, doing very good work, and we found much to admire and little or nothing to criticise.... We ventured into Germany.... We flew over the Ruhr, a scene of desolation which absolutely beggars description. Subsequently we went into Holland.... and had a good view last Sunday of Rotterdam. The signs of hunger were very obvious there. However the city is still a going concern.... The destruction everywhere is appalling.... So far as Germany is concerned, all government has come to a standstill. There is neither post, telegraph, telephone, railways nor any other form of communication....

It was very satisfactory in Rotterdam to see hundreds of German prisoners being marched out of the town on foot on their way back to Germany. The population watched them go I thought with great dignity and restraint, but the poor little Dutch children with their spindly legs mocked them freely.... It is unfortunate I think that neither America nor England has had the experience of deported prisoners and of nationals who have been imprisoned in the Concentration Camps. I personally met in Paris people who have been in the camps and many of their relations. Nothing you have read in the papers can equal the abominations that were practised in them. There is a great streak of sentimentality in both our countries, and Mary Stocks and I have come home feeling little patience with the people who want to be kind to the Germans. Eventually of course they must be given a chance to win back their way into the European family, but for the moment there has got to be very stern treatment until they show some signs of repentance and horror for the enormities that have been committed in their name.

3 June 1945 28/45(VI)
VM to Nan Carruthers

.... The Domestic Service Report was published as a White Paper, and I am sending you a copy. It has had a very good press, which makes me the more incensed with the Ministry of Labour for sitting on the scheme for a whole year and doing damn all nothing about it.... I had hoped to have the Institute ready to catch women demobilised from both the Forces and the factories, and I regret the delay the more because its a very big task to get a venture of that kind started and requires a great deal of preliminary work....

The USA had just terminated Lend-Lease.

27 August 1945 28/45(VI)
VM to Nan Carruthers

.... Food is scarcer than I have ever known it. You can't get coffee any longer except with great difficulty. You can't get soap or matches. Rice has disappeared, cheese is microscopic. Our clothes ration has been cut again.... So that when America chooses this particular moment, without one word of warning, to give us not so much a kick in the pants as a firstclass kick in the stomach its only natural we feel both resentful and astonished! We have thrown everything we possess into this war, we have destroyed our export trade to fight it; we come up gasping to the surface, more impoverished and harder hit than we have ever been for clothes and food, and you to whom as Churchill said we have been a faithful ally choose this moment to try and push us under again! .... In your letter of August 5th you wrote how sad and anxious you were in the United States about the result of the Election, that you were not going to give money to underwrite a socialised Britain as you didn't hold with that kind of thing. So it's idle to pretend this isn't a hit at the Government....

12 October 1945 12/2
VM to Mary Smieton

.... Many people feel that the Ministry [of Labour] is missing the moment of demobilisation and though girls in the Services might have considered domestic employment under the scheme of the Institute, they will certainly not return to the old haphazard methods. The situation in countless households remains acute and there is still great suffering among individual householders.

Various private schemes are being put forward to meet the need, the latest apparently by the Women's Adjustment Board, a body of fashionable ladies who give tea parties at the Dorchester as the first step in reforming the world. Judging from the notices in the Press they appear to have adopted wholesale many of the recommendations in the Report....

22 October 1945 12/2

Mary Smieton to VM

.... The major stumbling block about it is that if the profession is to be made attractive the wages which will have to be paid will be prohibitive to many households in need and a solution to that involves important issues of social and financial policy. It is these with which we are still struggling....

2 December 1945 28/45(VI)

VM to Nan Carruthers

.... I attended a large meeting at the Albert Hall last week in aid of starving Europe, presided over by the Archbishop of York. Two things became clear to me as the meeting went on. The expulsions from Eastern Europe for which Russia is responsible are the main cause of this welter of human misery. Some people in this country think we ought to have a general cut in rations in the interest of Europe. I am entirely opposed to this.... But I would support and contribute to a *voluntary* scheme, though it can only be a gesture....

The 'Save Europe Now' campaign, launched in the autumn of 1945 was spearheaded by the Jewish publisher, Victor Gollancz. His aims were to prevent further expulsions from the east and to avoid starvation.[3]

16 December 1945 28/45(VI)

VM to Nan Carruthers

.... It was settled last Friday that U.N.O.'s permanent home should be in the United States. Pesonally I think it a mistake, for the United States is too far removed from the problems and the atmosphere they create. I fear that

---

[3] Ruth Edwards *Victor Gollancz: A biography* (Gollancz, London, 1987) p 411; John Farquharson, '"Emotional but influential": Victor Gollancz, Richard Stokes and the British zone of Germany, 1945–49', *Journal of Contemporary History*, vol. 22 (1987), pp 501–519.

meetings will turn into an orgy of guzzling and drinking. When Europeans are let loose on your food I hardly fancy they will take much interest in any other matter.

.... nothing very violent is said publicly, but don't be under any illusion. The name of the United States is *mud* on this side of the Atlantic.

.... This year the cupboards and shops are emptier than ever, and we have the pleasant sense of being handed over as economic bond slaves to the Americans.

20 February 1946 12/2

VM to Eveline Cooper

.... I do not think the future of domestic work is at all rosy from the point of view of the employer, but I am sure that the only way is to get an extension of day work .... We have experienced the greatest revolution in history and its consequences have fallen heavily on the employing class. The 'good old times' will never come again. We have to make up our minds to do with a half-loaf, or indeed a quarter-loaf, instead of the full supply we had in former times.

8 March 1946 12/2

VM to Mary Smieton

I hope it is true that your Department is considering the question of allowing the introduction of foreign women as domestic workers and that some of them will be available for private houses. I know the difficulties about ministering to the idle rich, but honestly I do not think that a handful of drones ought to stand in the way of alleviating the sufferings and trials of people in a far more modest state of life..... You would, of course, only admit foreigners under licence and with a special passport, and you could attach certain conditions to their service—that they should only be employed in households, say, of not more than 2 (e.g. a nurse and a general). If they were furnished with a passport of a special colour they could not go off and take employment in any other form of work. There are plenty of continentals who would be glad to come and work here and since, so far as I can judge, the demobilised girl is even more unwilling than she was before the war to undertake domestic work, they would certainly not be getting on the tail of another woman's wages....

20 March 1946 25/92
Sir Alfred Zimmern to VM

The circumstances of these people[4] are terribly hard. I have nothing but sympathy for them but the Home Office has a very severe man in the shape of Sir Frank Newsom in charge of these questions. I have never yet succeeded in getting any request about an alien favourably considered....

29 March 1946 26/49
VM to T.H. Tilling

Tilling had recently been demobbed and returned from Germany where he had commanded one of the British teams investigating war crimes. His HQ had been at Belsen. Markham was replying to a letter he had written about 1,000-2,000 people liberated from the camp who could not return to their previous countries. They were almost all young Jews between 18 and 35 years who had lost their parents. He suggested to Markham that they should be brought over to the UK as domestics. Markham sent copies of the correspondence to Elizabeth Macadam and Sir Arthur Salter.

....few people are more tragic than these 'forgotten' nationals and displaced persons for whom no future seems available....The question of domestic service does not, I think, arise. Jews proverbially make very bad houseworkers and in view of the attitude of the Home Office which is utterly rigid and unimaginative there would be little chance of any wholesale admission of foreigners....

In fact, there were schemes at this time to bring over displaced persons and 'surplus' German women to work as domestics and nurses in the UK. When this source of labour dried up, a campaign (now better remembered) was launched to recruit workers for low paid and unpopular jobs from the New Commonwealth and Pakistan.

29 March 1946 12/1
Notes VM made for a BBC discussion programme on domestic service

No girl can be better employed than in helping another woman to bring up her children & make home comfortable for the breadwinner.

During the course of the programme Markham commented that there should be more home helps for working-class women and

---

[4] Germans wishing to join relatives in the UK.

.... this is really a problem for women. Because it's a field where women have exploited women in the past. And if the difficulty of getting housework done is not solved, women won't be able to make their contribution in the world.... We want professional women and women writers and artists to be able to make their contribution to the national life. Above all we want family life with its loyalties and affections to be made safe, and *home* not an apartment house or residential hotel, the centre of it.

29 April 1946

12/2

VM to Mrs James

.... I am more and more satisfied that the only solution is to create a public service which shall be available primarily for the sick, the old, and the mothers with young children, but on which any householder can have a call in an emergency. Such a service would have to operate on a means test and employers would have to pay as much as they could reasonably afford, the balance being made up by the State.

7 August 1946

25/51

VM to Harold Macmillan[5]

Being personally concerned in my abrupt removal from the [Assistance] Board to make a job for Mrs Adamson I couldn't agitate in the matter. But I was none the less grateful to you for drawing attention in the House of Commons to what had taken place. I only received the Prime Minister's telegram two hours before I heard the announcement on the wireless. The office were never consulted and were only told the same afternoon. Attlee's reply to you [on 25 June] that I took the salary of £750 at my own request was not correct and I wrote and told him this and that it had been an agreed salary between the office and myself. My predecessor was a full time Civil Servant of high rank who was Accounting Officer to the Board. His salary was, of course, not appropriate to me. The new position made no difference to the work I was doing and the post of Deputy Chairman since Strohmenger's time has been and remains mainly honorary. There was no justification of any kind for doubling the salary. With the change over to National Insurance the Board will lose a million pensioners in October & are shutting down over 50 offices.

[5] Harold Macmillan (1894–1986), Conservative MP for Stockton-on-Tees 1924–29 and 1931–45, Bromley 1945–64. 1940–42 Parliamentary Secretary, Ministry of Supply, 1942–43 Parliamentary Secretary, Colonial Office, 1942–45 Minister Resident in North Africa and the Mediterranean, 1945 Secretary of State for Air, 1951–54 Minister of Housing and Local Government, 1945–55 Minister of Defence, 1955 Secretary of State for Foreign Affairs, 1955–57 Chancellor of the Exchequer, 1957–63 Prime Minister.

The real point I would ask you to watch, however, in the future is the composition of the Board which looks like becoming a dumping ground for Labour supporters. Three recent appointments have all been members of the Labour Party.

.... It is contrary to the whole spirit and intention of the Assistance Board that its membership should consist of party nominees who will necessarily bring a party and not a detached view to the difficult and controversial questions with which it has to deal....

I think I should add Jimmy Griffiths,[6] who strikes me as a very good fellow, had nothing whatever to do with the Adamson affair. I understand it is Attlee himself who is concerned in these appointments.

9 August 1946   25/51

Harold Macmillan to VM

It is indeed a tragedy to think of this deterioration in standards. It looks as if we are going to revert to a spoil system. I suppose the truth is that the aristocracy and the new democracy are equally corrupt; it is only the middle class, like you and me, who have these higher standards of probity.

24 November 1946   25/6

Sir Norman Birkett to VM

I would like to broadcast about Nuremberg but Convention holds me fast....

The whole trial is, of course, open to grave criticism .... on balance it was a step forward if only the League of Nations will build upon it.

29 June 1947   25/83

Janet Trevelyan[7] to VM

It was partly, I think, that she was by nature a Conservative and never a real democrat, so that each big increase even in the male electorate caused her some concern, and then I think her aesthetic sense was outraged by the type of women who were running the Suffrage cause in the years before 1914! Not only the Suffragettes; even the rank and file of us — always excepting Mrs Fawcett, for whom she had a *great* respect.

Something in her Oxford make-up, something too in her work for London children (especially the cripples) made her long for the able women to devote

---

[6] James Griffiths (1890–1975), Labour MP for Llanelli 1936–1970. 1945–1950 Minister of National Insurance, 1950–1951 Secretary of State for the Colonies, 1964–1966 Secretary of State for Wales.

[7] Daughter of Mary Ward and her first biographer.

themselves directly to *that* instead of descending into the vulgar scrum. She thought of women as the *civilisers*, rather outside the scrum, but of course it was an impossible ideal and before her death I think she came to see that it was.

After Germany had been defeated in the early summer of 1945, the government of Germany was carried on by the four occupying forces, the Soviet Union, Britain, France and the USA. The British zone was run by the Control Commission for Germany (CCG). It aimed at creating a liberal democracy which would ensure a stable and internationally safe Germany. German women were a key target of this strategy.[8] The aim was to promote 'democracy' and 'citizenship' among the women, at first to counter the influence of Nazism, but almost immediately to provide a bulwark against the feared ideological encroachments of the Soviet Union's communism. The British were conscious that there were many more women than men in Germany, and women would therefore constitute the bulk of the electorate. Further, the Nazi party had discouraged women from taking an active part in politics, their prime role being seen as breeding machines for the perfect Aryan race; some of the British recognised that the ideology of women's proper place being in the home had preceded the Nazi era. Moreover, although there is no agreement among historians (mainly because of statistical problems) as to the numbers of women mobilised in Germany during the war, the British in the late 1940s certainly believed that German women had not entered industry in the same numbers as British women, and that if the German economy was to recover it would require many more women taking up paid employment outside the home. If the economy did not recover it was feared that discontent would make extremist parties more attractive to the Germans. A series of ad hoc projects, rather than a pre-planned and comprehensive programme, were developed by the Foreign Office and the CCG. The CCG appointed women's affairs officers, who encouraged German women to take an active part in their local politics and in women's organisations. Tentative Anglo-German exchange schemes were launched. A number of British women went over to Germany to speak to groups of women about the importance of taking an active part in public life, and in the case of Violet Markham, to make recommendations about future British policy.[9] The appalling living conditions in Germany immediately after the war, and in particular during the bitterly cold winter of 1946–47, had already been well publicised in the press by Victor Gollancz. Markham recorded her impressions of her visit in a diary, and wrote an unpublished report on her experiences. Her views are typical

---

[8] A similar policy was pursued in the American zone and both Britain and America were criticised by the French.

[9] Before Markham went to Germany she was summoned to see Queen Mary about her forthcoming visit.

of the attitudes of British women who visited Germany during the occupation (although there were those who believed that the older women were more interested in politics, not the younger ones, as Markham suggests).[10]

11 January 1948　　　　　　　　　　　　　　　　　　　　5/26
Markham Report on German tour

I flew to Germany on Tuesday, December 2nd, and returned to England on Friday, December 12th. The tour included visits to Hamburg, Düsseldorf, Cologne, and Berlin, and during its course I addressed six groups of women including middle-class, professional and Trade Unionist women. Among the latter were some Communists. I had in addition many interviews with both C.C.G. officials and individual Germans.... I was impressed with the energy with which officials of the Education Branch of the C.C.G. are working. Pioneers of a new order, they are confronted with incredible difficulties of material shortages of paper, books, etc., and of wide-spread spiritual disillusionment. Re-education on an empty stomach presents a hard task for teachers and pupils alike.... The hope lies of course with the younger generation for it is unlikely that much impression can be made on their elders whose mentality has long been fixed.

The German women as a whole made a poor impression on me. Their energy and political experience are on a low level. This is understandable as the old feminine tradition of subservience to the male and his ideas had never been shaken and demolished as in England.... It is only since the defeat of National Socialism that they are beginning to emerge from nooks and corners but handicapped at the moment by food, fuel and housing shortages, and the bare struggle for life these impose. Allowances consequently must be made for the listless and dispirited attitude of the older middle-class women with whom I spoke.

So far as German women are organised at all, they drift mainly into groups within political parties — Catholic, Protestant, Socialist. There is much bitter feeling between political parties and these rancorous differences permeate the whole field of work and are a great obstacle to collective action. This inability to come together voluntarily for the general good throws light on the facility with which Germans hand themselves over to dictatorship. It is not surprising, therefore, that the women, weighted by a long tradition of subservience, have little capacity for independent action or thought. They are very conscious of their own misery but little conscious, so far as I could judge, of the world-wide misery provoked by Hitler's war. There is an

---

[10] See Helen Jones, 'Creating good citizens: British attitudes towards women in Occupied Germany' in Alan Bance (ed), *The cultural legacy of the British occupation in Germany* (Berg, Oxford, 1995).

equal lack of any spirit of co-operation between classes. Not all Germans are living on one uniform and low level of poverty. Some better-to-do people, I was told, still exist whose circumstances are much easier. I did not gather that such people play a conspicuous part in the relief of their poorer neighbours or indeed show any sympathy with them. Similarly the agricultural population as a whole shows scant appreciation of the plight of the towns....

Generally speaking, the older women I met had flung in their hand. Any suggestions I made about the value of getting together for mutual aid were met by a series of negatives. I found them personally friendly and eager to talk. The more sensitive are keenly alive to the spiritual and intellectual isolation in which they have lived for years. Even contact with an ex-enemy who comes from the outside world is an event to be welcomed. It was, however, difficult to rouse them from their apathy and make them feel that their country's future demanded efforts from them on another plane than that of the daily fight for food. I had hoped to interest the groups I met in organisations like Women's Institutes and the Townswomen's Guilds. But this I found impracticable and the literature I had brought remained unused throughout my visit.... Formal lectures and addresses are not, I think, of much use in Germany to-day, especially so far as the older women of the Frauenring, Frauenauschauss,[11] Frauen-club, are concerned. On the other hand, I found informal discussion meetings at which they could express their own views very profitable.

But for my recollections of the First Occupation, I should have been puzzled by the friendliness of the groups I met and the entire lack of any bitter feeling when talking to a member of the victorious nations. What proportion my audiences formed of women as a whole and how far they were representative, I cannot of course judge. I was only conscious, had our position been reversed, of the very different reactions any group of organised English women, either in town or country, would have shown to advances from a well-meaning German visitor who came to expound a new way of life.

I felt more hopeful about the younger women especially among the Socialist and Trade Unionist organisations. Here I found a much higher level of intelligence and interest than among the middle-class women. There was a greater keenness to hear and to learn and more desire to work for the future.... Apart from personal relations, German women admit that they learn much from contact with women's organisations in this country and their methods of conducting business....

The whole problem of the German women strikes me as most seri-

---

[11] Women's committees formed spontaneously by women or in some cases appointed by the Oberbergermeister in order to give women an advisory role in local affairs.

ous.... They form a great block of inexperienced, politically inert electors who would certainly provide the raw material to be exploited by any new and unscrupulous leader should such a personality emerge. It is claimed that the women's vote put Hitler into power — an ominous warning which should not be forgotten.... I agree entirely with the view [Dame Caroline Haslett][12] has expressed that amid the warring philosophies of the hour the safe path towards developing a more responsible sense of citizenship among German women is the approach through work. This is a critical moment for German women in industry, and every effort should be made to secure for them a proper status in factory work as in other branches of national life. There is much talk about equal pay for equal work, but I did not feel satisfied as to the reality in application of the formula. Training as urged by Dame Caroline is essential if the women are to play their part efficiently in industry and to be eligible as workers in the more highly skilled jobs. Visits to this country of German vocational guidance officers and the setting up of training centres are, I think, excellent and practical suggestions. I also agree that so far as industrial life is concerned the stress should be on personnel management not on welfare, often a nebulous term.

Visits of German women to England, sponsored either by Trade Unions or by responsible women's organisations in this country, are a very desirable bridge between the two countries....

Careless talk in England which represents the C.C.G. as a corrupt welter of spivs and drones should be dismissed as silly and slanderous....

So far as Women's Affairs are concerned, I am clear that the section merits a position of greater *authority* than what it holds at present.... As stated earlier in this report there are grave social and economic problems bound up with Women's Affairs in Germany. The status of the section, therefore should be proportionate to the importance of the work it has to carry out....

The condition of the children in many respects is puzzling. In the schools I visited there were children whose appearance did not differ materially from those to be found in the schools of an English town. Others showed very clear signs of malnutrition.... Shoes are an acute problem in every family. Educational difficulties impose a shift system of instruction but, in addition, some children have to stay home while their brothers and sisters go to school in the available foot wear.... I was told by the head teacher that parents form themselves into voluntary squads and from time to time clean schools.

---

[12] Dame Caroline Haslett (1895–1957), electrical engineer. 1919 First Secretary of Women's Engineering Society, 1924 founder of Electrical Association for Women. 1947 only woman member of British Electricity Authority. Served on numerous public bodies, including Industrial Welfare Society. Part of team of women who went to Germany after the war to lecture to German women. 1950 President of International Federation of Business and Professional Women.

Another matter about which, with very little evidence to go upon, I nevertheless felt uneasy was the welfare of the British women on the C.C.G. staff, especially that of the younger girls. By welfare I do not mean the organisation of dances and sing-songs, but the presence of officers who make careful enquiries about billets, health, hospital arrangements, and the general care of the women staff. Young girls, separated from their families and living among such conditions as obtain in German to-day are in special need of the oversight of some older woman to whom they can turn in any difficulty as a friend and who will watch with sympathetic care over their general moral and spiritual well-being. I was definitely informed in one area that such conditions were not fulfilled.

British wives in Germany

....How are they occupied? Servants are plentiful and, for most of the new-comers home duties are probably far less exacting than those they have left in England.... Is there not some contribution the wives, well fed and well housed in a desolate and hungry land, could make to the needs of the country where they are for the time being domiciled? .... Not all the wives, military or civilian, are idle. Some are already doing very good work, but many more might come forward if an appeal was made.

....the sea of distress is deep and widespread, and it is unpleasing to reflect on any body of English women living in idleness and indifference among scenes of so much suffering. This is not a question of an occasional treat or party got up for children, but of steady and constructive work carried out with regularity....

The problems of the Occupation.... thrusts itself on the attention of every visitor.... Black market is universal and here, as elsewhere, its presence is destructive of elementary standards of honesty and fair dealing.... The visitor is assured that the towns are sinks of immorality.... [There is] a moral whirlwind so destructive of the very basis of morality.... prevalent in Germany today....

After her visit Markham got together with a number of other women who had recently visited Germany in order to coordinate a response to the Foreign Office. Their main recommendations were that the Churches in Germany should be encouraged to play a more prominent part in the revival of Germany, visits of German women to England should be better coordinated, juvenile offenders should be treated in a more enlightened fashion by the German courts, there should be more industrial training for women and three high-powered women should be appointed to the CCG to oversee policies in relation to the churches, industrial training and the training of women in civil affairs. All the suggestions, except the last were already being pursued to a greater or lesser extent, and the final suggestion was ultimately rejected.

21 November 1949 25/7

Violet Bonham Carter[13] to VM

Like you I hoped & wished for the best when this Government got in. I have been bitterly disillusioned not only by their economic muddles but by their betrayal of Liberal values and of the old idealism of the Labour movement. Slave Labour of P.O.W.'s, closed shop, paid informers and the attitude of the T.U.'s towards Refugee workers all offend me in my inmost beliefs — It is a tragedy for Liberalism that the *quality* of our 10 surviving MP's has been so poor — that they have so frequently voted in different lobbies (both from each other & from the *far* abler and more sensible Liberal Peers)....

25 November 1949 25/7

Violet Bonham-Carter to VM

....About the P.O.W.'s — there was no excuse for not *paying* them for the work they did. (Even if we kept them.) As you know every farmer paid the Govt £4 a week each for them & the Govt made 60 million a year out of them.

It might well have been urged — as you suggest — that Germany should rebuild what she had destroyed. But the manpower should then have been requisitioned for a fair cross section of her male population.

The whole burden & sacrifice should not have been laid on a scratch lot of soldiers — many of them boys of 18 — who had the bad luck to be taken prisoners — & many of whom were impounded by us when the Canadians & Americans had sent them back to Europe to be freed.

We did it for our own convenience and we cannot get away from the fact that they were slaves — and that this was one of the offences for which we indicted Germany at Nuremburg

17 May 1950 25/20

VM to Lord Denning[14]

....So with all the changes and improvements in women's political and economic position and all the talk about her emancipation & her entry into this or that profession, home-making remains overwhelmingly her largest job.... I deplore that any young mother should be caught up in factory life

---

[13] Violet Bonham-Carter (1887–1969), a Liberal, daughter of Asquith, much interested in international affairs. In the 1930s she was a strong supporter of the League of Nations and critic of the Nazi regime.
[14] Lord Denning (1899–) 1944 High Court Judge, 1948–1957 Lord Justice of Appeal, 1962–1982 Master of the Rolls.

by the demands of full employment. What the average woman wants is not work, but husband, home and children....

1 May 1953   UCT BC 643 B18 63
VM to Joyce Newton Thompson

.... the only ground on which the N[ational] P[arty] or any English party can make a fighting stand is to accept & act upon Milner's dictum—'not race not colour but *civilisation* is the test of political rights'... you can make the test as high as you like & in my opinion the test should be very high. These savages should *prove* themselves before claiming the heritage of centuries. But that is an approach fundamentally different from what the Dutch openly, & the majority of English secretly & at heart believe, about the relation of the races....

In 1953 Markham's autobiography was published. She died six years later.

Index

Anderson, Adelaide, 80
anti-suffrage campaign, 1, 7, 8, 34–40, , 41–55, 59
   1912 Albert Hall Rally , 6, 7, 20, 41, 48–50
Asquith Margot, 39
Astor, Nancy, 107–108
Auxiliary Territorial Service (ATS), 163, 165, 166, 179, 185

Barker, Lilian, 105, 107
Barlow, J.A.N., 112,
Belgium, 31, 185
Bell, Gertrude, 8, 47, 55
Betterton, Sir Henry, 118, 123, 125, 126, 135
Beveridge, William, 92
   Report 172
Bevin, Ernest, 157, 161, 172, 177
Birkett, Norman, 155, 156, 191
Black American servicemen in Britain, 169, 170–171
Bonar Law, Andrew, 92
British Broadcasting Corporation, 20, 166–167, 178
Brock, Laurie, 60, 75, 158
Buchan, John, 7
Canada, 8
Central Committee on Women's [later Training and] Employment, 1, 3, 10, 12, 99, 105– 106, 107–109, 110, 111, 112–113, 114–115, 122, 141, 157, 158, 174
   see also unemployment
Chamberlain, Neville, 9, 59, 85–87, 88, 89, 90, 115, 118, 141, 153, 154
Chance Lady, 36
Charity Organisation Society, 5, 46, 63, 70
Chatsworth House, 154
Chesterfield, 1, 8, 67–68, 99
Churchill, Winston, 153, 177
Colville, Cynthia, 9, 170
Coventry, 80
Creed, Capt., 46, 48
Cromer, Evelyn Baring, first Earl of, 7, 9, 36–37, 38, 41, 42, 43–45, 46, 47, 83
Crowdy, Rachel, 178
Curzon, George Nathaniel, Marquess of, 44, 53, 54, 82

Dawson, Geoffrey, 79
Dawson-Scott, Grace, 72–73
Derby, Edward George Villiers, Earl, 68
Derby Lord, 9, 78, 88, 93, 97
domestic service, 3–4, 11, 12, 17, 99, 106, 108, 109, 122, 139, 158, 172, 173–174, 175, 177,

180, 181, 186–187, 188, 189–190
see also Central Committee on Women's Training and Employment, employment, unemployment
Dublin, 79, 95
Duncan, Sir Patrick, 8
Dundee, 141, 142

Edinburgh University, 1
employment
　middle-class women, 11, 17, 100, 103–104, 109, 163–164
　working-class women, 11, 17, 99, 163
Factory Inspectorate, 11, 84, 103–104, 109
First World War, 8, 57–98
　National Relief Fund, 8, 9, 58, 60, 62, 75–76, 79
　National Service Department, 8, 9, 10, 59, 83–84, 85–90, 91
　Soldiers and Sailors Families Association (SSFA), 58, 60, 61–65, 76
　unmarried mothers, 10–11, 57, 61, 63, 65–70, 73
　women's morals, 11, 57, 58–61, 65, 67–70, 73, 80, 96
　women patrols, 67, 80
　women's paramilitary activities, 11, 59, 70–74
　women's war work, 59, 74–75, 78, 79, 83, 84, 96–97
France/French, 12–13, 95, 102, 162, 165, 183, 184–185
Furse, Katharine, 79, 91

Geddes, Sir Auckland, 86
Glasgow, 61–65, 119–122, 144
Gollancz, Victor, 187, 192
Greville, Lord, 42, 44, 45
Guest, Frederick, 77

Haldane, Elizabeth, 11, 14
Harcourt, Loulou, 53
Harcourt, Mary, 41
Hart, Heber, 47
Haversham, Lady, 37
Hayes Fisher, William, 42–43
Hensley Henson, Herbert, 34
Hills, John ('Jack'), 41
Hoare, Samuel, 154
Hodge, John, 88
Hyde, Mrs Clarendon, 37

Innes, Mitchell, 47

Jersey Lady, 37, 53
Jessel, Capt., 47
Jevons Dr, 42, 44, 45
Jones, Thomas, 8–9, 112, 123, 140, 144

Kitchener, Horatio Herbert, Earl, 73

Lansdowne, Henry Charles Keith, Marquess of, 77, 78
Lawrence, Susan, 42
Lee, Sir Arthur, 54
Liberal Party, 1, 14–18
　see also Markham, Violet
Liverpool, 119–122, 140, 144, 146–147
Lloyd George, David, 9, 66, 77, 83, 87, 89, 93, 99, 107, 124
London, 5, 41–43, 44, 45–46, 47, 136–138, 140, 148, 178
Long, Walter, 75–76
Lothian, Philip, Marquess of, 156
Lyttelton, Alfred, 7
Lytton, Constance, 39

Macadam, Elizabeth, 5, 189
Macarthur, Mary, 10
McKenna, Reginald, 75–76
Mackenzie King, William Lyon, 8, 12

Index

Macmillan, Harold, 191
Macnamara, Thomas, 107–108
Mallet, Bernard, 78
Mallett, C.E., 47
Manchester, 140
Mansfield, 5, 100
Markham, Arthur, 5, 11, 14, 29, 34
Markham, Violet
  anti-suffrage attitudes and campaigning, 6–7, 10, 13, 15, 26, 31, 35, 41, 45–46, 48–53, 80–83
  Carruthers, James, (husband), 1, 3, 7, 12, 66–67
  citizenship and duty, 2, 5–6, 10, 12, 13, 14, 27, 30, 82, 93, 94, 110, 112, 183, 192–196, 198,
  early life, 2, 3, 4
  educational work, 5, 12, 13, 14, 26–29, 32, 33, 36, 102, 179, 182, 183, 192–196
  First World War, 6, 8, 9, 10, 11, 57–98
  foreign affairs, 12, 13, 15, 99, 101, 105
  gender issues: views on, 1, 3, 6–7, 8, 10, 11, 12, 13, 14, 15–21, 26, 30–31, 32, 33, 57, 70, 90, 98, 100, 102–103, 109, 110, 111, 145, 189–190, 197–198
  see also Central Committee on Women's Training and Employment, domestic service, First World War, Second World War
  1918 General Election, 11, 14, 15, 20, 100
  Germany and Germans, 11–12, 13, 104–105, 156, 168, 181, 182, 185–186, 192–196
  imperialism, 7–8, 33, 55
  liberalism and Liberal Party, 4, 11, 14–18, 94, 99, 106–107
  Mayor of Chesterfield, 12
  philanthropy and local politics, 4–5, 8, 12, 13, 23–34, 36, 40, 46, 57
  Second World War, 12, 148–182
  unemployment, 9, 12, 99, 113–114, 115, 116, 119–122, 124, 133–135
Masterman, Charles, 60
Middleton, J.S., 66
Milner, Alfred, Viscount, 7, 10, 79–80, 87
Ministry of Food, 91–92
Morant, Robert, 8, 9–10, 66, 77, 91–92
Morrison, Herbert, 161, 172
Mothers' Union, 68–69, 149
Murray, George, 75

The Netherlands, 185
Northcliffe, Alfred Charles William, Viscount, 70, 93
Northcote, Henry Stafford, Baron, 44

Open Door Council, 17

Pankhurst, Sylvia, 20
Personal Service League, 40, 117, 130–131, 152
Phillips, Marion, 105, 107
Portsmouth, 65

Rathbone, Eleanor, 19, 20, 102
Reading, Stella, Marchioness of, 130, 164
Rhondda, David Alfred, first Viscount, 92
Riddell, Sir George, 8, 77
Runciman, Hilda, 14,
Runciman, Walter, 39

Salter, Sir Arthur, 12
Save Europe Now, 187
Second World War, 148–182

Air Raid Precautions, 143, 154, 158
bombing, 148, 161–162, 163, 178–179
evacuation, 148, 149–152
women's morals, 12, 165, 166, 175
18B Advisory Committee, 12, 154–155, 156
Shackleton, Sir David, 77, 88
Sheffield, 32, 119–122, 176
Sheffield University, 1
Smith, Constance, 83
social work, 5, 93–94
Somervell Mrs, 37
South Africa, 7–8, 13, 32, 33, 34, 55, 56, 198
Soviet Union, 13, 164, 187
Spender, J.A., 9, 70, 73, 84
Stevenson, Frances, 9, 87, 88
Stockton, 119–122
Strachey, Philippa, 118–119, 127–128
Strachey, St Leo, 38–40, 70, 76
Talbot, Meriel, 110
Tennant, May, 8, 84, 88–89, 91, 111
Tennyson, Mrs Lionel, 37
Terry Lewis, Lucy, 47–48

Thomas, J.H., 77
Tomes Miss, 42, 45
Tuckwell, Gertrude, 105
Tunbridge Wells, 73

unemployment
Unemployment Assistance Board, 1, 3, 8–9, 113, 119, 120, 121, 122, 123–124, 125, 126, 133, 135–140, 141–142, 143, 145, 146, 149, 152, 156, 159, 160, 161–162, 163, 178, 179, 181, 190–191
women, 99, 113–114, 136–138, 139, 140–141, 144, 146–147
United States of America, 3, 157, 163, 168, 169, 170–171, 175

Wales, 113–114
Walsh, Stephen, 86
Ward, Dorothy, 42, 53–54, 191–192
Ward, Mrs Humphry (Mary), 34–35, 37, 38, 41–43, 44, 45, 47–48, 53–54, 191–192
Wilson, Mona, 62–65, 88
Women's Army Auxiliary Corps (WAAC), 59, 85, 88, 94, 95, 96
Women's Voluntary Service (WVS), 152